THE
BEST
WOMEN'S TRAVEL
WRITING

2010

TRUE STORIES
FROM AROUND THE WORLD

WOMEN'S TRAVEL LITERATURE FROM TRAVELERS' TALES

100 Places Every Woman Should Go

100 Places in Italy Every Woman Should Go

The Best Women's Travel Writing series

Gutsy Women

Gutsy Mamas

Her Fork in the Road

Kite Strings of the Southern Cross

A Mile in Her Boots

Sand in My Bra

More Sand in My Bra

A Mother's World

Safety and Security for Women Who Travel

The Thong Also Rises

Unbeaten Tracks in Japan

Whose Panties Are These?

A Woman's Asia

A Woman's Europe

A Woman's Passion for Travel

A Woman's Path

A Woman's World

A Woman's World Again

Women in the Wild

Writing Away

TRAVELERS' TALES

THE BEST WOMEN'S TRAVEL WRITING

2010

TRUE STORIES FROM AROUND THE WORLD

Edited by

STEPHANIE ELIZONDO GRIEST

Travelers' Tales
an imprint of Solas House, Inc.
Palo Alto

Art direction: Stefan Gutermuth
Cover photograph: © Mark Lewis
Page layout and photo editing: Cynthia Lamb using the fonts
    Granjon, Nicolas Cochin, and Ex Ponto
Interior design: Melanie Haage
Author photo: Alexander Devora
Production Director: Christy Quinto

ISBN 1-932361-74-X
ISSN 1553-054X

First Edition
Printed in the United States
10 9 8 7 6 5 4 3 2 1

We travel, some of us forever, to seek other states, other lives, other souls.

— ANAÏS NIN

For my HB,
with all my love

Table of Contents

Introduction

My great-great uncle Jake was a hobo who saw all of America with his legs dangling over the edge of a freight train. My cowboy cousins chased cattle across the Wild Horse Desert of South Texas. My father drummed his way around the globe with a U.S. Navy band. Growing up, I dreamed of someday telling stories that rivaled those of the men in my family:

"Once, in Marrakech...."

"I'll never forget that time in Burkina Faso when...."

But how? I could envision buying a ticket and boarding a plane, but what would I do after it landed?

Then, during my senior year in high school, a neighbor triumphantly returned home after a semester abroad and introduced me to the magical world of hostels, backpacks, and Lonely Planets. She was only a few years older than I and—unlike my other adventure role models—female. If *she* could roam in foreign lands, perhaps I could too.

When I enrolled in college that fall, I studied the language of the farthest country I could fathom (Russian) and then jetted off to Moscow. Thirteen years later, I'm still feeding my travel addiction. My sleeping bag has been unfurled upon a Kyrgyz mountaintop, the Mongolian steppe, and the dungeon floor of a renowned Chicago dominatrix. I've marched with Zapatista rebels, belly danced with Chinese Uighurs, and sipped mojitos with Cuban hip-hop artists. Though I've explored thirty countries and all but three of the United States, I ache for more.

This is why Travelers' Tales publishes an annual anthology of women's travel writing: so we can prove to each other that yes, we can do this. We don't have to wait until our college loans are paid off, or our kids are grown, or our bank account is stabilized (because really—will that *ever* happen?). We don't even have to wait until the perfect travel companion strolls along. We can quit our jobs—yes, even the one with dental insurance—kiss our beloveds goodbye, and fly. And this anthology shows just how supremely we capture the adventures that ensue.

Our journey begins and ends in Ecuadorian wilderness: Mary Caperton Morton takes us on a treacherous climb up an icy volcano, while Marisa Handler fills our glass with rum and sends us dancing around a table. In between, we attend the birth of a child in Bali, befriend a mujahideen in Kabul, create edible art in Tehran, and watch a dissident performance in Mandalay.

Myriad motives inspired these adventures. Johanna Gohmann wanted to make a special contribution to the English art world, while Erika Connor wished to nurture the street dogs of Rajasthan. Maliha Masood, Jennifer De Leon, and Valerie Conners hoped to unearth their ancestral roots in Pakistan, Guatemala, and Italy. Alison Stein Wellner aimed to find a food so hot she'd ignite on contact (as she once watched her grandfather do). Diane Caldwell sought another kind of heat involving a desert and a certain sexy Bedouin.

Although many of our authors left home with a carefully set intention, they discovered something else entirely. One came to terms with being lesbian. Another tossed out the shoulder pads that previously lined the B-cups of her bra. A third realized that yes, she really is Jewish, no matter how seductive New Age practices like channeling and energy healing may be. They all learned to walk the world's passageways with ever more confidence, and returned home with a renewed sense of wonderment.

So maybe you're stuck in a can't-quit job, or you have an especially needy family. Maybe the economy has dealt a nasty blow, or you've gone back to school for another degree. These stories will speak to you as well. They demonstrate how we can take whatever fate crosses our path. If Kellen Zale can survive that never-ending Chinese Communist Party banquet with a host whose English consists entirely of Madonna lyrics; if Kendra Greene can swallow that caterpillar; if Mary Caperton Morton can crawl to safety with three cracked ribs and two ruptured spinal discs, then we can probably handle our grouchy boss, unruly child, or ill and aging parents.

Revel in these stories, then plan your next journey. Mother Road is waiting.

—STEPHANIE ELIZONDO GRIEST
Iowa City, Iowa

ॐ ॐ ॐ

The Suffer Fest

A mountaineer expands her inner terrain.

From around the road's bend: a shriek of metal, a cloud of smoke, and a bus careens at our van, head on. We swerve madly for a near miss. Then I see the accident: a blue truck in pieces. A man lies in the road, very still. Our van squeals to a stop on the shoulder, and our guide asks if anyone has gloves. We all step out. A crowd has gathered. Somebody has covered the man's face with a bright blue jacket. All I can see is an outstretched hand, lying very still in a pool of darkening blood. I stare hard at the hand, desperately willing it to move, willing it to grab the jacket away, willing the man to rise. He doesn't. A bystander walks towards us, shaking his head. "There is no suffering here."

At 10:30 my alarm goes off, rousing me from a fitful sleep. It takes a few seconds to remember where I am: in a bunkhouse in Ecuador, 16,000 feet above sea level. I crawl out of my sleeping bag. It's 10:30 at night, but time to get up. I have a mountain to climb.

Bleary eyed, I reach for my headlamp and pull on layer after layer of clothing. It's high summer on the equator but the snow-capped peak outside is nearly 20,000 feet above sea level and it's frigidly cold up there. Around the bunkhouse, my climbing mates stir and start cocooning themselves in layers of fleece, down, and Gore-Tex. Nobody talks. We don't want to disturb others still sleeping, but there's electricity in the thin air. Excited and nervous, we are about to climb higher than any of us has ever been before: Volcán Cotopaxi, one of the highest active volcanoes in the world.

I linger on the short walk between the bunkhouse and the dining hall. It's a clear night and the mountain, visible high above camp, is glowing in the moonlight. Cotopaxi is crowned by a smooth, very steep, nearly symmetrical cone of perpetual ice and snow. Located in the Andean mountain chain, southeast of Ecuador's capital of Quito, Cotopaxi is among the largest of thousands of volcanoes that circle the Pacific tectonic plate along the Ring of Fire. It is also one of the most active and deadly. Incan legend has it that the volcano roared to life in 1534 to protest the Spanish invasion, killing scores of conquistadors. Since then, the mountain has erupted more than fifty times. The most recent blast in 1903 narrowly spared Quito but strong winds blew tons of searing ash southward, smothering thousands in nearby Latacunga. Chances are good Cotopaxi will erupt again soon, though probably not tonight.

The dining hall of the climbers' hut is candle-lit and smells of starchy food and mountaineers. One of the long wooden tables is piled high with junk food and surrounded by my nine other teammates and our five guides. A few have dropped out, citing the shock of the accident earlier that morning. I'm not hungry, but force one last meal of oatmeal and cookies into my uneasy stomach. It will be too cold on the mountain to stop and eat much more than snacks, but my body may burn up to 15,000 calories in the next few hours, so I've been gorging on carbs and high-calorie food, storing fuel for the climb. Even here, the altitude is already wreaking havoc. I'm sleeping poorly, coughing, nursing a spreading bruise of a headache. Altitude sickness is a very real danger at these heights. Crushing headaches, nausea, and disorientation are only the beginnings of high altitude cerebral edema: potentially fatal brain swelling.

Rodrigo, one of our Ecuadorian mountain guides, stands at the head of the table and reads out our rope teams: two to three people per guide. Instead of being roped to the mountain, we will be roped to each other. If one of us falls, we have to trust our teammates to catch us. Having successfully summited another volcano, 18,400-foot Cayambe last week, I am assigned to a rope with three experienced mountain men. I'm in good hands and thrilled with the vote of confidence in my climbing abilities, but aware I will be our weak link. I top off my water bottles with boiling water to stave off freezing, stuff a few candy bars deep inside my layers, and shoulder my backpack. Ready or not, it's time to climb.

A rough climb over sharp red volcanic rock takes us to the foot of Cotopaxi's glacier. It's now 11 P.M. Most successful summit trips take between ten to twelve hours of continuous climbing to get to the top and back down. Since the midday equatorial sun softens the snow and makes it slippery and dangerous, we are starting before midnight to ensure we are off the slopes before noon tomorrow. Soon we reach the edge of the glacier, strap our crampons onto our boots, and rope up. My team is ready first and we step out onto the ice. Little do I know, we won't see the rest of our group again until the following afternoon.

Climbing at night by headlamp is encouraging: it reduces the mountain to a more manageable size. The darkness keeps me from worrying about how I will survive the next twelve hours and forces my focus on the bright patch of snow illuminated just in front of me. As I climb, my mind thinks only of my next few steps. The pace of mountaineering is slow and agonizing, almost elderly. It is too cold to stop and rest, so we must keep moving upward, always. I fixate on the tortoise's mantra: slow and steady, slow and steady. With each step I plant the spikes of my crampons firmly in the ice and take a breath. Then I move my axe, impale it deep in the ice, and take another step and then another breath. I continue on like this for hours, not climbing a mountain, but merely crossing a narrow circle of light.

The four of us are spread along our yellow rope about fifteen feet apart. I am second in line after Bryce Green, our Californian mountain guide. Behind me is Colin Hamel, a videographer making a promotional video for our guiding company, and then Matt Hardy, trip coordinator for Johns Hopkins University's Outdoor Pursuits program. Bryce continues upward like a machine, slow and steady and never pausing. We climb for what seems like hours before I figure out that if I need to rest, I have to ask. I speak up for a water break and we stop just long enough for me to dig out my already slushy water bottle and take a few sips. Stopping is precarious. The slope is steep enough to reach out and touch the snow in front of me without bending over. Bryce is not so much ahead of me as *above* me. Stopping on such a steep slope doesn't give my calves a break and without the balance of forward motion, I feel like I'm about to tumble over backwards and off the face of the mountain. By the time I get my water bottle back in my pack, I'm already shivering. Bryce calls down *"¿Listo?"* We respond *"¡Sí!"* through chattering teeth and continue following him up the endless ladder of ice and snow.

The moon is full and the stars are magnificent. The Big Dipper hovers over the slope ahead of us, so close that once we reach the top, it seems we can climb right into the ladle and up into the night sky. Here in the southern hemisphere, we have a different view of the stars, including the prominent Southern Cross, which none of us has ever seen before. My rope team is moving well and we have passed several other teams of climbers laboring up the slope, their faint mumblings in Spanish and German and Russian fading into the night. I concentrate on my pace, on taking a controlled breath with each measured step. Every now and then, Bryce yells over his shoulder for our numbers. A one means you're about to die, while a ten is euphoria. At this point, I'm a little tired, but elated just to be up here, so I yell back: "Ten!" There's plenty of light from the moon, so I turn off my headlamp and keep going up, step by step, feeling confident, climbing a mountain.

I'm not wearing a watch, but I know the hours are passing because the stars are moving and the moon is sinking. As it slips behind the mountain, I reluctantly turn my headlamp back on. The next time Bryce asks for my number, I reply "seven" and ask the time. It's 4 A.M. We have been climbing upslope for five straight hours now and my legs are shaking and numb with exhaustion. With every step I have to hunch over my ice axe for balance and my arms and shoulders ache from the effort. My back hurts worst of all though, throbbing like it hasn't in years. Not since my accident.

As a teenager I was thrown off my horse and speared into the ground at top speed. Upon waking from blunt unconsciousness, I tried to move my hands to take off my helmet but found only searing numbness. Later I would learn I had broken several vertebrae, cracked three ribs, and ruptured two spinal discs. All I knew then was that pain scorched my spine, leaving me unable to do anything but lie still, gasp for breath, and fight off panic. Hours passed before I willed my hands to move again. All alone and miles from help, I began dragging myself home—face down against the earth—in a state of shock. I remember every inch of that journey, every rock and root that ground against my broken ribs, every clump of grass I grabbed to pull myself along. Every inch brought new pain, but the suffering was welcome. It meant I could still feel something, that I was still alive. I had left the barn in the early morning and it was well past dark when I finally reached the edge of the spotlight on the driveway, where somebody later found me.

If that was the hardest day I had lived, this is a close second. Bryce warned us yesterday that mountaineering is "one big suffer fest." With the moon gone, darkness sets in and it seems colder than ever. I'm exhausted, painfully cold, and approaching utter misery. But even if I turn around, I would still have hours of dangerous downhill climbing to return to camp—and most mountaineering accidents occur on the way down. Worst of all, my teammates would have to turn around with me.

The wind picks up, whistling in my ears. I can no longer hear the crunch of my rope mates' boots. We are all silent, saving our breath for the increasingly difficult task of gulping the thin air. I trudge on and on, feeling alone on this miserable mountain.

The saying "the darkest hour comes right before the dawn" is never truer than in mountaineering. With the moon gone, it is pitch black, except for the feeble light from my headlamp. My body gave out long ago and I'm running solely on stubbornness now. We are around 18,000 feet when I completely forget the name of the mountain we're climbing. I know it begins with a "C" but that's it. The air up here holds half as much oxygen as it does at sea level and it must be taking a toll on my brain, along with my lungs. We stop for a break on a rare level section and I collapse on the snow, convinced I'll never move again. Bryce asks us our numbers. I mumble "four" and my rope mates aren't faring much better. I want to lie here forever, but prickling cold sets into my hands and feet after a minute or two. I rub my gloved hands together and suddenly I'm back on the road, staring at the hand, the dead hand, just lying there on the road, not moving and I'm standing there, wishing it would move. I know it never will, but I can, so I shake my head clear, stumble to my freezing feet, and climb on.

Looking at his watch, Bryce has good news and bad news: dawn is coming soon, but we still have at least three more hours until the top. Three hours! I cannot conceive of three more hours of this. The wind has died down and Colin, sensing our dark moods, offers to tell a story to get our minds off our misery. He begins a tale about two mice, the details of which I sadly cannot remember. But it works and our numbers rise a notch or two. As he wraps up his story, the first glimmer of dawn peeks out from behind the mountain. Then the dark sky lightens to a robin's egg blue with streaks of red. For the first time, we can see what we've been climbing. Below, our tracks switchback across the endless snow, down and down to where the clouds swirl far below us. Gazing back at the way we came, the name "Cotopaxi" comes back in a flash. I am as exhausted as I've ever been in my life, but dawn flooding over the Andes is beautiful and it rejuvenates my resolve not just to make it to the top, but to enjoy the journey. Not everyone gets to summit mountains.

Daylight brings a newfound fascination with this icy, alien world. I don't know if it's another wind, or my change in attitude, but I'm finally able to embrace my miseries and enjoy this experience. We continue climbing, marveling at the massive ice caves, towering seracs, and bottomless crevasses along our route. Occasionally we have to cross one of these giant cracks in the glacier, and each time I hold my breath, try not to look down, and leap across. On one crossing, Colin misses the edge and falls into the crevasse up to his waist. I dive to the ground, shoving my axe firmly into the ice to anchor us and he climbs out.

A while later, we stagger around a towering pile of snow and ice and suddenly, just above us, the mountain stops. The summit lies atop a twenty-foot pile of corniced ice and snow. I follow Bryce up, climbing vertically hand over hand. Swinging my axe and hammering my toe spikes into the snow, I drag myself up, inch by inch. When I reach the edge I rest a moment on my knees, eyes bleary, unable to summon enough energy to focus, let alone stand. But then, Bryce tugs on my rope and says, "Welcome to the four-mile-high club." It makes me laugh. I open my eyes wide and stand atop one of the highest volcanoes in the world. It's a clear day and it isn't just the thin air that makes me gasp; the view from the summit is breath-stealing. Other snowcapped Andean peaks dot the green valley far below and I can actually see the curve of the Earth against the horizon. The volcano's black crater lies just below us. The smell of sulfur is strong, but somehow the thin air up here is still pleasant to breathe. Colin and Matt join us and we all take pictures, holding our axes high in triumph. Just then I remember a note from my guidebook: Cotopaxi sits near the equator and here on top, we are closer to the sun than anyplace else on Earth.

All too soon, the clouds start rolling in and the cold wind forces us to take our leave. After scrambling down the cornice, we face directly down slope, kicking our spiked heels deep in the ice and start descending. Along the way we pass other groups, but nobody we know. Once our radio finally comes back into range, we learn that everybody else turned back sometime during the night because of altitude sickness or exhaustion. As the sun keeps rising, the air heats up and for the first time in hours I am comfortably warm. We stop occasionally to slather on sunscreen, peel off layers, and eat candy bars. Three hours after we left the top, we spot the edge of the glacier below. It's late morning and what was ice last night is now soft, slippery snow. The final leg of the descent is by far the hardest. My body is on the verge of collapse and I just can't kick my feet into the slope any-more. I slip and fall most of the way down and have my rope mates to thank profusely for preventing me from flying off the mountain. Finally, we stagger onto the red rocks that we left nearly twelve hours ago, remove our crampons, stow our axes, and trudge back to camp.

The physical toll of scaling big mountains is terrific: in the course of three such climbs over two weeks, I lost nearly fifteen pounds. Breathing the thin air left me with a tightness in my chest that lingered long after I returned home to sea level. When it finally cleared, though, I was sad to feel it go. The psychological effects of that trip lasted even longer. Cresting that summit left me restless for rare heights, and gave me the fortitude to scale them. I have climbed many mountains since. Every now and then, I still see that smoking bus hurtling at me in dreams, but after Cotopaxi, the accident has become less of a nightmare and more of an inspiration. That day on a wending mountain road in rural Ecuador, a blue truck was crushed by a bus and a driver was killed instantly. But a pack of climbers lived another day to scale another mountain.

❧ ❧ ❧

Mary Caperton Morton is a freelance science and travel writer with degrees in biology and geology and a master's in science writing. She spends her winters in an off-the-grid Earthship in rural New Mexico and summers in the Sapphire Mountains of Montana. Everything she owns, including her border collie/Newfoundland mix Bowie, fits in a little Volkswagen, and everything she really needs fits in a twenty-five-pound backpack.

࿐ ࿐ ࿐

Not-Surfing New Zealand

A writer learns the Tao of the waves.

M y guy Michael is an avid surfer. Crazed, actually. His boards (one long, three short) are festooned like fine art around the house. His wetsuits (a selection) are arranged with reverence in the closet, a rubbery all-sea, all-season wardrobe. His feet are radically callused and his kelp-proof hair buzzed short, all in service of his sport. And this obsesses him mind, body, and soul, much more than any girl—even his girl, *this* girl.

So when he invites me on a ten-day surfing "safari," I am stunned yet thrilled. I mean, it's not like we are more than four, maybe five months into the relationship. I slightly suspect my purpose in coming along is less to impress him with my travel savvy and romantic charms and more to do with my job: sitting on the beach to oversee the safety and well-being of Michael's flip-flops while he frolics in New Zealand's legendary surf. Yet I

cannot help dallying with the fantasy. There we'll be,
Michael and I, strolling hand-in-hand along the sand,
laughing together during moonlit midnight skinny dips.
Maybe—just maybe—our tentative, mincing romance
will be goosed forward by the island's balmy beauty.

And so, here we are, screaming out of Auckland in
our rental campervan. Michael's boards (one long, one
short) joyride along. We are no more than fifty-three
minutes off our thirteen-hour flight from San Francisco.
It is 5 A.M. New Zealand time, dead-of-night dark, and
already my Kahuna is dressed for his baptism in the
local waters, that is to say, naked but for some boardshorts. Come dawn, the scenery gets heart-stopping.
Volcanic, wind-swept, desolate: here in New Zealand
the descriptive "pristine" isn't kidding. Wild, clean, and
everywhere, the sea; each twist in the road reveals a vista
of startling beauty.

We speed north along the Whangaparaoa Peninsula
until we screech up to a beach our guidebook calls
Pikiri. I am almost speechless at the spectacle. It is an
arc of flawless white sand fringed in ferns and flowers;
it unfurls, I swear, for forever at the edge of a dazzling
turquoise-green bay. We are completely alone but for
a far-off fisherman, who bobs in his boat beyond the
frothing breakers.

"Oh!" I manage to squeak.

Michael fairly squeals, "Let's check it out!"

We hop from the campervan and the snap of salt air,
the smile of the sun, make me giddy. Call me a hopeless
romantic, but come on! We have arrived at paradise. We
trot onto the beach and Michael, rapt, gazes out to sea.
His hands are raised to shield his eyes from the glare and
I am not at all sure he is breathing.

"All right!" I say. "Here we are, we made it. Have a great time!" I of course expect the excited surfer to grab his board and fly into the water, and I cannot wait to be abandoned to my beach towel for hours, nay, days. Curiously, however, Michael simply gazes; then gazes some more. He scans the water left, gazing, and gazing still, he scans the water right. He mutters something, that is, if I'm not mistaken.

"Excuse me?"

"Wind's onshore," he mumbles.

That's surfer speak for *I'm not going out*. But why? Before I can ask, we pop back into the campervan and peel away from Pikiri, fluffing dust along a dirt-and-gravel road, the kind that in remote New Zealand makes up most of the off-highway byways. Up ahead lies Mangawhai Heads. "Good beach and bar breaks" are here, according to Michael's surf guide. Our campervan careens into the parking lot. Here, the waters are all sun-shimmery and full of blue maomao fish and bottlenose dolphin. Out we hop. Jogging over to a desolate dune, Michael assumes the stance while I pop back into the campervan to bikini-up and prep for a nice, long beach flop. I am just winding up my tedious SPF-30 routine when he appears at the sliding side door.

"Right's not right," he says.

Pop back into campervan. We fluff more dust for some miles and next pull up to Te Arai Point, stop, and again hop out. Beautiful, droopy kowhai trees bright with brilliant yellow flowers—New Zealand's national bloom—frill the beach with the sort of foreign-looking flora that says we are far, far from home. I have barely inhaled the heady kowhai scent when I am hustled back into the campervan, so fast I lose a hair clip and an earring. "Right's all right," Michael says, and guns the engine. "But a left would be better."

I mean, really. Does this make sense?

Then we arrive on a breezy bluff above the beach at Mangawhai Heads. The surf unfurls below in elegant foamy curls that look like pure possibility. The solitude is stunning: just us, the gulls, and the dawning concept that I am the only surf bunny in the world who doesn't get it. When will there be some *surfing* in this surfing safari? I look over at my "dude," in the parlance, and surreptitiously inspect him for signs of funk that all our driving around checking things out has not yet resulted in a surf. We have traveled thousands of miles to practically the end of planet Earth, after all; the beaches we have seen have looked idyllic for hanging ten, carving-up, or showing off the whatever-it-is that makes big-wave riders, like my guy Michael, experts at their obsession. I am so hoping to hear it just once from him: the "L" word, as in "Later, Babelini!" Yet, the guy seems eerily fine with all our hopping-and-popping along the coast; he appears downright pleased with his not surfing the best of New Zealand. I do a mood check to be sure.

"Are you having fun?" I ask. Michael is frozen in his not-breathing, sea-staring stance. He seems not to have heard me.

"ARE YOU HAVING FUN?"

"Are you kidding?" he says. His jaw drops into *duh* position. "I am absolutely stoked."

"So, then, go!" Teasing, I shove him in the direction of the water. "Surfers surf, no?"

There is a long—very long—comatose moment. Michael then replies, although not in so many words: No.

"Needs south wind."

Pop we go, back into the campervan. We hop and pop our way north, ever north, and the beaches become a blur, each to me more perfect than the previous. There is Whananaki ("a local favorite," according to the surfer's guide), and Mimiwhangata Park ("will have waves when other beaches are flat"). The guidebook tells us that seductive Sandy Bay, on the Tutukaka Coast, is hot hot hot for world-class scuba diving around the offshore marine reserve of Poor Knights Islands. But when we careen off the road, pull up to the beach and hop out, I am no longer the wide-eyed surfer's girl who in all innocence expects "Cowabunga!" to be the next word on the wind. Am I the fool who believes there will be a cry of "Surf's up!"? As if.

Surfing must be something like love. A careening hunt from beach to beach fueled by a heartload of hope that up ahead lies, at last, The One. Here at Sandy Bay, a small surf beach that venturing north along the Tutukaka Coast kicks off a succession of bays where there's even more opportunity to surf (or not), I ponder the possibility that traveling with a mostly-naked man in relentless pursuit of something elusive could be teaching me something important. Something it would be good to get. Something maybe like love: the perfect wave to seek and seek yet never ride.

"Wow," I say at first sight of the beach. Faster than the syllable slips my lips, my travel companion goes, you guessed it, pop, back into the campervan. "Michael, come *on*." This time I whine. Yet I am astounded when in a wordless rush he does not flip the ignition but instead wiggles into his wetsuit, wrestles a board off the top of the van, waxes it to high stickiness, and runs, dashes, to the water's edge.

Between us lies an expanse of powdery sand, lavishly gilded by billions of tiny, perfect shells in the palest of peaches and pinks. The sea shimmers in a rhapsody of aqua and green. It is my turn now not to breathe. What a gorgeous spot to flop for hours! I load my beach bag— hat, glasses, snacks, trashy tell-all—and dance my happy feet to a spot among the shells where, should he catch a wave, which of course he will, I can rave over Michael's display of surfer mojo. "Yay! Go you!" I'll hoot. The last thing I see before drifting...dreaming...snoozing the drooling, snore-filled snooze of the jet-lagged is Michael crouched in the sand, eyes on the sea, hands raised against the glare. He's gazing.

What is it, twenty minutes, twenty days later? I am jolted awake. A body drops beside me with an *oaf*. "It's closing out," Michael croaks, winded. He isn't even wet.

On surfing safari, a girl owes it to herself to rework her notions of romance. To be sure, volcanic islands along the Pacific Rim of Fire, like New Zealand, may promise a lot of, well, heat in the love a couple ignites or renews on them; the balmy subtropical climate may woo one into a woozy state of "I'm in love!" when it's really confusion behind the daze. What does it mean that Michael won't surf? I look for the metaphor. Does this portend doom for our relationship, a sign that down the road there will be no *let's just go for it*? As the day grows long, we do more not-surfing around the daz- zling Bay of Islands, where the pretty British Colonial town of Russell charms me but doesn't soothe my fear. The map says we're zooming toward Cape Reinga, New Zealand's northernmost tip. Here, the native Maori believe their spirits leave the island at death. Michael and I in the campervan aren't talking much. I am alone with my foreboding and he focuses dead ahead on the

road, which now winds toward the town of Kaitaia and
the phenomenon called Ninety Mile Beach. Ninety cur-
vaceous miles of beach it is, indeed—a surfer's Shangri-
La where honestly, I'm thinking, there has to be a spot
right enough to entice my reluctant Kahuna into the
water. Ninety miles is ninety miles! Surely here a surf
will happen. Our campervan careens into Kaitaia, and
after hopping out per usual, Michael and I plop down
on stools at a beach shack that serves fish and chips
wrapped in newsprint.

"Good on ya, mate," says a mostly-naked fellow two
stools over. I can tell he's a kindred spirit to Michael:
his boardshorts are sea-battered and salt-worn. I eat;
they chat. And before I know it we are going pop, right
into this Kiwi's campervan for a ride that rockets this
way and that until eventually, here I am, flying along
the beach in a topless ATV called a "quad." Up front
Michael and his new best friend speak Surf, while in
back their boards bounce as high and hard as my der-
riere on the crooked seat. I try not to fall out. The ATV
whips to a halt on a remote rock shelf. Little glistening
pools hold tide creatures—anemones, starfish, crabs.
Surf spray spits salty drops on my face as the waves rise
higher and higher until they curl and crash and foam.

"Right's all right, mate," says Michael.

"Right, mate. Left's right right as well," says his
friend.

"Right."

"Right."

And just like that, they're in the water. With hoots
and "Wahoo!" they surf the waves breaking left. With
joy and "Banzai!" they ride the waves curling right.
The endless hours of sea-gazing that have led to this
moment are not pointless, the careening drive from

beach to beach far from a waste of time. The surf guide
tells me that Michael's comatose act on shore is really a
crucial part of the sport. For if a surfer is not considering the waves before he (and by this I mean he or she)
rides them—how they're timed, in what configuration
they arrive, whether or not there are onshore or offshore currents or riptides—how will he know, really
know, the soul of the swell to which he is committing
his efforts? A surfer must hold in his heart the wave
that will demand his greatest skill and answer his highest desire. Otherwise, how will he live its thrill when, at
last, it arrives?

"All riiiiiiiiiiiiiight," comes a cry from the water. I look
out in time to see Michael dancing in the surf on a wave
so smooth and well-curling and perfect—so right—that
even from the beach their dance looks like love.

That's when I get it, this lesson of love and life and
surf: never settle for less.

*   *

*Colette O'Connor is Michael's ex-girlfriend, living and work-
ing and definitely not surfing around the Monterey Bay area in
California. Her lifestyle features and travel essays have appeared
in publications ranging from the* Los Angeles Times *to* France
magazine *to other Travelers' Tales titles:* Paris, Sand in My Bra,
Whose Panties Are These?, *and* The Best Women's Travel
Writing 2005.

❧ ❧ ❧

The Heat Seeker

Mission: Cranial Flare-up.

*I*t started with the currywurst in Frankfurt. That's probably not the best place to commence a quest for the hottest food in the world, but nonetheless.

I was in Germany for work and had met Carl, a California-born expat. He told me about Snack-Point, which claimed to serve "The Best Worscht in Town." Currywurst is a sliced sausage served in ketchup with added chile powder and other spices. Snack-Point makes this available in varying degrees of heat and even serves one sauce made with Red Savina habanero powder, which held the Guinness record for the hottest chile in the world until 2007, when it was displaced by India's *bhut jolokia*, which is sometimes used as elephant repellant.

Carl ordered for us in German and, in chivalrous deference to my feminine taste buds, ordered for me

something from Snack-Point's mid-range of heat. We
stood at the tall tables, under an awning, in the rain, and
speared the meat with a plastic pick. It was delicious,
and my mouth felt hot and tingly, but my head did not
ignite.

And that was disappointing, for I wanted to replicate
something I'd witnessed in elementary school. I'd often
spend weekends with my grandparents and various
extended family members, driving around to tag sales,
flea markets, and junk shops in the New York City suburbs. This was my grandmother's second-favorite pastime (arguing being her first). One Sunday, our family
descended on a Westchester strip mall for a traditional
Jewish Sunday dinner: Chinese food. I was deep into my
chicken lo mein when my grandfather missed the duck
sauce and instead dunked his egg roll into the dish of
extra-hot mustard. He flushed from chin to scalp and
rose a few inches from his chair, while his hands flew
into the air and then clapped down hard on the top of his
bald head—as if to keep it from exploding.

This impressed me. I'd never seen a person turn that
shade of purplish red. As he sat there shaking his head
and saying, "Hoooo boy, man oh man," and some other
things not to be repeated in polite company, a desire was
born within: I wanted to eat something so hot that I
would risk a cranial flare-up.

I have since joined a long tradition of people who
have, to a greater or lesser extent, structured their voy-
ages around spice. The most famous heat-seeker was
Christopher Columbus, who mistook chile peppers,
which originate in South and Central America, for
black pepper. (This is why we call chiles "pepper" even
though they're not botanically related.) Columbus and
other explorers took their plunder, with chiles among

the booty. In ships' holds, chiles made their way to the cooking pots of Asia and Africa. Today, it's no easier to imagine the fiery cuisines of India, Thailand, Sichuan, Ethiopia, and Morocco without chile than it is to think of Bolivian, Mexican, or even New Mexican food without those hot pods imported from the New World.

Unlike my historical compatriots, I will not pillage, steal, kill, or enslave on my mission. Instead, like any traveler pursuing an interest on the road, I seek out crimes of opportunity: Wherever I find myself, I seek out restaurants known for their fiery cuisine; if an item on the menu is labeled "hot and spicy," I order it. When given the option, I always, always ask for it extra hot.

I realize this is an odd thing to pursue, the feeling of heat in the mouth so intense that it mimics the most extreme pain one can stand. It's probably important to say that in no other way do I relish things that hurt. I am, in fact, quite a wimp.

But heat provides no ordinary sensation of pain. Science tells us it's an "ambiguous neural response," one that we did not evolve to properly interpret. When you bite into a chile pepper, your body knows one thing for sure: it's experiencing an intense sensation. Panic ensues. This may be a very dangerous situation, your mouth may actually be on fire! And yet none of your sensors register actual heat, as measured in degrees Fahrenheit or Celsius. Just in case, your brain registers what's happening as swallowing fire, and creates a full-body response. You flush, you sweat, you rise from your chair and clap your hands on your head.

Some people hate this, and some of us find it pleasurable in the same way that some people find a horror movie or a roller coaster pleasurable—it's fun to simulate the physical reaction we have to actual danger without the real risk of it. Eat hot food and you get all the fun of setting yourself on fire—including the surge of endorphins to help ease your theoretical third-degree burn—without getting the least bit singed. Eating spicy food is an adventure sport. The currywurst in Frankfurt was obviously the junior leagues. I was ready to push myself to the limits.

I had expected that my global search for the spiciest food would be something of a private mission, one that would only capture the attention of others at the split-second at which I achieved my goal: feeling like my head was going to explode. And for a while, it played out as I imagined. I did not gain a second glance in Louisiana's Cajun country, for example, as I downed fiery gumbos and Tabasco-spiked ice cream, nor did I merit extra notice in Hong Kong, when I dug into tiny dumplings bathed in orange chile oil on a side street in Kowloon.

On my first night in India, though, my private adventure sport started to morph into a spectator event. It was nearly 11 P.M. by the time I'd threaded through Mumbai's maze of cars and haze of crowds and arrived at Masala Kraft, a contemporary Indian restaurant. It happened to be located in the Taj Mahal Palace and Tower, which, at the time of my visit, was still months away from the terrorist siege of November 2008.

A waiter brought out the first two courses, both house specialties: Delhi-style corn on the cob, roasted and rubbed in lime, cilantro and a mild chile powder, and amazingly tender Lucknow lamb kebabs, a dish first prepared for nobles who were too lazy to chew. He deftly transferred each course in succession from serving dishes onto my plate, and hovered nearby, in order to intercept any forward motion I might make towards the serving dishes. So his vigil would not be interrupted, a more junior waiter ran my dishes out from the kitchen.

But when it came time for my chicken-and-rice dish, which I'd ordered extra hot, there was a commotion. My waiter was ushered aside, replaced by a young man in a dark suit. Was he the manager? The maître d'? In any event, he was someone of greater authority. During my first two courses, I had been sized up, and I was deemed to be in over my head.

With a flourish, he presented a bowl of chicken, a bowl of rice, and then a bowl of something white and creamy.

"The chef sent this out because he thought it would be too hot for you," he explained, spooning *raita*—a yogurt and cucumber relish—onto my plate. "This *raita* will be your savior, and then also the mango chutney."

He pointed each out to me, seeking comprehension. I assured him that I was really into the spice, and he assured me that there was no way I could possibly imagine the heat that they could deliver from the kitchen. My mind flashed to the McDonald's and the Subways that I'd spotted en route from the airport. Judge U.S. cuisine by those standards, and it's easy to understand how anyone could reasonably think that we Americans are a nation rendered taste-insensate. I thanked him, and he took a couple of steps backwards and joined my waiter and a busboy. They watched me.

I took my first bite.

Nothing! Not hot at all. It was delicious, and I loved it, but it was savory, not spicy. The manager came forward as I swallowed and anxiously inquired how it was, whether he should return it to the kitchen and fetch something more mild. I strove for diplomacy. Delicious, loved it. It's not you, it's me.

He frowned, then brightened.

"Oh, you've just tried the chicken," he said. "The heat will really be in the rice."

So I had some rice. He could tell by my face that it hadn't made a ripple.

"Well really," he said, laughing, "you should eat it like an Indian!"

He explained, as if to a child, that if he were dining that night, he would eat the chicken with a stack of raw chile peppers beside him, alternating bites of each. He was just kidding, but of course, now I wanted to try it that way. He attempted to dissuade me, but with a sigh, sent for the chile peppers. They arrived, three of them, thin and green, on a white plate.

Again, the staff gathered to observe. The manager had become my coach.

"Eat it from the thick side, where there will be fewer seeds, the heat is in the seeds," he advised. (Actually, I found out later that the heat is most concentrated in the membranes between the seeds, but that's a small distinction.) "Take a bite of food, then a bite of pepper, just a tiny bite! The tiniest of bites! Then more food!"

I wondered whether he was going to fetch a towel to wipe my brow—or his.

No turning back now. I took a bite and chased it with chicken.

This was no joke. It was hot. How hot? You don't have to be a chef or a biochemist to know that tolerance for spicy food varies. In chile peppers, the heat comes from a substance called capsaicin. Genetics determine our sensitivity to capsaicin, which means that individuals experience heat differently. In 1912, a pharmacist named Wilbur Scoville was frustrated with the inexactitude of this, and found that no technology could detect capsaicin as effectively as the human tongue—namely, his. He dissolved extracts of different types of peppers into an increasing quantity of sugar water, until he could no longer detect the pungency. He then assigned scores, expressed in Scoville Units, to each pepper, starting with a zero for a bell pepper. Until quite recently, food companies selling things like spices and salsas would employ a panel of trained Scoville tasters, and used an average of their assessments to assign a Scoville unit rating. This highly subjective objective measure continued until the invention of the High Pressure Liquid Chromatograph, which measures capsaicin levels precisely.

I don't travel with a chromatograph, so I'll describe the way I experience heat to you another way. You know how it feels to take a nap on a beach on a sunny day? The sun is warm on your face, but there's a cool breeze so you're not hot, and you're certainly not sweating. That's how it feels inside my mouth when I'm getting what I would consider a basic level of heat. Now imagine the breeze dies down a bit, so now you're noticing that you're getting a bit toasty, and it would sure be nice to have a cool beverage or duck under a beach umbrella. That's what was delivered by the chile pepper I had at Masala Kraft.

While I was short of my skull-thumping goal, it was still a pretty fantastic experience. Capsaicin renders the mouth exquisitely sensitive, so that you can feel the precise texture of what you're eating—each grain of rice, each shred of chicken. It also commands attention, a trait I value in a life lived in a state of quasi-Attention Deficit Disorder. When you're eating heat, you cannot read, you cannot watch TV, you can't even really carry on a reasonable conversation. Each bite is its own experience, each bite requires a breath, a preparation, a question of whether this morsel will burn as much as that morsel. I ate the entire plate of chiles and retired to my room upstairs, where my stomach burned until the sun rose the next morning.

As I traveled through India, I noticed a common denominator among the people who wouldn't serve me sufficiently spicy food: they were mostly male. India values modesty in its women. As journalist Amal Naj reports in his book *Pepper: A Story of Hot Pursuits*, even before the days of the pornographic Spice Channel, spice and heat have long been associated with carnal pursuits. African women bathed in pepper-infused waters to enhance their attractiveness; in Swahili, *pili pili* is the name for pepper and also slang for penis; a Peruvian prison banned peppers believing it aroused the inmates. Indeed, at least some of the physical effects of eating hot foods—flushing pink, sweating—are also likely to show up between the sheets.

There is something a little bawdy about being a woman who likes it hot, and perhaps, then, my search for it could strike men as being somewhere between unseemly and a little slutty—a quest that a decent man shouldn't encourage in an apparently respectable married woman such as myself. And quite possibly, a quest that a young man would not like to engage in with an older woman, and find himself lacking.

Which may be what happened in Honduras, which is not at all known for its spicy food, although plenty of chile peppers grow there, both in the wild and for export. I'd set off on a nature tour of the Welchez, just outside Copán Ruinas, not far from the Guatemalan border. I was traveling with a group that happened to be all female, and my stammering requests in Spanish for hot sauce had already made clear my penchant for all things hot. Our guide was a young man with a wide smile topped with the bare beginnings of a wispy moustache. He was somewhere between giggly and giddy, clearly amped up by the idea of leading a bunch of girls around the tropical rain forest.

As usual, I lagged behind the crowd, snapping pictures of the otherworldly beginnings of banana pods, red hibiscus blooms, and bright green berries that would turn into my morning joe. The group rounded a corner ahead of me, and I heard my name being called. I caught up to find that everyone had stopped.

There, hanging from a bush, were chiles—red, skinny, to the best of my identification abilities, tabascos. It emerged that I would now be expected to eat one of these, or at least try it. Of course, I didn't need a lot of convincing.

The young guide plucked a chile and handed it to me. "Wait a minute!" he yelled.

He tore off into the jungle. I stood there holding the pepper, feeling vaguely idiotic. The group formed a semi-circle around me and the chile bush.

He came back clutching something green—mint, he said, for after.

I took a mincing bite from the thick end, remembering that the seed membranes on the thin end held most of the heat. And I chewed and swallowed.

My husband and I have an old friend, a guy we knew when we were in high school, and not that long ago we reconnected with him for a rainy afternoon of margaritas. I'd gone off to the restroom, and when I returned, he was in the middle of regaling my husband with an off-color guy story. I encouraged him to continue. Really, I said, you can't shock me. The rest of the day, he did his damndest to curl my hair with ever-escalating tales of lewd debauchery, which apparently reached their crescendo during his days on a rugby team. After each tale he'd look at me expectantly—but although my eyebrows were tickling the inside of my skull, I maintained a Zen-like countenance and calmly sipped my margarita.

As I stood there in Honduras, with my young guide staring eagerly—and the group training their cameras on me—I re-evaluated my stated mission. Although I really wanted to have heat that was more than I could stand, I didn't want *this* moment to be my head-banging moment. No matter how much this hurt, I decided, I wasn't going to create a spectacle.

But it wasn't going to be easy. The burning started with my lips, then shot like a pinball machine throughout my mouth. I could feel the pepper's progress as it slid into my digestive system. It felt like I had actually swallowed fire.

Somehow, though, I did not sniffle, I did not cough, I did not cry.

"Not bad," I said, attempting nonchalance. I hoped no one would ask me to take another bite.

The guide simply couldn't believe it.

"This chile must have lost its heat!" he said. He grabbed the pepper from my hand and popped the whole thing into his mouth, chewed three times, and swallowed.

It was too bad everyone had put their cameras away, because here was the show they were waiting for. First he gasped, and then he started coughing and then wheezing, shaking his head rapidly side to side like a wet dog. Then he was crying, gasping, and laughing at the same time. He crashed off into the jungle in search of a stream and drank from it, returning with his plaid shirt soaked. He clutched a handful of mint in his fist for the rest of the tour, chewing on it pensively. He kept his distance from me. Which was fine because I wasn't talking to anyone, either. My mouth burned for the rest of the day. His mouth must have burned for a week. Could that have been my ultimate heat experience, my definitive tribute to Grandpa's head-thumping moment? I didn't know—my pride got in my way.

જ્જ જ્જ જ્જ

Alison Stein Wellner pursues many tasty adventures from her home in New York City. She's the culinary travel guide for About. com, a blogger for Luxist, and has contributed to Business Week, Glamour, Men's Journal, New York Magazine, Robb Report, Yankee, *and* Yoga Journal, *among other publications.*

In the Half-Light

Love in the land of phantasm.

There was Carson, who I knew I'd fall in love with. There was Bonnie, who ran away to perform puppet shows on Nevsky Prospekt. There was Alexei, eighteen and effeminate, with wide ears and an obsession with hand washing. There was Irina, the ecologist, who always wore heels and some oddly bright color. There was David, the Russian major, who knew everything, even more than the Russians.

There was St. Petersburg, looking like somebody blew a cigarette on a nice painting until it sort of melted and turned gray.

There was Hostel Ostrovok, where a Russian I didn't know dropped me off in a car like a tin can. Hostel Ostrovok was leaking things, dripping with disease, lust, and the smell of sweat. It was surrounded by two liquor stores, mud, a dead cat, a stillborn bird, lots of lonely-looking men, abandoned vehicles, chicken wire, and a playground with more crippled dogs than children. All the buildings looked like this one, hundreds stretching for miles.

There was the elevator we took to the thirteenth floor of Hostel Ostrovok. It was the size of a kitchen cabinet. There were usually about five of us in there sharing the same breath of cigarettes and booze.

I was second to arrive after David. He had thinning blond hair and suffered from a degenerative bone disease sure to leave him crippled and blind in ten years. I met the Russians, Alexei and Irina, downtown and hated them both for their sense of better days. I met Carson, heroin-eyed and hungover, in the pee-yellow glare of the hostel's only bathroom. I met Bonnie sitting on the windowsill in my room, the dying green sky her backdrop, smoking with her eyes down.

"My mom forced me to smoke my first cigarette when I was thirteen," she said with a languid movement, as if she had practiced saying this. "I've been chain-smoking ever since." She sat on the bed and stared at me. "I'm leaving tomorrow. I just came to get the visa."

Bonnie, with oddly large blue eyes, came and went silently. Carson and I watched her leave and we respected her for this.

Both Carson and I lied to get in the program, an environmental studies volunteer project better left unnamed. We found it on the internet on a website with photos of women catching fish. It said we could help Russia, and the Russians, and the elk and trees and especially the tundra. Neither of us spoke Russian.

On the third day I moved into Carson's room. I wrapped a sheet around my body and left him naked on the bed. From the hotel balcony, I watched the world unfold thirteen stories down—the red soviet bricks, a babushka stretching, that pack of crippled dogs panting in the playground—and I waited for him, to come to me, to be aware of my movements; the way the sheet formed against my back. When I asked him a question, he nodded and turned his head toward the TV. The blue glare lit half his face, and I stood in the sun with nothing to behold me. That night, before bed, I turned off all the lights in the room. I didn't want him to be an image anymore, just a feeling in the dark.

One morning, when the dogs were sleeping, we went to play on the monkey bars. As the air warmed and the dew dried, the dogs rose like corpses and surrounded us.

Afternoons we took the metro downtown where old ladies sold vegetables, shoes, clothes, guinea pigs, a piece of dried meat. In the corners were puddles of cigarettes, curled beggars, abandoned dogs, groups of amputees wearing camo and singing love songs.

The metro and the Russians became our daily routine: wake up early, go down the elevator, walk a mile over last night's drunks, kick half-full beer cans, poke the dead cat, or check to see if it had been relocated (it had), stop at a kiosk and buy ten-cent beers. At the metro we'd find Irina, waiting. She was always alone in the middle of the metro clutching folders full of information about lead contaminated soil. David loved Irina.

Carson and I always sat next to each other on the metro, letting our eyes bulge in and out of our heads. An old man got robbed next to us and that was the first time Carson held my hand.

When no one else showed up, we took the overnight train north to the Kola Peninsula, above the Arctic Circle. It's home to taiga forests, migrating peoples, man-eating pigs, Santa's house, and men named Orlof. On the map it looks like something being born.

On the train a beer can rolled from one side of the car to the other, shaking with the rhythm of a screaming child, a curtain flapping, a drunk man hitting the wall, the roar of doors opening and closing between cars, everything followed by gasps of silence.

It smelled like everything Russian: a palpable mix of sausage, vodka, and musk. A smell like an untended costume store, a diner, a smoky but quiet tavern, a very old lady.

An overcrowded room of men sang and slurred Russian pop music. One of them raised a hand at me, decorated in gold rings, as if to excuse the behavior.

The food tasted like eating a cigarette. It lingered on your teeth and spread to the pits of the stomach.

I went to the empty sleeping room and tried to fall asleep. I pressed my hand against the wall knowing Carson was on the other side. I knocked and the wall vibrated with a hollow echo. He returned the knock and I traced his imagined silhouette with my hand.

In the morning the windows opened for the smokers. I stuck my head out like a dog, letting the wind dry and water my eyes. We passed swastikas, graffiti that read Fuck America, a dog with three legs, piles of burning things.

I hung out with a Russian guy by the window and we talked, he in Russian and I in English. They never seemed to mind if you didn't know Russian. They just kept on talking and you kept on talking. He handed me a coin. It was some keepsake coin celebrating the first Russian in space. He said America wasn't first. He told me to bring it back and stick it up George Bush's ass. They always knew a little English.

A woman named Sveta, beautiful and red-haired with blue eye shadow, met us at the train station and drove us into the nature reserves with a man named Roman who never talked.

There were no restaurants, no gift shops, no paved roads, no fences, no warning signs. To get in, we needed special permission and a passport. Driving through the entrance we got a salute from a ripe old Russian in an army hat, his eyes saying something else.

It was midnight but still bright as noon. We stayed in a cabin by a river called the Svir, as lifeless as a chlorinated pool. In the place where the waves broke was a halo of glittering vodka bottles and diapers.

Carson and I shared a room that was tiny and dirty and had two single beds. The green curtains cast a morbid hue on our skin. We pushed the two beds together under the window and sat there with our heads down. Irina and David shared a room. Alexei stayed in a room at the farthest end of the hallway.

The park ranger was Igor. The only man who would hire Igor was Vasili, the park manager, whose right arm was missing and whose left thigh was one big scar from the afternoons he spent whittling. Vasili lived in a yellow house with a wife who we only saw through the window on dark nights, sitting on the couch and staring.

Igor carried a knife, three packs of unfiltered cigarettes, an orange lighter, a notebook, a silver flask of absinthe, a walkie-talkie, and a pack of menthol gum. He arrived as a refugee looking for work after he escaped the Chechnyan military. At first I only saw Igor in the distance, appearing and disappearing like a strange fog. He always wore a mesh camo top, camo pants, aviator sunglasses, and a gold chain.

When it rained Carson and I went swimming in the

Svir and everything smelled metallic. Things morphed behind the rain: oil tankers with their loud creaking moans, Carson disappearing and reappearing in the grayness. We would dive underwater and look at each other. Our hair standing on end, our cheeks puffed with air and leaking, our skin looking green, and our bodies swaying. Each time we dove deeper, holding hands, and our skin turned a different shade: green to purple to blue and then just black and two white eyes.

When it was hot, Igor tanned on the beach. He sat in a rainbow foldout chair and watched us. Carson and I talked about how no one we knew or would ever know would come here.

One time we had to help an ecologist catch fish. She lived in a small cabin on the edge of the river. We sat in two small fishing boats that smelled like moss, paddled out into the deepest part of the river, and threw nets into the water. Then we just waited, sat in the sun, and slept. We only caught two fish and then we ate them with salt.

We were there two months and the nights started turning dark in August. We could see the moon late at night. It woke us up. Carson and I would lie together under its light.

Sometimes we would sit in this light and the only sound would be Igor and his pull-up bar and the struggled gasps that accompanied it.

Sometimes Carson and I locked ourselves in the room. We drank warm beer and made serious plans about running away to Moscow or Helsinki or Prague and then immediately forgot them.

Sometimes I tried to make my breathing the same as his breathing so that maybe if he noticed he would think there might be some connection between us.

Sometimes I sat by the window looking at nothing and my fingers found their way into the dust on the sill and I'd start writing his name. When he opened the door, it all blew away in a quick rain of glimmery fly carcasses and blue wings.

At night we met Igor and we drank. I forgot why I was there.

One night when the sky was purple and the mosquitoes were thick, Carson and I went swimming and the water was gritty and pink like chalk. We tried to imagine where on a map the river Svir started and ended. Then we dove underwater, held each other, and let the current take us somewhere else.

We washed up on shore a few minutes later and sat down in the sand. Two rangers named Sasha and Sasha walked by and invited us back to their cabin. Along the way, three more rangers named Roman, Grecia, and Roman joined us. Igor was there pouring Russian Cocktails (vodka mixed with beer). The smoke was so thick that everyone's face seemed to melt and wander around underneath it. They took a shot about every fifteen minutes. They played Rammstein.

We sat down next to Igor and with a thick accent and a voice too high for his looks he whispered, *Russian extreme*, really emphatic and slow-like. He told me about Russian extreme with hand movements and serious eyes and some description about a tiny boat in the sea and a not so tiny tornado. This was followed by long pauses, teary stares, and collapsing arms.

He said he was married four times but it didn't work out. He said once he lived in the woods with just his knife, a picture of someone he loved, and that pack of menthol gum. He told us to be careful, how we should never leave the Svir.

The night continued like this: loud German rock music, smoke thick like butter, a lot of useless talk, everyone camo-clad, chain smoking, and slamming vodka.

The first Sasha was missing teeth and smelled like pond water. A stomach protruded from his body like a tumor. I watched him turn from happy to sad in a moment. He rolled onto the bed. We poured him a beer, took his picture, left him where he passed out—a sad heap of a man.

We wanted to let Sasha sleep so we headed up a blurry trail to another ranger's house. It looked the same, smoke and camo and dark wood and lots of fishing supplies. When we ran out of alcohol we drove to a twenty-four-hour liquor store where I peed behind something I don't remember.

On the way back we stopped at a bridge over the Svir and everything looked black and white, and everyone was smoking. The woods and sky and water took on a strange permanent stillness, the kind of stillness and silence and permanence that makes you feel alive in a sort of strange, sick way. I balanced on the edge of the bridge in the half-light, looked down and wondered what it would be like to jump into that water. The rangers danced and Carson's feet hung out of the back of the car. We drove back to the cabin.

Carson made a bed on the floor, curled slowly into himself. The first Roman leaned against a window, closed his eyes and fell asleep, still smoking. The other Roman was missing. Grecia just stared at the wall. Igor was on the table, his face flat against the wood, one eye gazing up toward the ceiling.

There was no more music, just the odd movement of smoke.

There was me, just sitting there watching all this happen, not really a part of it, not really separate from it, just knowing that this was very fun and disturbing and sad.

There we all were, lying there in the quiet, some of us snoring, some of us sleeping, none of us dreaming.

I got up to leave and walked out onto the trail toward my cabin. Igor followed. He grabbed my arm and stood behind me. He let out a half moan, took off his shirt, and handed it to me. He set it in my hands where it hung slack and cold like a dead animal. I slipped it over my arms and let it fall onto my torso. Igor walked back into the cabin with the other rangers and lay among them.

I went to my room and lay across the bed, a cold sheet hung over one leg. I left my eyes open, glaring brainlessly into the moonlight. My body was loose and felt heavy and nothing was moving except for my hand that scratched at the shirt. I lay there in bed clinging desperately to this world, and thought of Igor in the cabin, hand clasped around a shot, clinging forever to another.

♫ ♫ ♫

Jennifer Percy grew up in the high desert of central Oregon where much of her childhood was spent listening to Garth Brooks and eating T-bone steaks. Her most recent adventure took her to Serbia and Bosnia-Herzegovina where she wrote about the influence of aphorisms on post-war identity. Currently, she is an MFA candidate at the University of Iowa's Nonfiction Writing Program. Her essays have appeared in such magazines as The Atlantic, The Indiana Review, The Literary Review, *and* Brevity, *among others. She has received scholarships from the Bread Loaf Writers' Conference, the Iowa Arts Foundation, the Stanley Foundation, and the University of Iowa Museum of Art.*

ॐ ॐ ॐ

Design a Vagina

She finds something new for the mantelpiece.

One cozy night at home, while enjoying a pizza dinner, I flipped on the television just in time to see a close-up shot of a woman's labia being "trimmed" by a surgeon.

"Look!" I shrieked at my fiancé, involuntarily crossing my legs. "How can they show that on regular TV?!"

David glanced up from his pepperoni, barely raising an eyebrow. "It's educational," he shrugged.

Yes, you could say that the Broadcasting Commission in Ireland is a bit more relaxed than our ol' FCC in the United States. Since I moved to Dublin last August, I am constantly throwing a hand to my mouth à la Goody Proctor, shocked by what the Irish can get away with. Janet Jackson could not only flash her nipple here, she could shave it and cover it in creamed corn, so long as it was educational.

But back to the vagina trimming: the program was called "The Perfect Vagina," and while it put me off my Hawaiian pizza, it was a fascinating look at the latest cosmetic surgery craze—labiaplasty. No longer satisfied with merely having the boobs of a porn star, women now want the whole package. They are paying doctors to "sculpt" their vaginas into what they believe is a more aesthetically pleasing look. In the U.K. alone, the number of labiaplasties has doubled in the past five years, and—never one to miss a trend—the surgery is quickly gaining popularity in the U.S. Girls as young as fourteen are approaching doctors for consultations.

I was grateful when the program shifted to a more inspirational note: a segment on Jamie McCartney, a British artist working on a sculpture he calls "Design a Vagina." Using only volunteers, he is making casts of 200 women's vaginas and displaying them together in forty block panels. He wants to show people that where vaginas are concerned, "the variety of shapes is endlessly fascinating, empowering, and comforting."

Indeed they were. As I stared at his sculpture work, I was astonished. I had no idea there was such a smorgasbord of vulva out there—and I've seen my share of porn. Apparently the porn industry really does adhere to a strict labia code, because I'd never seen such variety. I squinted at the screen, wondering which one most closely resembled my own. And that was when I realized, with a blush of shame, that I had absolutely no idea. And I am thirty-three years old.

Sure, I've done the ol' crouching with a mirror fandango. I have a vague idea of what I look like. But the truth is—and I am more than a little embarrassed to admit this—I'm a bit...shall we say...bashful about my lady parts. I consider myself to be a pretty open, sex-positive person, and yet, for most of life, I've treated my vagina like I would my credit score—I only look when I absolutely have to. As a result, I don't even know myself well enough to pick myself out of a lineup. Men, on the other hand, could probably do a pen and ink drawing of their penises while blindfolded and clutching the pen in their teeth.

The only reason I'm not more embarrassed about being so vagina-shy is because I have plenty of female friends who are the same way. And these aren't creationist child brides with twelve-inch braids swinging down their backs. These are strong, independent, open-minded women who suddenly go Victorian when the topic of vaginal examination comes up. We could be chatting about all sorts of things *related* to vaginas—vibrators, tampons, you name it—but mention the girly garden itself, and out come the painted fans and smelling salts. (Granted, these women are straight. My lesbian friends are on much friendlier terms with the vagina.)

I could sit and *tsk tsk* those women having surgery all I wanted. But I wasn't exactly Eve Ensler when it came to vaginal confidence. Which is when I got to thinking... David and I had been wanting to take a trip to London... Why not pop over, see Big Ben, pose with a charming red phone booth or two, then hop a train to Brighton and participate in "Design a Vagina"?

The next day I Googled the artist. I found his web page and sent a nervous email. Did he still need models? I was half hoping he'd respond with, "Nope. I have all the vaginas I need, thanks." No such luck. He wrote back that afternoon, with a friendly note saying that he did indeed need a few more models. His tone was so mellow and affable. I was expecting something more formal, but he sounded like we were arranging a drop-off for an old

futon. We debated times and settled on the second weekend in January.

Convincing my fiancé was astoundingly easy. I was
prepared for a smallish row over the idea of letting a
stranger pour plaster into my vagina. David has a bit
of a jealous streak, and has more than once gone into a
huff over the length of my skirt. He also is a software
engineer from Northern Ireland, and the nerd factor
combined with old timey Irish-ness can at times be a bit
A Beautiful Mind meets *Cinderella Man*. He is a Russell
Crowe box set, basically.

And yet when I posed the plan to him, he barely
flinched.

"You're sure you're O.K. with it?" I grilled him.
"Because I want to be absolutely sure you're comfortable
with it." I was half-hoping he'd be terribly uncomfortable with it, of course.

"Well it's your body. If you're comfortable with it,
then I guess I am." He shrugged.

Oh dear. How dreadfully supportive and diplomatic.
He must *really really* have wanted to see the London
Eye.

And so, we booked our so-cheap-the-plane-must-be-
powered-on-prayer Ryan Air tickets, found a hotel, and
were set. We would officially be kicking off the new
year with "Design a Vagina."

A couple of days before we left, I booked a full bikini
wax, as the artist said this would yield the best results. I
hunted down Brazilia, a salon in Dublin that promised
"luxury waxing," and made an appointment for "The
Hollywood."

The morning of my wax I decided to do a little pre-
wax pruning. I flipped on the shower radio and, instead
of the usual U2 tribute, some station was inexplicably

playing "Feed the Birds" from *Mary Poppins*. I stood naked with my scissors, thinking of what a fitting nod this was to my London adventure. Although I didn't know if Poppins would approve.

Tuppence…a…baaaag!

I arrived at Brazilia rather nervous. A few weeks earlier I'd gotten an eyebrow wax at a different salon, and my eyes had swelled shut like I'd gotten a pint glass to the face. I was concerned that I was somehow allergic to Irish waxing methods, and envisioned arriving for my vagina sculpture with genitals like a blowfish. But Trish, my friendly Irish waxer, shooed away my concerns. "Nah, the wax was just too hot. You'll be grand."

With my legs hoisted into the air, she set to work with the precision of a sheep shearer. I casually steered the conversation toward labiaplasty. Was she by any chance familiar with the procedure?

"Ah sure. We have girls come in who've had it done. Young girls too. Like in their early twenties. It's too bad really…" she sighed.

I asked if, in her many years of waxing, she'd ever seen a vagina that needed to go under the knife.

"No, no, no! They're all different. But to be honest, in this job, after a while you don't even see vaginas anymore. All you see is hair."

Riiiiip!

Trish finished up, and after she left, I shyly gave myself a once-over in the mirror. My vagina now resembled a sad old man's wistful smile.

The morning we headed to the airport, I was feeling the usual nerves of travel—*Do I have my passport? Is my face wash in a baggie?*—as well as the not-so-usual nerves that come with having your genitals made into an art piece. Once the wheels left the tarmac, my head was buzzing with paranoia. *What are you doing? Your vagina on display? Are you insane? What if this guy is a totally gross pervert? Or what if your vagina has a reaction with the molding material, and you end up in an emergency room in England?* My mind refused to conjure the image of David making that phone call to my mother.

I leaned over to David and confessed my anxiety. As befits a man who grew up in Northern Ireland in the 1980s, he was unimpressed. "What's there to be nervous about?" he scoffed. "He's just going to put goop on your undercarriage, then take it off."

We arrived in London without incident, although we were greeted by the sight of a man in customs with about sixty boxes of condoms in his open suitcase.

"Don't know what he's thinking. The Irish accent will only get you so far with the ladies in London," David observed.

The English accent, however, had us in stitches. I hadn't been to London since I was nineteen, and David had never been. Everyone sounded very Dick Van Dyke-ish to us, and we suppressed laughter every time someone called out, "'ello love!"

We located our hotel and, after a night of fitful sleep, I turned to David. "What if he shows me my sculpture and I scream in terror?"

"What if he shows it to you, and you have a penis?" David whispered back.

We arrived in Brighton a little before noon and summoned a taxi. The grandfatherly driver whisked us past the pastel-hued tattoo parlors and tourist shops, then dropped us off on the oceanfront. The Brighton Pier loomed before us in a haze of ghostly fog, and I could barely make out the amusement park at the end.

Opposite the pier was a string of little studios and art galleries, each located under a decorative archway. The place had a rather hippy, Venice Beach vibe, save for the people sealed into down parkas.

We located Brighton Bodyworks and gazed into the window. A cheerful sign advertised BODY CASTING, and on a ledge beneath the sign sat a rather ghoulish row of sculpted baby fists.

Oh dear.

I turned to David, my eyes wide, but he pushed me inside. The gallery was small, and we were surrounded by neon-colored abstract paintings. We gazed around and spied another sign with the words, BODYCASTING UPSTAIRS. We walked up a creaky spiral staircase and were greeted at the top by the sight of Jamie McCartney busily encasing something in bubble wrap. His head was shaved, and he was wearing jeans and a stylish hoodie.

"Hi. I'm Jo?" I croaked.

"Ah yes! You're here for the sculpting! Great!" He came over and gave me a friendly handshake.

"And this is my fiancé, David," I gestured.

"Ah, yeah, nice to meet you." He turned to David and gave him a smile. "So you're going to let her do this? You're crazy!" he laughed.

David and I exchanged tight grins.

"No, no, just joking. Here, take a seat and fill out the waiver, and I'll be right with you."

His sunny female assistant piped in, "Would you like a cup of tea?"

We declined, and I silently wondered if the English have yet to find an occasion where a cup of tea need not be offered.

Jamie got back to bubblewrapping, and David and I sat on two white cushioned cubes on the floor. On the wall behind us hung full body casts of naked torsos, both male and female. A ginger cat was meowing around the room, trying to wind its away around David's legs. Over in the corner there appeared to be a table made of actual goat legs. I struggled to focus on the waiver in my hand. My eyes immediately darted to a paragraph absolving Jamie of any responsibility should I experience an adverse physical reaction to the molding material. I gulped. Then I spied the line that said, "Sexual arousal may occur."

I stabbed the page with my finger and looked at David, fearful of a full-on *Cinderella Man* meltdown. Amazingly, he was the picture of calm.

Jamie returned. "So! Any questions?"

I mentioned the allergic reaction, and he explained that the molding material is the same stuff that dentists use to make casts. None of his models had experienced any problems, but he had to include that in the waiver for legal reasons. The same thing went for the sexual arousal part.

"This will likely be the most un-erotic experience of your life. As you'll soon see…" He gestured cryptically into the adjacent room, and I spied wires and a white tent constructed from a tarp. It looked like he was caring for an ailing ET.

"But because of the area I'll be working on," he continued, "I have to put that sexual arousal line in there. Really, the whole process only lasts about three minutes."

But um…I had to ask…did *he* ever get aroused? Not that I thought the sight of my vagina was going to drive him into a manic fit of ecstasy, but just out of curiosity… was it difficult, as a straight man, to stay professional?

He sighed and rubbed a hand over the shiny dome of his head. "I've done so many of these, it's really just a part of the body to me at this point. It could be a nose."

Judging by the slightly weary look in his eyes, I believed him.

I then voiced my last concern—anonymity. I was cool with my vagina being one of 200, but would be a little uncomfortable with a flashing neon arrow singling out "Johanna's Bits." Jamie assured me there would be no such arrow, and pointed out that anonymity was important to the power of the piece. It wasn't about whose was whose, after all.

And according to the waiver, mine might not even make the cut. There was no guarantee he would use my sculpture in the finished piece. Apparently, my vulva might not be riveting enough.

Well.

I took the pen and signed my vagina away.

Jamie sat down to chat, and after a few minutes I began to relax. He wasn't creepy at all. In fact, he was quite entertaining, and I began to feel like I was chatting with a fun new acquaintance at a house party—at a very oddly decorated house.

He told us about some of the people he'd sculpted so far: young women, post-pregnancy women, a post-op male to female transsexual, a sixty-five-year-old woman. He wanted to break the sixty-five-year-old barrier, but so far, he hadn't convinced anyone older to volunteer. He also was hoping to sculpt a woman who had undergone female circumcision, as he was really gunning to get as much variety as possible. He had already sculpted a woman pre-labiaplasty, and she was going to return for another sculpture after the surgery.

"I asked her after the cast was made, 'Are you sure you still want to go through with the surgery?' And she said, 'Oh yeah, definitely.'" Jamie shook his head. He blamed a lot of the cosmetic surgery craze on porn. "Women are more exposed to porn now. It's like in the '70s, when men would see porn and everyone had a twelve-inch penis, and they would think that's the norm. Now women see porn, and are critical of themselves."

Out of curiosity, I asked him how much it would cost to have a separate sculpture made to take home with me. You know, since I was a volunteer and all. He quoted me a heavily discounted rate: fifty pounds. We agreed that he'd make two casts. One for him and one for me.

"Of course," he said, "it won't be ready today. But I can put it in the mail."

I liked this idea very much, as I would be spared any potential awkwardness at Gatwick security.

And then the moment was upon us. David and I stood and followed Jamie into the room with the dying ET tent. We were now actually outside, standing on a huge veranda overlooking the ocean. It was brisk, to say the least. Sculptures were scattered around the room—there were a naked man and woman on the floor, and a voluptuous pair of breasts jutted from a wall. We eased our way around the bodies, and my heart began to rumba. Jamie ushered us into the tent. Inside was a single heat lamp and a workman's table. Lining one wall were rows of metal shelves filled with various body parts: halves of faces, more baby fists, a smattering of vaginas. It was all very Frankenstein's workshop. David tried to bumble his way into a corner and hit his head on a jutting penis.

"Oh yeah. I turned that one into a magnet," Jamie apologized.

He said he'd give us a moment to "get ready" and then left to fetch the molding materials.

Now or never. I yanked off my jeans, leaving on my socks and turtleneck sweater, and hopped up onto the table. I looked at David. He stood shivering in a corner of noses and labia, and I immediately got the giggles. I seemed to be experiencing a sort of pre-piercing/pre-tattoo adrenaline rush. Not that I had ever gotten either.

Jamie burst back into the tent. He was carrying a couple of buckets, and he accidentally slopped water all over the floor, causing David to bump into the heat lamp. Their Larry and Moe routine wasn't doing much for my nerves, and my heartbeat switched to flamenco. Jamie got to work mixing the materials, chatting away. He explained that it was a two-part process. First he'd make a cast out of the algaenate—the dental stuff. And then, using that as a mold, he'd make the actual sculpture.

The algaenate mixture turned out to be bright blue, and as he walked over to the foot of the table, I lay back, closed my eyes, and assumed the position: I spread 'em.

And despite the strangeness of it all—despite the fact that a man in rubber gloves was applying cold blue goop to my vagina while my fiancé looked on, despite the fact that it was freezing cold, and outside the tent I could hear children playing on the boardwalk, and somewhere in the distance, there was a chain saw—my case of nerves seemed to ease, and I suddenly felt strangely...comfortable. I mean, I wasn't ready to kick back with some chamomile and *The Story of Edgar Sawtelle*, but I also didn't feel that scandalous. It really wasn't much different from going to the gynecologist or getting a bikini wax. True, Jamie had no medical or cosmetology license, but he was an *artiste*. And there had certainly been people who were none of the above whom I had allowed to see my glory. And while the cold goop wasn't what I'd describe as pleasurable, it was a walk in the park when compared to hot wax or a speculum.

Once Jamie slathered the goop on, he had to let it set, so I had to lie still. The tent fell quiet. *Ho Hum. How about those Mets?*

Suddenly, the ginger cat slinked into the tent. She eyed our activities warily, then made a hasty move to jump onto my stomach.

"NO NO NO!" we all cried at once, and David and Jamie both lunged for her. Jamie managed to grab her and shooed her out of the room. Whew. Relief. I tried to block out images of starring in one of those wacky AP headlines. *Did you see the one about the woman who got a live cat stuck to her vagina?*

"O.K., here we go," Jamie said. And I was shocked that it was over so quickly. It really did only take about three minutes. He began to peel the cast away. The sensation was akin to taking off a pair of bikini bottoms after a belly flop.

"There you go." He held my Smurf-blue vagina up for me to see.

Well! There I was. I was for some reason rather surprised. What was I expecting? Fins? It just looked so, well...small. And it was more symmetrical than I'd imagined. It was beyond strange, but also incredibly cool to see it in this three-dimensional way. It felt like I was finally meeting a beloved pen pal that I'd known intimately for years. And now at last, here we were, face to face.

Jamie put the cast on a counter to dry, and immediately set to work making the second one, which would be mine to keep. This one was made even faster, and without feline interruption. He placed it on the counter next to the first.

"All right, then. I'll let you get dressed. Take your time." He headed back inside.

I hauled myself off the table and was very happy to slip back into the warmth of my jeans. I pulled on my sneakers and joined David by the counter. He was peering down at my twin blue vaginas lying side by side. I could only imagine what was running through his head. No doubt, he was wishing he had long ago settled down in the Irish countryside, with a shy Siobhan or a blushing Nuala.

He looked up at me, eyebrows raised. "You can't give me a hard time about anything for at least a month." He smiled.

On the train back to London, David sprawled across from me, quietly killing aliens on his iPod Touch. I was still feeling a slight adrenaline rush, and my brain was buzzing as I tried to process what had just happened. Was it worth it? Yes. Absolutely yes. If that sculpture kept even one woman from going under the knife, then my six minutes under the goop was beyond worth it. I was suddenly overcome with gratitude. By God, I owed my vagina an apology. My body was amazing and beautiful. And so was the body of the woman sitting behind me. And the woman pushing the coffee trolley down the aisle. I wanted to stand and shout for every woman on the train to go and get their vaginas molded at once!

I turned to David. "Maybe we could will my sculpture down like an heirloom?"

He stared at me in horror. "Are you mad? Can you imagine being given your great-grandmother's vagina?" he shuddered.

I assured him I was only kidding. No, the sculpture would be a private art piece. I'd likely wrap it up in a pretty scarf and tuck it into the deepest recesses of my closet. It would serve as a unique memento of this place and time. A reminder of my body at age thirty-three, of my wonderful fiancé's infinite patience, and of the time I was given a full introduction to a place that had always held such mystery.

If I ever wanted to, I could take it down off the shelf, unwrap it from its little shroud, and give it a friendly pat.

"'ello love!"

♪ ♪ ♪

Johanna Gohmann has written essays, articles, and reviews for Bust, Elle, Red, The Irish Independent, *Babble.com, YourTango.com,* Publishers Weekly, *and other publications. Her essay "The Vagina Dialogues" was selected for Best Sex Writing 2010. A native of Indiana, she resides in Dublin, Ireland.*

❦ ❦ ❦

Bosnian Blues

After a breakup, a woman seeks answers
in her lover's homeland.

My friends are concerned.

"Why are you going to Yugoslavia?" they want to know.

"There is no Yugoslavia." I reply. Like the pop star, Prince, who for a time changed his name to an unutterable symbol, the word *Yugoslavia* can now only be invoked when preceded by the phrase *formerly known as*.

"Why are you going to *former* Yugoslavia?"

Does one need a reason? The travel ads on CNN rave about the "sights and sounds of Serbia." Go to Croatia, they promise, and you'll "discover the Mediterranean as it once was." Isn't that enough?

"I'm going because I can no longer stand not going."

They fear that I will indulge in unnecessary *dwelling*.

I don't tell them that visiting former Yugoslavia is actually an act of revenge.

I always called you "the Bosnian," even after it became clear that "the Serbian" would have been more accurate. And though you complained, I think you liked it. There was pride amidst all the confusion. You were from a war-torn land and I knew nothing about it.

"We'll go there together," you said. "We'll rent a car and head west from Belgrade. You'll see what I love to see when Vlasenica appears around a bend in the road. You'll see how beautiful my country is." I vowed silently that I would go. But I knew even then that you would not be with me.

You had already been to my home, unannounced and uninvited. I was in Las Vegas, the city where we began. After a long last night talking about our villages and our dreams and our regrets, you finally left. (You were always coming and going, and somehow, most of the time, it felt like you were already gone.) A few weeks later you left a message on my phone: "Hey, how are you? I'm in Three Rivers. It's beautiful. The Sequoia trees are beautiful. I've talked to some people who know you. I'm calling from the pay phone by the Village Market..." The Village Market? My Village Market? Where I used to beg my mom to add a candy to the cart? I felt invaded—thoroughly and lusciously invaded.

In Dubrovnik I sip wine, swim in the ocean, and walk on the walls surrounding the city. Though under UNESCO protection, Dubrovnik was hit hard in the war. Over two-thirds of the buildings in the old town were shelled by the Serbian and Montenegrin remnants of the Yugoslav People's Army.

But you'd never know it now. She has a brand new face, built to look old, the result of rigorous plastic surgery using traditional techniques and materials. Dubrovnik's white limestone buildings and tiled roofs are beautiful all over again. A local looks left and right before drawing circles on my map of the city. These are the spots that haven't been made over; these are the places to peek at bombed-out buildings. Surely this is not why I've come? To rubberneck at other people's ruins?

In any case, the most lasting scars of war are borne not by buildings but by people. I see a hint of it each time I ask a question. They flinch and hesitate, then give staccato answers impeded not by any difficulty speaking English but from an inability to speak of the past. Or else they are so eager to talk that the words rush out in a torrent, colliding and contradicting as they fill the space around me, a foreign girl who has only read books.

On the island of Korcula I meet Ivo and Dora, a couple of well-educated and outspoken hippy types from Zagreb sporting half-shaved, half-dreaded hair-dos. They lament the European Union's refusal of admission to their club: "Croatia is very Western; the Balkans start at Bosnia." They attempt to translate jokes about the Herzegovinians, the hicks of former Yugoslavia, before moving on to the pretentious Slovenians: "They think they are better than the rest of us, they think they are Austrians." When I point out that there are similar implications in the remark that "the Balkans start at Bosnia," Ivo smiles and blushes. "It's true that we are part of the Balkans, I don't want to deny that."

They ask why I've come to their country. "I've been reading a lot about former Yugoslavia..." I finally offer, and they read the love-story-gone-wrong on my face.

"So," Dora asks, "does this meet your expectations?"

I admit that Dubrovnik and the surrounding area feel a bit like...Italy.

They laugh, "You see? The Balkans start at Bosnia!"
So I go east.

*In Amsterdam you stayed for a week in my canal-side
basement room and I pretended that you were mine.*

*"Hey, wake up, you're dreaming," you cooed, curling me
into your ripe mass—an amoeba gently enveloping a smaller
organism. "Were you dreaming of Bosnia?"*

"You know I've never been to Bosnia."

*I'd been there only in books. For months, when you
were gone, I burrowed through everything I could find in
translation—painfully tangled histories, classic Yugoslavian
literature from before the wars of the late twentieth century, and contemporary novels written by ex-Yugoslavs
with names that ended in C... Ugresic, Drakulic, Jergovic,
Arsenijevic...*

*Sometimes, I'm sure you remember, you'd take a book
from a pile and "read" to me in your language.*

*You read to me when I was pulling away, in the moments
when I sensed the danger and admitted that you would never
love me. Incomprehensible bedtime stories delivered in a
language more soft and dark and beautiful than any other
rolled me back to your side.*

My passport is forever at the ready on the bus ride
from Dubrovnik to Mostar. We wind our way inanely
back and forth across national borders that didn't exist
fifteen years ago—Croatia to Bosnia, back to Croatia,
then Bosnia again.

I eat at a restaurant on the western riverbank. I order
everything, enough for four people. I want to sample
it all. *Civapcici* with creamy *kajmak* ("not for diet!" Ivo
had written as a footnote in my journal while making

culinary recommendations); a spinach pie called *zel-janica*; filo pastry *burek* filled with cheese; pickled vegetables; Bosnia's version of baklava as well as *herma-sice*, a dense little cake soaked in syrup and nuts; thick Bosnian coffee.

I have drinks with Frasier, an American boy spending the weekend away from his new home in Dubrovnik where he sells smoothies and wraps at a backpacker's bar. He is in love with a Croatian girl. *Naturally.*

"Do you speak any of the language?" he asks.

I have two phrases: *Volim te* and *Havala.* Sometimes I grab the wrong one and tell the man who pours my beer, "I love you."

Frasier tells me about the Northern wind: "They say it is invigorating and healthy. But the Southern wind, called the Yugo, brings the sand from the desert and...bad things."

I laugh and lament that he is getting mystical on me.

"No, really! If an important governmental meeting is scheduled to take place but the Yugo begins to blow—"

"They postpone?"

"They really do. They postpone."

"Well then, I think I need a great big Northern wind."

"It was just here," he gushes, "two days ago, the big storm..."

"I was in Korcula."

"That was your Northern wind."

On my way back to the room I've rented, I realize that I'm drunk and lost. I walk down barely lit back alleys, pass once and then a second time the same men drinking beers and boys playing a nighttime game of street soccer. They watch me closely but they do not speak. I consider pulling out a phrase from my book, "*Eez-goo-bee-la sam se,*" but why? They can see that I am lost.

We spent a day walking in Brussels. You took me to a restaurant you'd seen before and wanted to try.

"Yugoslavian Specialties" it had once read on the door, but we could see that someone had tried to remove the word "Yugoslavian," presumably around the time that the country ceased to exist. Now it just said "Specialties." I was surprised to hear you speak French to the two men inside sharing a bottle of slivovica at the counter. Yes, we were in Brussels, but these were your people, right?

Later, as we ambled through the streets of the Marolles District, you launched into a fairly bitter tirade on the impossibility of speaking your native language in a Yugoslavian restaurant outside of former Yugoslavia. "I cannot ask, 'do you speak Yugoslavian?' because there is no such language. If I ask, 'do you speak Serbian?' I will offend a Croatian or a Muslim. If I ask, 'do you speak Croatian?' I will offend a Serb or a Muslim. If I ask, 'do you speak Serbo-Croatian?' I will appear too cautious, almost paranoid."

I might have pointed out that cautious (and paranoid) didn't seem too far off the mark. I might have mentioned, conversationally, that the officials at the Hague Tribunal trying war criminals from former Yugoslavia use the term BSC (Bosnian, Serbian, Croatian), or that Slavenka Drakulic has written that, "like refugees scattered across the continents, they usually do not specify; they call it 'our language' or nothing at all." But I said nothing. We will simply eat specialties that dare not speak their name.

We lay down in the sun on our coats. You slept, thoroughly but briefly—four minutes tops. It was enough. I cried just a little as you snored.

At an Irish pub, I both adored and detested the way you could seamlessly rave about the plight of your people, like a full-grown man, and then, when the waitress brought a fresh round of Guinness, lick the foam from your fingers like a little boy.

You told me about your father's adamant belief in what most of us would deem conspiracy theories. The Freemasons are ruling the world and sabotaging the Serbian agenda.

"It's so sad. He needs to believe in something to make sense of it all, the way that people believe in God when nothing else works."

I asked what answers you personally had come up with for the Yugoslavian question. You silenced me with the assertion that there is no "Yugoslavian question."

"But you have to speak French in a Yugoslavian restaurant..." I pushed.

You agreed that perhaps there were still some small difficulties with classification.

The girl tugs on my arm and points above my head. Grapes. I had not noticed them. I've been walking along a partially covered street through Kujundziluc, the old town of Mostar, and can see now that fat green grapes are dripping from the rickety rafters. She displays her palm for payment. I give her a one mark coin and instantly another girl appears at my side. I show the newcomer how to use my disposable camera. She takes my picture and I hand her a coin. A third appears. I give her a coin, too, and try to walk away but she follows. "I already gave to you," I laugh and try to reason. But she doesn't want more money, she wants to take my picture. I leave them then, but hours later in another part of town, the three girls find me again and silently follow my steps.

I take a picture of a billboard advertising Prima beer. A sleek, Slavic Barbie in a red bikini seduces me. Behind the billboard sits a building gutted and pockmarked by war, and, further still in the background, the baby-blue minaret of a mosque built hundreds of years ago.

The "new" Orthodox church was reduced to a pile of rubble in '93. Behind the rubble the "old" Orthodox church still stands.

"Is there a Serbian part of town?" I ask a man selling books.

"No Serbs here," he responds, looking alarmed.

"But there is an Orthodox church, there must have been Serbs living here at one time…"

"Not now," he insists.

I wanted you to explain things that I could never understand.

Lying in bed, your arm pressed against my stomach, I babbled about how my sister and I used to heat water on the stove for each other when the bath ran cold in our childhood house, as it often did. "Yeah, we used to do that during the war…" you replied, and made me feel foolish.

When you were a kid you collected empty cigarette packs. You and your best friend were in heated competition for the best collection in the neighborhood. The night before your family left in secret for Canada, you were allowed to say good-bye to this one friend. You gave him your precious cigarette packs.

"So your friend then had the very best collection in the neighborhood?" I asked.

"Yeah, I guess. I don't think about those times a lot. But yeah, with mine incorporated, he must have had the very best collection."

Later there were less palatable pillow revelations.

"She's my rock."

You would never have finished school without her. You admired her stability. You were a freewheeling far-flying gypsy and she chased away the nightmares of solitude and entropy that such a life naturally inspires.

But is it fair, I wondered, to make a person an anchor?

I snap a picture of Stari Most, the famous bridge, that almost perfectly matches the cover on my copy of Rebecca West's massive travel memoir *Black Lamb and Grey Falcon.* A local guidebook from the humble tourist kiosk informs me that Stari Most was painstakingly rebuilt after "evil forces" blew her up in 1993.

Evil forces? While in Croatia I had asked Ivo about the bridge. He cut me off before I could complete my cautious question—"Yes, yes, we blew up the bridge. It was a mistake. But let me tell you what *they* did to *us...*"

Years ago the Neretva River had marked an important boundary—Catholics to the west, Muslims to the east. Now all Bosnians are essentially free to walk where they wish. Tanned young things dive off Stari Most to the applause and tips of tourists. For most of the evening I watch them plummet to the river below, contribute my spare change (the euro, the Croatian kuna, and the Bosnian mark are all welcome), and decline the opportunity to have a drink afterward. I've had enough of Bosnian men.

But my Bosnian is not really Bosnian, is he?

You were difficult from the moment we met.

"Where are you from?" I asked, thinking it a harmless question that would initiate conversation in an uncomplicated way.

"Bosnia."

"Ah, you're Bosnian," I sighed.

"I am from an area of former Yugoslavia that, since the breakup of that nation, is now part of modern Bosnia and Herzegovina."

"O.K. Got it. Bosnian."

"Well...actually, I'm not Muslim. I'm Orthodox Christian."

"So you're religious. You believe in God, go to church, and all that?"

"No. I'm not religious. But my family is Orthodox Christian. My background is Orthodox Christian."

"So your family is religious..."

"What I'm trying to say is that I guess I'm Serbian."

You guess?

You don't like the way you imagine the world perceives the word "Serbian."

On my last night in Mostar, my hosts invite me to dinner in their candle-lit yard off the alley. The gathering looks warm and the food smells great, but I decline. I spend the night alone in my room with my notebook, surrounded by cans of cheap Bosnian beer and a half-empty bottle of slivovica. Yes, half-empty and not half-full. I spend the night alone in my room aching and scrawling.

Djordje, Djordje of the gypsy jungle.

Djordje, my 6' 5" hulk of a Balkan boy.

Djordje of the painfully perfect white teeth and nappy hair.

Djordje of the giant man-paws that didn't look the least bit capable of all they were capable of doing to the female body. Djordje of the nails perpetually encrusted with dirt from the work that he enjoyed and his father hated. (His father wanted him to work at a bank or something similarly respectable and lucrative, something that fulfilled the family's "Canadian dream," and that made the most of the fact that they were no longer in some part of former Yugoslavia that is now part of modern-day Bosnia and Herzegovina.)

I'm having trouble seeing the present. I'm finally here in the Bosnia that has always been for me a setting in books, and, like a zombie, I'm missing most of it. Everything takes me back to the past, *our past.*

But perhaps it's not so inappropriate. These tiny new countries have labored feverishly to rebuild and to rewrite their stories. *Yugoslavia was an artificial construct; finally we are free to be as we were always meant to be, separate and independent; what we did in the war was not as bad as what they did to us; what happened before is finished....* But no one has really forgotten. Everyone here walks with one foot tied to the past.

Cross-legged on the bed in my little rented room in Mostar, I realize that my trip is finished. There is no need to travel further, to Sarajevo or Belgrade. I will not go to Vlasenica. I will not make a call from a pay phone outside the market where Djordje used to beg his mom to add a candy to the cart. There will be no revenge. I see now that I have come to let go.

You wooed me in Spanish and French and the language that dare not speak its name, a language more soft and dark and beautiful than any other. (How did you know that I was Wanda, grinding against the banister while John Cleese's character danced below, spouting Russian, with underwear on his face?) Yet you never said, in any language, the words I most wanted to hear... Te amo, Je t'aime, Volim te. *These words were reserved for the one with whom you felt more easy, the girlfriend back in Montreal you had always referred to as your ex.*

I had merely denied the obvious and wrapped myself in the belief that if I could understand what happened in former Yugoslavia, then I could understand my Bosnian. If I could touch that part of you, then I would have all of you. It was ludicrous—a deluded hope dragged halfway around the world. Even had the premise been sound, it would not have worked. All my effort to understand what happened in former Yugoslavia only led to a state resembling something along the lines of "enlightened confusion."

I did not understand, but neither did you. You found it impossible to be Serbian; you found it impossible to be with me. You couldn't see the forest, for the trees were blown to bits by a war that had nothing and everything to do with you. What do you do with nostalgia for a country that no longer exists? The same thing, perhaps, you do with love left over when the relationship is finished—consign it to the warehouse of ache.

❧ ❧ ❧

After receiving a master's degree in English, Landon Spencer ran away from academia to join the circus. She's been touring the Western world with an acrobatic and equestrian show for the past four years. When she's not riding, she's writing.

ɾ϶ ɾ϶ ɾ϶

Grinding Saffron

Fresh herbs transport the author
to a sacred Persian kitchen.

I started chopping herbs when I was five. All the women of my family—plus my grandfather—gathered in my grandmother's small kitchen in Tehran, each with a task that contributed to the upcoming lunch feast. Jaffar, the young man my grandmother had hired to help with shopping and household tasks, would go to the market early in the morning and return with a basket full of fresh herbs bundled in newspaper. I was tasked with unwrapping the parsley, tarragon, dill, and mint, and searching the bundles carefully to remove the foolish snail or two who had clung to the harvested herbs. I would then rinse and sort the greens and set up my space between two of my great-aunts. One governed the sink with her tall, broad shoulders; the other towered near the stovetop, tending the rice, her pretty breasts poking

65

into the emerging steam, making it wrap in swirls like a car on a mountain road. Once the rice was boiling, she would lower the heat, drop in pats of butter, and wrap a cotton kitchen cloth around the lid before sealing the pot, so that excess water would be absorbed into the cloth, not back onto the rice. The heady jasmine-like rice scent filled every recess of the kitchen. It became my great-aunts' perfume, a scent released from their clothing in hugs given hours later.

Iranian cooking requires titanic quantities of herbs. I would often chop three to five cups of herbs for use in stews, sauces, rice, and meat dishes. After the herb chopping, I became the guardian of the saffron. A precious spice, I had to grind it as fine as possible in the brass mortar and pestle. No matter how fine I ground it—it felt like splitting atoms—one of my great-aunts, the Sink Governess, would inform me that I needed to take it to an even finer point. She would then lecture me on how much more mileage of color, flavor, and fragrance I could get out of these gold market-priced crocus flower stigmas. She was the more frugal of the aunts, always worrying about money, and her eye never left my mortar and pestle. I would take a few strands of Iranian saffron, a much more potent form than the Spanish variety, and place them in the mortar with a sugar cube. Added friction helped grind the stigmas even more finely. Herbs are chopped early in the game, then added to a lamb stew for their bright and complex flavors. Saffron is a latecomer, added at the end to color a dish as much for that unique nasturtium-nectar-and-mud taste as for visual drama.

For some reason, I loved chopping herbs—the knife and board's rhythms, the green fragrance emitted from the cuts—but I hated grinding saffron. No matter how long and hard I ground, it was never fine enough for the Sink Governess. I felt as if my arms were going to fall off. My mind wandered. There was no trance state as with the herbs; it was just hard work. I would also grow hungry, ready for us to gather around the big table in the next room and listen to my uncles and grandfather talk about men's topics: mystical poetry, music, politics, how to repair a pipe.

My grandfather was a great lover of gadgets—he was often in his basement workshop inventing wondrous, Dr. Seuss-like gizmos. In his happiest times, he was working on an idea that would use the quiet energy locked in gravity to run an engine. He was fully enamored with the idea of an oil- and gas-free world and his idea was partially prototyped in metal and Plexiglas in his basement workshop. He often let me join him there, giving me my own tools and materials and letting me invent alongside him.

Beyond his Tehran basement workshop, the kitchen was his favorite room to accessorize. He especially liked the juicer, with which he would make his daily health tonic of carrot or apple juice. My prized tool was comparatively low-tech: my grandmother's chopping knife. My grandfather carefully picked it out in a kitchen supply store in Tehran, where we had walked hand in hand, chattering along the way. We picked out a large carbon steel butcher's knife. It could reduce the chopping effort by 40 percent, he explained, if applied to herbs instead of meat. Its handle and wide blade made it an ergonomic dreamscape.

Back in my grandmother's kitchen, I took that shiny new butcher's knife and the large, worn, green-stained wooden chopping block, and forged a space between my great-aunts. Standing on a stool, I chopped and chopped until I was part of their world, a child privy to the banter of strong women.

My deepest adoration went to my oldest great-aunt, Khanoum. She was the rice-maker and the most independent and outspoken one. The other great-aunts seemed to argue with each other as much as they laughed together, and competed in couture as often as they helped each other pick complementary colors. Not Khanoum: she dressed beautifully but didn't make it a topic of conversation, preferring to discuss mystical poetry, music, politics, how to repair a pipe. She was independent, forthright, courageous, and opinionated in ways Iranian women were not. She had become a dentist—perhaps Iran's first woman dentist—and later a teacher fiercely dedicated to improving the lives and opportunities of her students. Though married twice, she had no children. When I knew her, she was retired, enjoying her books of mystical poetry and her garden. She owned her own house and lived there alone, though her home was never empty. She always had one or two young people around whom she had adopted and to whose education she tended. She liked to teach anyone of any age how to read, and held weekly literary classes at her house for the neighbors. Her home was largely an outdoor garden surrounding a cozy and functional abode. Pathways meandered among rose bushes, towering trees, fragrant herbs and mulberries. In the center, her private garden nook, she could be found in a cotton housedress, relaxing on a reclining chair, reading the newspaper or a book of poems, her reading glasses far down on her squarish, shapely nose. A strong, dark glass of tea would be perched next to her on a small table.

𝒮𝒯𝒢 𝒮𝒯𝒢 𝒮𝒯𝒢

My memories of Iran last only as long as childhood.
I was born in Boulder, Colorado, to parents who had
immigrated to the United States in the late fifties. Their
Iran was a cheerful turquoise-colored nation, a place at
peace with the rest of the world. Their immigration was
one of choice, for adventure and possibility.

I visited Iran several times on summer vacation before
the 1979 revolution. I cherished the two idyllic worlds
in which I existed: the warm, tender world Iranians
gave their children, and the hippie, open-minded world
Boulderites created for themselves. After 1979, one
of those worlds was no longer available. The scent of
cooking rice could send me into apoplexy; the crisp,
verdant edge of chopped herbs, into a deep longing for
two strong shoulders to flank me and tell me the world
was not so cruel. From my birth city's utopian perch, a
self-consciously created city of liberals, in time I came
to formulate my own ideals, often in the form of older
family members I would never see again. Khanoum
topped that list. She was my icon. On the verge of my
own independent life, I held her fast in my mind as the
sort of archetypal woman I wanted to become: rather
than a slave to fashion, a student of the soul; rather than
an unquestioning member of society, a discerning prac-
titioner of compassion and free will.

Countless relatives and friends visited during those
leisurely lunches in Iran. As they gathered around the
long table in the neighboring room, my grandmother
would take the rice from Khanoum and arrange the
fluffy, free-falling, butter-coated grains onto a large oval
serving platter. At the bottom of the pot a crisp crust had

developed from the slow, patient heat. My grandmother
would arrange pieces of this crust around the edges of
the platter. As the finale, the Saffron Hawk would take
my hard-ground effort and dissolve it into a glass of hot
water, mixing the liquid amber with a cup of cooked
rice. She would then splash the yellowed rice across the
top of the rice mound in the platter, creating an edible
van Gogh.

Khanoum would carry the rice to the table and join
the guests. Behind her, a procession: my grandmother
with an herb lamb stew further enhanced with kidney
beans and turmeric; my Saffron Aunt with a yoghurt,
cucumber, and dill salad; my mother with the plates; and
my brother with his favorite contribution to the meal:
the freshly baked flat bread from the bakery down the
street. Invariably, a corner would be torn off. He, like
me, could not resist sampling the fragrant warm bread
as it came out of the baker's oven. If you didn't tear a
taste, the one block walk home was torment.

All those people around that table made a child feel
totally enveloped in a warm wrap of affection and
encouragement. Maybe it's a blessing that all I know
of Iran is my childhood experience. If I had become an
adult in that context, a lot would have been expected of
me, a lot that I would have needed to fight in order to
lead the life I wanted. My role model would have been
gone by the time I reached womanhood: Khanoum
died shortly after the Iranian revolution, of old age, in
her home. She was surrounded by neighbors who loved
her and who would not let her die alone. She had many
children even though she had never borne one from her
own flesh. She remains a role model for me. Childless
like her, I know my actions, not my flesh, will determine
whether I live and die alone or with people.

To this day, nearly four decades later, when I take out my own chopping board and a very similar knife—one my mother gave me for herbs—and place my cleaned and rinsed herbs on the wood, images of my Tehran family rush to my side and I never feel alone. My kitchen is as small as my grandmother's was, and I like to think that I can feel the warmth of their bodies and their humor. I long for them to join me and tell me things about themselves and the family that I didn't have the wit to ask as a child. Between the swishing of the blade through the tender green leaves, I think I hear them whisper the answers.

I also don't mind grinding saffron these days. Even the unrelenting, frugal voice, *No, it's not fine enough, keep grinding*, is now a welcome reprimand. I'll turn the pestle, round and round, until the thump and rhythm brings back their voices. Sometimes, I can even conjure the feel of two strong bodies flanking me on either side, making me feel we never lose our connections with each other, even when time and space morph us into different energy and matter.

Some Sundays, after a full week, you can find me wearing a simple cotton housedress in the quiet part of my home that I've designated a sanctuary space, like Khanoum's peaceful garden nook. My eyeglasses will be riding down my nose as I read a favorite book. And yes, a strong cup of well-brewed black tea—Darjeeling to be precise—will sit upon my table, sending its steam up to the heavens.

෴ ෴ ෴

Beebe Bahrami (www.beebesfeast.com) is a writer and anthropologist. Her work appears in many publications, including Michelin

Green Guides, Transitions Abroad, Perceptive Travel, *National Geographic books,* The Pennsylvania Gazette, *and in* Bark *and* Archaeology *magazines. Her book,* The Spiritual Traveler Spain: The Guide to Sacred Sites and Pilgrim Routes, *reflects her specialty in writing on the western Mediterranean world of Spain, France, Portugal, and Morocco. This was the realm she discovered after the Iranian revolution in 1979 closed off visits to relatives there. Born in a progressive town in Colorado to parents who immigrated and have remained there since the 1960s, Beebe long ago discovered in Spain a place like herself, one that was a thorough blending of influences from both the East and the West.*

᪥ ᪥ ᪥

Woman in the Wild

On a camping trip, she discovers her own true north.

"Can I go with you?" I blurt out across the scratched bar top, interrupting Eric as he tells me about his bees.

With his long brown hair smoothed into a thick ponytail and secured with a piece of string, Eric is attractive, but what makes him even more so is that he brews his own beer and raises bees for honey. We met in biology class but have never formally hung out, maybe because there's something equally odd about him; something I can't quite place. Eric is a loner, and seems to prefer it that way. Still, he's leaving for the East Coast in two days and I want to go with him.

I yell louder over the din of rowdy college students: "I'm a good travel companion and promise I won't talk much!"

He quietly sips his beer, contemplating my proposition. By now I'm visually consumed by images of the crashing Atlantic at sunset, lighthouses, large Victorian homes, doilies, silver teacups, and Castle Rock—the fictitious town depicted in many of Stephen King's novels.

"I guess," he says. We sit silently for a moment. "But I'll be doing some backpacking," he adds. "Is that cool with you?"

"Oh sure, that would be great," I lie. I've never backpacked a day in my life. But maybe, besides Eric's long lean arms and dark grin, that is part of the draw.

For the next two days I wonder what kind of relationship might develop between us. He's asked me out a few times in the last year for a beer or to study, but nothing came to fruition and I never equated his asking with anything special.

"Are you bringing your own tent?" my friend Kate asks. "Or will you just snuggle up in his? What if he expects 'payment' for the ride back?" She laughs at her cleverness.

"Ah, he's not like that," I say, as if I actually know. Even if he were like that, I'd still go. *I need this.*

"Besides," I add, "I've made out with a lot worse."

Any attraction I have to this humble mountain man dissipates by the time we hit third gear. When Eric said he doesn't talk much, he should've clarified that he doesn't talk *at all*. And without a working radio in his 1989 Malibu, we have an awkward—and silent—3,300 miles ahead. At first, the silence frightens me. I look over at Eric frequently and he just seems so at peace—so *far away*—while I'm fumbling with my overactive imagination through countless fallow fields. How can I get to where he is?

After poking around Bar Harbor, Maine, for a day, we hop on board the Cat, a monstrous catamaran with a belly big enough for 250 cars. It tops out at 55 mph and sets off a fifty-foot rooster tail. We careen across the ocean to the thick accented hillsides of Nova Scotia. Our destination is Kejimakujik National Park, where we will backpack along an eighty-kilometer loop that equates to roughly sixty-five miles. That's sixty-five miles more backpacking than I've ever done in my life.

"You are in 'bear country' now," the attendant at the visitor center warns, eyebrows raised. Growing up in Wisconsin, I never had to worry about bears unless they escaped from the zoo. Anxiety balls in my belly. Suddenly I am worried about whether or not I'll be able to walk even five miles, overcome my childhood fear of the dark, deal with continued silence from my partner and, most of all, avoid being eaten.

Eric loses the rest of his charm when he announces that he'd rather backpack alone. "Nothing personal," he says. "It's the way I've always done things."

He points to a smudge of green on our trail map, eight miles away. "This is where we *should* end up tonight."

At first, I love my surroundings. Though we've only been in the country for a day, Nova Scotia already seems so *simple*. Last night, I was stunned by the darkness enveloping us. Every light and every store seemed to blink out right along with the setting sun. Gone, gladly, was the twenty-four-hour convenience I'd grown accustomed to. Even the houses were simple, not huge and overpowering. Everything seemed to have a purpose, a reason for being.

As I walk along the trail, I try to revel in the beauty of everything. The trail's undergrowth is a lush green, sensuous and ripe with smells. I am fully enjoying myself—until my back begins to twinge. I work at REI, an outdoor gear store—in the shoe department; they won't let me near the camping section—and so was able to rent my gear for free. What I failed to learn, however, was how to fit it properly. All fifty pounds of my backpack are now hanging off my shoulders.

After a mile of torture, my throat tightens. *I hate this!*

Then the sounds begin. The deep rustles and barely audible grunts. The bushes move just long enough for me to look in that direction before a sound erupts elsewhere. I feel eyes creeping over my body, violating, penetrating from behind every twig and stamen.

I decide to arm myself. I fashion a "bear bell" out of a rusted tin can and two rocks. I've read *Backpacker Magazine*; I know that if you don't want anything in nature to get too close, you make noise. Lots of it.

After hobbling into our camp at Lake George hours later, I'm dismayed to find Eric writing in his journal next to the creek bed, a look of contentment on his face. *Bastard!* We cook beans and rice over an open flame and Eric watches me plant the blue tent in the dirt.

So far, we've been cordial if not quiet with one another. I'm not picking up any vibes, but still, *this is it*. Our sleeping bags and warm, sweaty bodies will soon be snuggled close. But then he packs up his foam pad, headlamp, and sleeping bag. "You might want to move that tent," he says with a knowing smile as he heads toward the woods. "A bear can smell our dinner from a mile away."

The trees close in behind him and I'm left with a weak fire and weaker tea. *Where is he going?*

❧ ❧ ❧

The next morning I wake up in the small tent, which I shoved into the underbrush at the side of our camp, a good fifty feet from our dinner.

I had another dream.

I was at a party this time, lingering in the doorway, when I noticed her. She had long curly hair, blue eyes, and a tight shirt that accentuated every curve. She was sitting in an oversized ottoman chair, alone. In the dream I weaved my way toward her, through the mostly male crowd. She saw me coming. *So good to see you, Laura, I've been thinking about you.* She smiled—and that's what did it. The only invitation I needed. I crawled on top of her, pushed my hands beneath that tight shirt, and pressed my tongue between her lips.

Then I woke up.

It's the same dream over and over, and I don't know why I have it. Or rather, why I like it. Closing my eyes, I immerse myself in the still-warm memory. I shouldn't want those soft red lips and softer skin. I shouldn't want a woman at all.

I lie back down on my greasy pillow. I never learned how to masturbate, but now feels like the time to start. I always told myself I didn't need sex. I've never really enjoyed it with any of my five previous boyfriends. The recurring dream of the woman is the closest I've gotten to fulfillment in a long time.

Frustrated, I throw my feet out of my sleeping bag in one swift movement. Maybe I can like this Eric guy after all. He is kind of quiet, but he's fit, intelligent, and there are moments when he doesn't seem annoyed that I'm along.

I crawl out of the tent to see him scrambling enough

eggs for two. I put on my best sexy camp face and smooth down my tangled hair. "Can I help with anything?" I ask, awkwardly letting my hand fall on Eric's shoulder. We both flinch at this sudden contact. After too long, I feel him relax, barely. I sit down beside him on the tiny log he has found and try to think of something poetic or profound to share. Instead, a thick wad of hair falls in my mouth and when I blow it out, I catch a whiff of my own breath. Eric, who had been looking curiously at me, quickly turns away. Now what?

This is useless. I don't *feel* it for Eric. We eat in silence. I envision more girl-on-girl fantasies while I wait for him to get ready. When he sees me fidgeting, he says, map in hand, "Go ahead. I'll meet you tonight."

Our next camp spot seems placed in another country, far on the other side of the park in a deep tangle of woods ripe with berries (and, I fear, things that like to eat them). We'll be descending deeper into the park, farther away from humanity and emergency services and telephones. Always the tomboy and the stubborn little girl, I bite back my tears. What do I expect, for him to hold my hand? To be my prince? Instead, I hoist my ill-fitting backpack onto my aching shoulders and step away from the warmth of our campsite into the cold shadows of the trees.

I've been attracted to women all my adult life and most of my teenage years as well. About the same time girls my age were having make-out sessions with their boyfriends, I was barely letting boys touch me, equating their sloppy kisses to onion breath. It's not that I wasn't attracted to boys in high school and beyond; I just didn't experience that electrifying *bolt* some of my girlfriends generated.

I was elected to the prom court along with a gorgeous guy named Jonah. We went on a few dates and every time he dropped me off, I opened the door before the car even stopped and tore across the front lawn of my house. I knew I looked foolish and thought (hoped) he would never call again. But he always did. Every damn time.

On prom night, as midnight drew near, our friends shuttled us into an empty bedroom. As I fumbled for him in the darkness, drunk (the only way I could do it), Jonah grabbed my hand. The macho captain and pitcher of the baseball team suddenly seemed like a scared rabbit. He couldn't kiss me, he whispered, shaking. He couldn't have sex with me, and was so so sorry. "I think I'm, you know," he whispered. "I think I like guys."

"Really? Well, I've always thought your sister was hot."

After a moment of terrifying silence, we collapsed into laughter. We *did* spend the night together, mentally undressing our entire high school class and declaring our most-wanted lists. We only "dated" for another month, after which I developed the imaginary boyfriend tactic to deflect admirers, essentially making up a boyfriend that didn't attend our school. "Nate" was my longest imaginary boyfriend; we dated for a year. That way, when guys would ask: "You have a boyfriend?" I could say yes as I watched another girl's ass pass down the hall.

The second day in "Keji," I walk sixteen miles. Alone. I finally figure out my backpack's waist belt, which transfers the weight to my legs. After years of playing college soccer, they are my best assets.

We are nearly two days into this unfamiliar mini-jungle and I haven't seen another soul except Eric. I desire human interaction to such a degree, it's making me neurotic, desperate. "Take a picture of me!" I want to say around every bend. In front of the deep blue lake, by the boulders strung across the mirrored streams, atop the mossy undergrowth, beside the wildly phallic red and purple mushrooms lining the sides of the trail.

As I mope along, sulking in my loneliness, I kick up a real bell to attach to my makeshift bear bell. A little jangly silver ball that must have fallen off someone's pack or bear alarm device. Either way, this new discovery deepens my desperation for companionship. I start thinking about my manager at REI, which is even more worrisome. Sure, I've had crushes on gorgeous women—Hollywood actresses, folk singers—but not on actual *lesbians*.

Julia has a mullet, chains her wallet to her pants. It's not so much that I want to have sex with her, but I want to ask her how she does it, what makes her do it, is it worth it? And—does she have any friends?

I revel in the fact that I don't *appear* gay, with my long hair and imaginary boyfriends. Eric keeps asking why I don't have a boyfriend. *A pretty girl like you.* He knows of at least a few guys who asked me out during the last semester, and I shot down each one, unmercifully.

But in the same way that I'm terrified of those miles and miles of wilderness and secrets, of being eaten or tortured by wildlife, I'm even more terrified of being gay.

The second night, I have blisters on both feet and am so exhausted that when I find what I think is our campsite, I collapse and fall asleep. Eric finds me an hour later and laughs. Earlier in the day, we'd actually run into one another, purely by accident. Keji is a preeminent paddle-

and-portage area, a haven for canoeists because of the abundance of lakes. At the edge of one of these pristine lakes, Eric and I met eye-to-eye, or rather, eye-to-ass. Eric was naked when I came upon him.

"Oh, shit, sorry," I said, turning my head, ripe with red-faced shame. Here I was, a female flush with hormones and all of the essentials of baby-making, yet still I felt uncomfortable as I caught sight of Eric's lean, muscular back and firm butt. I felt as if I'd just come across my brother.

"Huh? Oh, hey." Eric was facing the lake, the sun making him squint before he waded in quickly, sucking in his breath. "You coming?" he yelled before disappearing in a fleshy blur.

I watched him paddle out to a huge, smooth rock and haul himself onto its surface. Watching him out there, I got annoyed, then angry. Annoyed that I was too afraid, shy, self-conscious—whatever—to follow him. I have a good body, an athlete's body. Still, the thought of hauling myself onto that rock in front of him, of being exposed, was too much. Eric stretched out in the sun and was so comfortable, so nonchalant, that I grew angry. Not at him, directly, but at life. He *knew* he'd marry a woman—*would be able to marry a woman*—wouldn't be labeled with derogatory statements; wouldn't have to come out to his parents and disappoint them with zero grandchildren.

I packed up my stuff and left without saying goodbye.

Travel mates for a week now, I still know very little about this quiet man. But one night he opens up. After we get a thick fire roaring, he pulls out a healthy-sized flask of whiskey and I wash most of my cares away as he tells me about his girl, Mari, back in Madison, Wisconsin. He misses her more than he thought he would, and now he hopes to get centered for the task at hand: proposing to her. I'm not surprised by this confession. Nothing could surprise me at the moment. My city skin is slowly sloughing off, and a deeper epidermal layer is emerging, fresh and curious and unscarred.

After that night, there are many good moments with Eric, sweet moments like when he brews me his special tea; like when he confesses that I am the first person he's ever been backpacking with; like when he seems to genuinely appreciate my company. But his faraway look has more to do with dreams than dissonance, and his obvious love for his girl makes me feel more alone than ever.

On our last morning, I wake up with my hand down the front of my long underwear. I haven't consciously been masturbating, or even *trying* to masturbate, but suddenly I realize my fingertips are wet. Even as I contemplate this, I feel my hand move down, through the forest of pubic hair to rest faintly on the warmth emanating from that region. On the brink of that foggy dream world, I imagine Julia rolling over next to me, nuzzling into my neck, saying *good morning sweetheart*, pushing her own hand deeper down. I moan a little, a tingling eruption pulling every neuron awake.

"Pancakes or oatmeal?" Eric asks through the blue film. I'm grateful I put the rain fly on the night before, or he would've seen more than dewy leaves. Who knows how long he's been standing there. Yet my tough new skin doesn't seem to care about exposure. With his daily absences and frequent silences, Eric has given me a gift

I've both coveted and feared. After packing up, I brush past him and hike straight out of camp.

I'm walking at a good clip, swinging the bell loudly, humming a made-up song, when suddenly the twigs start breaking. I stop in my tracks and grip the bell to quiet it. I can't tell where the movement is coming from. Adrenaline surges through my body, pricking my heartbeat and inducing a small wave of nausea. I swallow the lump in my throat. Up ahead, I see movement, something dark and swinging. *This is it! A bear! Come and get me motherfucker!* I push back into the thick growth at the side of the trail.

A painfully slow minute ticks by, then I see the cause of my fear: two people walking down the trail toward me. As if sensing my need, the forest clutters around me. My backpack disappears at my feet under the thick groundcover of leaves. But in that split second, something happens. The breeze feels good; the sun feels warm. *Simple.* I realize I could keep hiking forever, as long as I didn't have to hike *back*.

I throw my bear bell off into the distance, the tin can shattering into rust and dust. I still fear being gay, still fear my first sexual encounter with a woman. Yet I have released those fears just enough. Waves of desire and submission roll over me. Moving far off the trail, I sit on a mossy rock beside a glorious white and yellow mushroom and close my eyes. For the first time in my life, I pray for everything to come to me.

After bidding Eric a fond farewell, I wait along the Atlantic shore for a friend from Boston to pick me up. Eric's obvious love for his girl back home breaks my heart a little. Breaks the ideology I've grown up with. I want to be *with* a woman, and even more, I want to be that giddy human belting out love songs into the wind.

I end up in Boston a few hours later. I tell my friend that I just can't sleep inside, not now. I don't want the city's skin to muck everything up again. I pitch my tent in her backyard and dream of Julia, or someone like her, under the competing glares of Fenway Park and the full, lovely face of the moon.

Laura Katers lives in Denver, Colorado, and is a freelance writer for several magazines and journals, and a contributing editor for Matter Journal. *She recently spent several years teaching environmental education and nature writing in Australia, New Zealand, and California, as well as leading backpacking trips in Colorado and Alaska. A frequent contributor to various publications and causes focused on sustainability, bike culture, sexuality and diversity, she has published essays in* More Sand in My Bra, Going Green: True Tales from Gleaners, Scavengers, and Dumpster Divers, *and* The Best Travel Writing 2008, *among others.*

❧ ❧ ❧

The First Day

While searching for her roots, she finds her core.

"**I**'m going to Guatemala," I announced to my parents on Thanksgiving. Though I was twenty-eight years old and my passport bore stamps from five continents, a veil of me seeking their approval still laced my words.

Nothing.

"For six months," I added before stuffing a toasted roll in my mouth.

Still, not a word.

I decided to wait until we scooped seconds of turkey and gravy onto our plates to inform them that I had also quit my job—the one with superb benefits. They didn't need to know that I broke into my savings account to fund this return-of-Saturn trip, at least not until after the pumpkin pie. In our family, such an act would be equivalent to getting pregnant and not knowing the father.

"You gonna get killed," Dad said plainly. He chewed and stared at the wall.

"Go somewhere else," Mom piggybacked. "Italy?"

Their comments did not surprise me. They are from the very place I seek to live. Both left Guatemala in 1970 to flee rising political tensions and to pursue economic opportunities in the United States. Aside from a vacation here and there, neither returned.

I arrived in Guatemala City on a Tuesday night. As I pushed my swollen luggage on a cart, I spotted Dad waving his arm behind the yellow gates. I grinned like I was four years old and it was bring-your-parent-to-preschool day. We hugged, but then it was right to business. How was the flight? Your mother called. Be careful here. Watch the taxi. Did you hide your money in different places?

"Yes, O.K., yes, sir!"

He didn't laugh. "Stop speaking English," he snapped, ushering me through the crowd like I was a celebrity. Dad's brother, my *tío*, pulled up to the curb in his red Honda. My shirt clung to my sweaty back as we lifted my suitcases into the trunk.

When my father suggested meeting me in Guatemala (read: he gripped a round-trip ticket in his calloused hand), I was offended. What would Gloria Steinem say? A nearly thirty-year-old college-educated woman's father treating her like a toddler? When that cloud of thought passed, I remembered: I love my father. This journey was a "roots trip," so why wouldn't I want to bring the root with me? At least for the first week. My primary intentions for traveling to Guatemala included: to write, to finally correct my Spanish grammar, to write some more, to travel, to write more and more.

Unfortunately, I left my laptop's power cord back in Massachusetts, amidst the abandoned Balance bars I could not stuff in my suitcase, despite having sat on it half a dozen times. I decided I would go with the flow. My needs in Guatemala were already so much more basic: food, shelter, clean drinking water, bath. Perhaps it was like this in Boston, too, but I had skewed vision.

We arrived in Villanueva, a gated community on the fringes of the capital, and Tío parked the car. I looked up to see that each coral-colored casita mirrored its neighbors. Tía greeted me in whispers and handed me a glass of orange juice and *pan dulce* with a block of mystery cheese. I thanked her, carried the food to my room, and plummeted onto the rollout cot. It felt like I had only been asleep for five minutes, but at nine the next morning, Dad knocked on my door.

"Listen—"

"Well good morning to you, too," I said, wiping my eyes.

"This is very important," he ignored me.

When my eyes adjusted to the million-watt bulb of a sun spilling through the windows, I took inventory of his outfit. At home he wears faded t-shirts and Lee jeans he has owned since the nineties. Here: a button-down collared short-sleeve checkered shirt, khaki pants, and a belt.

"Yeees?"

"When you go to take a shower, whatever you do, don't touch the top wires. You can get electrocuted." He paused. "Yes, your *tío* almost died yesterday."

"Say what?"

"And come down for breakfast soon. They eat around 9 or 9:30 here." He pivoted. "Oh—" he added like I was in trouble. "That Pert Plus in there," he pushed his lips toward the bathroom, "that's mine. You can use it. It's two-in-one."

When I came down for breakfast, I immediately felt under inspection. The grammar errors in my Spanish, my too-American clothes, the way I didn't offer to pour Dad more coffee when I got more for myself, the books I carried around with me (¿*Qué es Lonely Planet?*), if I tried to read outside (¡*Que creída!* separating herself from the group) or inside (the light is no good, you're going to ruin your eyes). It was endless. At least Tía spared me any boyfriend questions. I should have knocked on wood because soon the telephone rang with calls—and boyfriend questions—from relatives in the capital. I explained to one aunt that these six months were not about those kinds of goals. She paused before nervously adding, "You have time."

Now that we had fried eggs, frijoles, tortillas, and coffee in our stomachs, the wide-open hours awaited. I had highlighted museums in my guidebook, circled restaurants and markets, and was eager to breathe in every scent and sight in between. So I was surprised when Dad said our first stop would be the tailor. He needed to pick up a pair of pants.

In the tailor storefront, a wrinkly short guy with a silver tooth chatted us up. The woman sitting beside him on the couch asked where in the U.S. we were from. How did she—"Boston," Dad replied. She asked what part. "Jamaica Plain," he said. She asked what street. Soon they were talking about the Cubans and the Jews "up there" and how small the world is, how it has changed. We walked to a nearby market afterward and two steps before the entrance, Tía reminded me, "Don't talk. They'll raise the prices if they hear your accent." So I only mouthed *Oh my God* at the sight of elderly *indigenas* in traditional textiles, kneeling on stacks of newspapers beside their fruit stands, folding spices in dried plantain leaves, all while gossiping into their cell phones. We bought some fruit and vegetables I recognized—cantaloupe and coconuts—and some I didn't—*zapotes* and *güisquils*. Later, on our way back, Dad pointed out a pair of young mothers pushing strollers with older, heavier, darker "nannies" taking smaller steps behind.

"You see," Dad said, "here, when you have a little money, you hire someone. You know, to help." It's like that everywhere, I wanted to say, but was realizing more and more that he wanted to be the one to explain things, and me to listen.

The next few days swirled with bright moments—Dad meticulously thumbing my traveler's checks as if I had never stepped foot in a bank before; visiting poor relatives who offered us soda and saltines and asked us to hold their babies to bring them good luck; meeting rich relatives who made it a point of impressing us with meals containing pricey varieties of meat, and who boasted spiky hair-dos complete with red highlights and side parts. We listened to stories. One *tío* shared how he was recently held up at gunpoint at a traffic light and they stole his new motorcycle. Another *tía* explained her job in the baby garden. The what? "*Sí, sí,*" she explained, as she bobbed a baby on her knee. "We take care of infants who are put up for adoption while the paperwork is settled in the other countries. Sometimes we have them for nine months, or eleven." Ah, yes, I remembered that 1 in 100 babies born in Guatemala are adopted by families in the United States, and that often, Guatemalan women are coerced into doing so. *Tía* ordered one of her children to fetch a photo album. I nodded at the glossy photos of this baby's "parents" in Ohio and his new house in the vanilla suburbs. His big brother, however, was also Guatemalan. *"Por lo menos,"* she said, pointing to the toddler in the picture. At least this baby would have one relative who shared his heritage.

In the evenings, we watched television and stayed up talking with our hosts. Dad talked more than usual. I loved hearing stories from his childhood—riding horseback with his mother to run long errands, how he broke his arm falling from a tree his five brothers dared him to climb, how their grandmother would rub coffee and spider webs into their wounds. "Spider webs are full of antibiotics," he clarified, anticipating my question.

Then came the time for our long-awaited drive to Xela, the nickname for Quetzaltenango. It was a part of the country neither of my parents had ever visited, and now it would be my home for the next several months. My plan was to study at a language school and live with a host family for one month before writing full-time for the next five. For my parents, while growing up poor, the luxury of travel within a country the size of Louisiana was just that: a luxury. I knew this was a special drive, the kind that I would look back on for years, decades, and maybe tell my own children about someday. The plan was for Dad to drive me to Xela before returning to Guatemala City and eventually back to Boston.

We drove in one direction: west. Having slept only one hour the night before due to a merciless mosquito, I fought my drooping eyelids all the way through the states of Escuintla, Mazatenango, each of the small pueblos, past the little boys and old men selling pineapple chunks, mangos, and coconuts with straws poking out. Huge trucks growled past, some carrying bundles of sugar cane that flicked off and looked like branches in New England autumn. We passed a car accident—a blue truck strewn on the side of the road. I caught a glance of a body, its limbs awkwardly stretched out on the black turf. Shiny blood. Dad immediately covered my eyes with his right hand and continued to steer with his left. "Don't look! Don't eh-even look." I squinted underneath this blindfold, the palm of his hand.

We drove until the sun stood directly above us, until it folded behind us. At one point we literally drove through a cloud. "The mountains are near," he said. Yes, I could see, but more, I could feel the gargantuan stature and spirit of the highlands emerge with each kilometer. I wanted to press pause, to live this over and over again. The closer we got to our destination, the more I ached for my own childhood memories of Guatemala. Playing *avion* (the Guatemalan version of hopscotch) with my cousins in dirt alleyways, building castles on the dark purple sand beaches on the Pacific, eating frozen choco-bananos in the open-aired courtyards while our mothers prepared a potful of sweet corn drink—*atol de elote*, and *mixtas*—basically hot dogs with tortillas instead of buns. But then a storefront yanked me back to my American youth: Domino's Pizza.

"You wanna stop?" he asked.

After a week of frijoles and tortillas, mozzarella cheese suddenly sounded appealing. I nodded.

Upon returning from the bathroom, I saw Dad sitting at a round table, his belt high up on his waist, his white socks peeking out of his black Payless shoes. His shoulders hunched, he held the receipt in his hand and bit his lower lip the way my *abuelita* did. I wanted to cry and laugh and hug him and go home. Back to our old house, back to my pink Huffy bike he taught me to ride on the field at Walsh Middle School, back to the smell of our home barbecues, back to a comfort I had forgotten, one I yearned for in this moment.

We ate greasy pizza. Got lost in Quetzaltenango for an hour. The narrow cobblestone streets and one-way signs didn't help. Eventually, we found the school. Dad rented a room at a nearby hostel. I lent him my flip-flops for the night because the communal shower was far from his room. I would stay with my host family. We were both relieved when they greeted us. A young woman in a wool sweater and jeans introduced herself and her four-year-old daughter, who cheerfully pushed around a play stroller and doll. The little girl was non-stop chatter, and she kept touching my arm and hands and ducking her head to the side while making funny faces. We learned that I would have to pass through the garage, living room, kitchen, stairs, and two brothers' bedrooms in order to reach the bathroom. Dad had *Hell no* written all over his face, especially because one brother had spiked gelled hair and a tattoo. In Dad's eyes, hair gel + tattoo = bad guy. To be more specific: a gang member.

In need of a distraction, I suggested we walk to the *parque central*. A massive pre-Semana Santa (Easter) processional complete with incense and chanting derailed us for an hour. We almost lost each other amidst the young couples with hands tucked in one another's back jean pockets, families of four crawling like amoebas beneath fuzzy blankets, and tourists with gaping mouths and stringy hair. The floats, which were carried by men and teenage boys, consisted of saint statues displayed on beds of flower petals or maroon fabrics. They swayed in a zigzag pattern up the narrow streets and circled the park where market vendors sold plastic rosaries and fried donut balls. Dad bought plastic sandwich bags full of sticky, sweet candies made of condensed milk, coconut, almonds, marzipan, and his favorite: sesame seeds. I heard foreign languages—German, French, and one I could not identify. "They're speaking K'iche'," Dad pointed a crispy candy in the air.

The farther away we walked from the *centro*, the darker the streets became, the less swooshing of sandals on the uneven concrete sidewalks. And soon, not a sound. Soon, not a shade other than dark. We were lost. After walking past the same stone archway three times, we finally saw a gringa. Fortunately, she redirected us, but not before Dad asked her how safe she felt walking alone at night. "I don't," she said. "Actually, my friends just walked me halfway but I usually never walk alone late at night. Really, I'd say, especially for women." I tried to make eyes at her, like, no, no, please stop elaborating. She didn't. "Sometimes there are robberies, and for the women," she looked at me, "rapes." O.K.! Thanks, chica. Dad's anxiety hit record proportions. His cheekbones in the moonlight gleamed like stones. The girl left. Eventually we found our bearings. He walked me home and said, "I don't know why you get yourself in these situations. You could have practiced your Spanish in the U.S."

All I could say was "Well…." He had a point, albeit a moot one. I was already in Guatemala and there was no way I was returning to Boston. That much I knew.

In the morning, after I clicked shut the white-painted iron gate of my home-stay, there stood my father in his striped sweater and jeans. Children in school uniforms trotted past him, with their young mothers trailing behind. He looked like he had been standing guard there on that street corner all night. Up until then, we were a traveling team. When I realized he would be leaving for good in a couple of hours, it was like a splinter sliced me in half. I was one thought away from choking-crying. "Let's go to the school," I said.

The school coordinator welcomed us in Spanish and we took our seats in plastic chairs arranged in a semi-circle. She led the orientation, answering all questions (most of which had to do with money and medicine and the internet) before giving a brief history of Guatemala. During the break, we met more instructors and sipped our coffee. I ate three pieces of *pan dulce* in a row. The cry was back, clotting my throat, strangling my vocal chords. I curled my toes to distract myself. My father would be heading out soon.

"O.K.," he said in the way he says it, o-kay. My face felt purple. I wished I were anyone or anything else: the manzanilla tea in the tall aluminum pot, the *profesora's* hair scrunchy, the silver spider on the wall. "Well," I managed to say, "let me walk you out."

The sun in the courtyard touched my face. I heard maestros gather their students and begin their one-on-one lessons. All this, until my stoicism finally crumbled. Some teachers looked my way. I didn't care. Yes, I'm twenty-eight years old and my father is dropping me off at school and it's the first day and I don't want him to leave and I am crying.

"Come on," he patted my shoulder. "It'll be O.K. You'll get used to it."

"I'm O.K.!" I bawled. "It's you."

"What?" His eyes glassed behind his wiry frames.

There was so much I wanted to say to him. How I was sorry that I originally thought he had hijacked my trip; how I was sorry that I was so blinded. Of course he wanted to go on this journey, too; of course he wanted to go with me. I didn't realize—all this time, in all my preparation—that traveling to Guatemala would have been incomplete without him.

"I know," he said, even though I had not said a thing.

So there we were. My dad. Me. We. There was nothing else to say or do. So we hugged. So we held on. So tight. Until we didn't.

✺ ✺ ✺

Jennifer De Leon's fiction, poetry, and essays have appeared or are forthcoming in Ms., Poets & Writers Magazine, SOLSTICE, Kweli Journal, *and* Guernica. *She teaches creative writing at the Grub Street Independent Creative Writing Center and the University of Massachusetts-Boston, where she is completing her MFA in fiction. Jennifer is the recipient of fellowships from the Bread Loaf Writers' Conference and the Macondo Writers' Workshop. She is working on her first novel.*

❧ ❧ ❧

Winter with Dogs

One stray traveler cares for others.

idden between the Araveli mountains of Rajasthan, behind long stone walls and thistle, is a shelter for street dogs. It looked unremarkable when I first saw it from the road: just a few flat white buildings that housed the kennels, surgery rooms, and office, and some outlying mud-brick sheds. Hundreds of dogs were baying, calling me in, as the desert wind swept across the yellow dust.

The yard dogs had once been kennel dogs. They had survived and found their ways into the hearts of the hospital staff: Three-Wheeler who guarded the gates, pesky Fly with crumbs on his nose, head-nodding Bruce, shy spirit Julie with the bead amulet necklace. They lived on the grounds, on the manure piles, in bushes, and if they could get through the gates to the office they'd curl up on the wicker chairs, on the night guardian's charpoy, in the file closet. They got into the bags of rotis people brought as donations. They went baying after cows, donkeys, goats, bicycles, herder girls, anyone who dared cross the land.

In the kennels were strange breeds, like hyenas and jackals, foxes, composite Salukis, Rampur greyhounds, rat terriers, shepherds, Labs. They were the color of sand, spice, clay, or tiger-striped, brindle, speckled, with short coats, soft as skin, long elegant legs, rat tails, long faces, flat heads, flesh-colored noses. They were dogs with crusted eyes, flea-bitten noses, half-eaten mouths, open neck wounds, maggots, mange. They were hairless, feverish, paralyzed, three-legged, one-eyed, dehydrated, suffering from distemper, parvo, or fatal rabies.

During the two months I volunteered there, I learned not to ask whether the dogs lived or not, or why they were here, or where they were going. But I wondered whether I was caring for the half-living or the half-dead. Nothing had quite prepared me for this—not my time in wildlife rehabilitation centers back home in Canada, or my youth spent in the forests observing life and death. I was grateful for Audrey, mother of the young woman who had started this charity and gone back to England for a needed rest. We laughed that maybe we were part of the dogs now, wondering if we had fleas in our hair or ticks or mange. Hand-washing blankets and sacks and draping them on the rocks to dry, welts and hives itching down our arms, brushing out the kennels with water and bundled straw, washing paralyzed dogs, bandaging wounds, warming orphan pups in our arms like mothers, taking the dogs out to the light. We talked more to the dogs than anyone else. We took on their smell in our clothes, our hair. The baying and howling in the kennels was the insistent song of life. Swollen ticks, maggots, open wounds were part of the beauty of survival. Their gentleness amazed me; a dog that had never lived with humans would lay his paw in my hand in recognition.

Sanam the intern drove us home on the moped, five kilometers to the village, where we lived with Anjou and her family. We carried four newborn puppies in a pink plastic laundry basket as we wove through cows with painted horns—green, blue, red, some with polka-dots; camels pulling carts, plodding on the pavement, bells jangling on their ankles; the great black water buf-falos coming up from the river, their heavy curled horns like shells, ancient spirals.

Anjou's soft bells tinkled in the evening as she met us at the gate. She moved so quietly sometimes I thought it was Raja, the little tortoise-shell street cat that the chil-dren had laid on my legs the first day after my arrival, sleeping off the strange night drive from Delhi.

A half moon hung from the dark sky and temple music rose from all sides of the village. Anjou and the children sang "Jende Mama," a song for the moon, dancing in the courtyard. She lit an incense stick off the gas flame of her stove and stuck it in a potted sage plant wrapped in orange veil. The electricity had been off since sundown. The night smelled of roses. We sat in a circle in the moonlight with tiny syringes of milk, puppies crawling across our toes, all of us transported, giggling. The little beige pup fell asleep in Anjou's lap, across her speckled green sari. Later, with the basket at my bed, I fell asleep to their squeaking, snuffling, and rumbling, and woke every hour to piercing squeals. Even in my exhaustion I was softened by the smell of milk on my hands, their warm bodies, white-tipped tails, and white paws, beige and black, pink noses, little white needle claws that scratched across my raw chapped skin.

In the morning, Sanam arrived and we rode to work in the chill winds with the basket of puppies, our eyes watering, the sand hills on either side beginning to glow red in the dust air, towering cactus spires, thorn trees, and gray-headed crows. The yard dogs summoned our arrival and escorted us in. The accountant, Vikram, sat in a wicker chair by old Nandi's dung fire doing the paperwork, untangling the confusion of dogs, kennels, and illnesses.

"Madame, full *sardi*," Nandi said calmly, lighting his bidi on the coals. Full cold.

"Full *sardi*," I repeated and everyone laughed.

The boys were waiting for the first chai. Someone impatiently threw on some straw and it blew up into flames and a great cloud of ash blew into the new boy's face so that his hair turned gray. Great uproar of laughter. These were the boys who went fearlessly into kennels of angry dogs and hauled them off to surgery, then laid them gently on the stone. They made up the food and water bowls, cleaned kennels, washed laundry. Turtleneck boy, cool laughing boy with the jeans and baseball cap who sang to the dogs, Ravi who called himself "dog-catching genius," Aladdin, the night watchman, guardian of the gates. In the caste system, animal handling was relegated to the lower echelons, along with street sweeping and clearing garbage. But here everyone worked for the dogs.

I did the rounds of the kennels, the noise ringing in my ears. I was surrounded by wolves. Sometimes the singing hit a certain pitch that vibrated right through me. Sparrows went flitting down the corridors and passed through the bars. The little dogs who wagged their tails at me, the hunted ones, the angry ones, the fearful, everything was spoken in the eyes out of darkness. They were not human nor animal but something in between, a lost race. A monkey stretched his black hand through the bars and took the apple from my hand, but his hands were numb, useless. He couldn't bring it to his mouth, so he let the apple drop to the ground and ate like a dog.

Explosions from a nearby farm rocked the earth. Pieces of concrete fell from the ceiling and the dogs went silent for a moment. The rescue vehicle came in after a night on the prowl with a load of street dogs, slavering and drooling in fear. All of the kennels were full, and the dogs just back from surgery lay dazed in the corridors with their raw sutured wounds, their new tattooed ears. The vets were doing the medication rounds and I saw the dreaded bottle of orange soap and the tray of clear liquid bottles and syringes on the floor.

Sushanta was singing a sweet mournful tune while he injected the clear liquid and then the orange into the veins of a skeletal mange dog deep in coma, caught between the living and the dead. He was not coming back.

"Sorry pup," Sushanta said.

I lay my hands on the cool gray mottled skin and felt the being leave. To where? My hands felt the precise moment. They lifted off like a magnet had released me.

I took my peaceful white-and-black dog out to the cactus hill where he sank his paws into the sand and sat and I laid my hand on his neck, soft as rabbit's fur. He looked at me with his soft brown eyes. He was healing from cancer, but nothing showed on the outside. I was trying to avoid the herder girls who were passing through with their speckled goats, their ornamental veils and heavy silver anklets, their flirting goat calls, laughter.

"Hallo, hallo. Give me your watch."

One girl carried a long pole with sharp metal scythe fastened to one end that she raked through the tree branches slicing off living green for her herd. Sometimes they climbed up barefoot and every day the trees took on new forms.

Crows floated in and out of the shed where the cows lived and descended on their withers in search of fleas. The young vet Darpan and the boys were holding down a cow with a maggot wound. The young vet vaguely wrung his perfumed hands. He never seemed to want to touch an animal but with the tip of his sandal. Nandi sat on the cow's head, smoking a bidi and softly talking, it seemed, to the cow. I felt drugged, sleepy, unable to understand the moaning, howling, weeping of the dogs back in the kennel, or that I seemed to have no natural wisdom but the laying of light in my hands. Wasn't there something like that? Learning to release the shadows and the walls within me?

In our courtyard of convalescents, the mynah birds had pockmarked the eggs we left on the wall to cool. A female peahen's broken leg was splinted with a piece of X-ray film paper and white bandage. She nestled against a male peacock like he was a pillow, shimmering turquoise breast and neck, marbled waves of dark greens and blacks down his back and the tassel headdress that the yard dogs always tried to pull through the cage bars. Lady, our grandmother dog that had once been paralyzed and could now walk, sat in the middle of cardboard boxes and cages of puppies, alongside a cat that shared his milk with the puppies. She watched over them all with her broken-tooth grin like some kind of healer.

We climbed the precarious bamboo ladder and ate lunch on the sunny roof with the men, among all their tiffin boxes of rotis and dal. Cell phones rang joyfully with Indian music. Sanam's made the sound of a cuckoo to remind him of his fast for the new moon. From above we could see the land like a map, the milling goats and the herder girls' red veils, the sound of a pump and the flow of water gushing, an old man walking barefoot, following the head of the water and opening the gateways with his hoe, an egret following him from channel to channel.

There was to be a caesarean procedure on one of the cows with a stillbirth. Everyone rushed through the last chores to come and watch, all the boys, the three vets, and a visiting transvestite in red veils with a gold hoop through one nostril. Nandi squatted down with a bare foot resting on the cow's cheek, his fingers rubbing her gums to comfort her. Someone held the IV pole and watched the tubes and the dripping liquid. Stately Dr. Aakash waved everyone back and performed the cut through all the layers down to the uterus, all of us kneeling before this ritual, silent, but for the transvestite's sensual voice giving us spiritual counsel. The smell of death. It took four men with Ravi, the driver, strongest of them all, to pull out the dead black-and-white calf by the hooves, and then we had to keep the yard dogs away. The uterus sat like a wrinkled folded bag on the cow's side. The young intern Dr. Darpan had to put it all back together and he was expert in this.

All the ringed fingers, silver and gemstones and bracelets and wrist watches, passed trays of iodine and instruments. Wrong instrument. The other one. He clamped the veins. Now the sutures. No 8. Wrong one. They passed him a new package. He pierced the curved needle through a layer of skin and pricked himself. Ah. He wove the thread in and out. His back was getting tired. He gently pushed the sutured lumps back through the hole and sewed it all shut. Then he looked up at me and smiled.

A grandmother was among us with two turbaned men. She showed me photos of her black-and-white cow, this one, now healed, that she had come to watch over. The photos were framed in glass, one with the family in front of their store, the other of herself and her cow. After they had gone, the stone was littered with matches and half-smoked bidis, green leaves rolled with string.

Later a herder girl came in with a wounded finger, an old piece of cloth plastered to her bloody finger. Sanam gave me some cotton soaked in iodine to dribble over it while I carefully pried it off. She winced softly. I looked at her face and stopped.

"Sanam, I can't do it. I can feel her pain."

He just smiled and told her what I'd said. He teased her, and she pulled the veil over her face. He made a gesture that I would just have to yank it off quickly. I gave her the iodine cotton and told her to keep working on it. When I came back it was off.

"Did you do it or her?" I asked Sanam.

"Me." He was putting on a new bandage in a fatherly, humorous way.

I asked her name and she read the blue tattoo lettering on the inside of her arm.

"Aneeta."

The red sun was sinking into the smoky hills. Wild peacocks scattered before us. Audrey and I snuck behind the cow house to gather cow dung and thorn twigs, our solution to having run out of stove gas at home. Who knew how long it would take for our order to come. Out in the yard before the hospital the yard dogs lay dormant

in the last light. The boys were hovering around Dr.
Aakash on his wicker chair throne, listening to a lecture.
No one noticed as we sped away with our bag of dung.

Next morning all the boys looked up solemnly from
the fire and Nandi intoned, *"Ney, tchaï."* No tea.

"That's O.K.," I said, and pulled out my little bottle
of Nescafé. They didn't know what to do with it so I
poured it into the pot of buffalo milk and everyone had
café au lait in little plastic cups, a novelty and yet in no
way did it compare to chai. Later, Nandi presented us
with a giant burlap sack of cow dung. Audrey and I
looked at each other and smiled. Nandi, caretaker of the
grounds, simply looked away and nodded.

Wounded-Mouth Dog lay convalescing under a huge
white lace blanket in the sun. She had staggered in one
day with a hole in the lower jaw and a bullet-sized hole
in the neck behind the ear. She walked right up to us
where we sat with the patients and looked at us. We had
thought she was one of the surgery dogs that had wandered off, drunk on anesthesia. But no one had seen her
before. The Wolf Pups now walked on top of her like
she was a mountain, and every time they went to look
under the cloth she made a whining fed-up growl. Tiger
Dog, a bony brindle shepherd with distemper, was now
able to walk around, tip-toeing on his long shaky legs,
looking at us with big bat ears up, piercing orange eyes
lined with black like kohl, looking for food. He stepped
into one of the pups' empty cardboard boxes, squeezed
himself inside, and fell asleep twitching softly, with his
head over the edge framed by a blue scarf patterned with
Indian kings on horses.

I was disturbed by some of the things I had seen, like
an aftertaste, like my dream of a haunted house where a
ghost girl came out of the darkness with a hatchet. The

next morning, in real life, I watched a goat herder girl get on the bus with her hatchet. It was like the image of the Goddess Kali and her many arms holding out the tools of life, a flower, a sword, to pierce the darkness with light. So many deaths at the hospital, puppies, dogs. And the peahen with the broken leg. I had taken her body in the evening up to the hill to dig a grave but the earth was all rock and dust, so I threw the bag up into the cactus trees where it caught on the thorns. Death had followed us home. We found our cat Raja dead outside our gate, without a mark. Was it rabies or poison?

I lost my black-and-white dog in surgery. "Of all the dogs here," Dr. Darpan said with a smile, "this is your favorite one."

Yes, the one I thought would never die. My head felt crushed. My lungs were char and fire. Audrey said she thought she was cursed, while we smoked on the roof in the evening wind, wrapped in our blankets. The prayers were coming in waves from the temple, echoing off the mountains. I thought there must be another explanation. The animals sensed they were dying and they came looking for a way to leave, or stay.

All life was sacred. Cows and buffalo wandered the streets, bus drivers threw carrots to the monkeys on the mountain, marigolds were strung on stones, in trees, in taxis, new houses were sung to. This was why our vets hesitated to put a suffering dog to sleep even when we pleaded. He had to be absolutely sure that it was in accordance with the universal flow of give and take. And then death ignited life; the moments were so pure.

In the cold Rajasthani winter, we warmed ourselves beside old Nandi's fire, eggs boiling in one pot for the needy dogs, tea water in another for us, and the great black pot of rice and lentils set aside for the dogs' dinner.

The Doberman amputee that all the boys were afraid of sat on my foot and looked up at me with warm amber eyes. Smell of spice, smoldering cow dung, Nandi's gruff voice, earth and smoke, his unspoken way with animals. Dust devils, swirling blowing dust. I could taste the grit in my mouth. I heard the trees talking and saw marigolds draped on the black stone in someone's field. I had a heightened sense of awareness that something greater than me was being played out, in this place where all life was one.

ॐ ॐ ॐ

Erika Connor is an artist and writer from rural Quebec, with a love of animals, nature, myths, and culture. She has taken care of wild birds and raccoons in rehabilitation centers, worked for the Humane Society's "visiting dogs in hospitals" program in Canada, traveled by white horse both in West Africa and Mongolia, observed wild horses in Mongolia, lived with the Fulani and Bambara people of the Sahel, and continues to lose herself between the worlds.

ℬℬℬ

The Angel of Repose

A writer is charmed by a devilish imp.

I had just settled into my attic bedroom when two young boys appeared at the door to say it was time for dinner. They took me by the hands and escorted me to the kitchen like prison guards transporting an inmate to the courthouse. Diego and Ettore, ages nine and six, were the sons of Marco and Bianca, my Italian hosts. None of them spoke English, and this was their first time housing a student attending language classes at the University of Perugia. Marco and Bianca thought the experience would be good for their boys. And I'd heard living with young children was the best way to pick up a language, since they tend to speak simply and repeat things more often than adults. I would soon discover the consequences of such traits.

Our first night together, I showed photos of my husband, Roger, our dogs Hannah and Baxter, and our ranch in California. Diego was convinced that everyone in the USA is a cowboy. The picture of my husband wearing a stetson, standing next to his horse, made it difficult to dissuade him. "Your *marito* is a cowboy! *Fantastico!*"

Ettore wanted to know every detail about my dogs. I told him Hannah was a German shepherd, "like Rin Tin Tin," and Baxter was a Norwich terrier. Unfortunately, Baxter had died shortly before I left for Italy. I tried to explain how he was run over by a rescue squad in front of our house, basically killed by people who normally try to save lives. But how do you say "irony" in Italian?

"Show me pictures of your children." Ettore said. This was something I was frequently asked when traveling around Italy. Even though Italy is near zero population growth, everybody expects married women to have children and they are disappointed if you tell them otherwise. Sometimes I carried pictures of my cousins' kids just to avoid looks of abject pity. But now I simply said the truth. "I don't have kids. My dogs are my children." Ettore nodded slowly, trying to grasp what kind of idiot I was.

The kids embraced their role as hosts and ad hoc Italian teachers with zeal. In the afternoons after school, we played board games like Clue and Monopoly. The Italian version of Clue was set inside a train station with rooms like the *Sala Cocktail* (Cocktail Lounge) and *Deposito Bagagli* (Left Baggage Claim). So a possible game-winning answer might be *Signorina Rosella nella die Biglietteria con la Corda*. (Miss Scarlet in the Ticket Office with the Rope.) I never really liked Clue, but the boys had their own rules that consisted of marching the characters around the board and pounding them with the various weapons. No mystery to solve. Everyone got murdered. It was much more fun that way.

On weekends, I'd join the family on outings to the *bosco* collecting chestnuts or mushrooms. Diego insisted I walk in lockstep between him and Ettore lest I get lost on the trail. Or run away, I thought, for unless they were sleeping, or at school, they rarely let me out of their sight. I began to feel like I was in that *Twilight Zone* episode where the father brings home a human pet for his daughter to play with.

Ettore constantly asked to see my pictures of Hannah and Baxter. *"Posso vedere il cani?"* Can I see the dogs? He'd point at the picture of Baxter and say—*"il morto"*—the dead one, and then repeat the story of how Baxter died over and over and over again. He was like a Lionel train on an infinite loop of track or an M. C. Escher drawing with no end, his brain a Möbius strip of obsession.

Each night at dinner he'd pose the same questions: "Which dog do you love the most?" Before I could answer, he'd shout, "The dead one. Right?" Then he'd say accusingly, "Why didn't you pick him up in your arms and breathe life back into him?"

I said I would have done anything to save that dog, but he seemed to be building a case that it was my fault. Then one night he said, "A child is better to have than a dog. No?"

What was with this kid? Had he been talking to my mother?

After a month of his nightly interrogation, I'd had it. "Ettore!" I said, *"Basta! Basta! Basta!"* Enough! *"Mi prefferito non parla tratta di mio cane!"* I really don't want to talk about my dog anymore!

He stiffened back in his chair, shocked at my sudden outburst. He glanced at his mother and father, waiting for them to reprimand me, but they said nothing. Ettore stared at me over the top of his tiny wire-rim glasses, a mixture of hurt and dismay in his eyes. I held his stare until he looked away. I felt terrible. In one exasperated moment, I'd moved beyond the careful, courteous exchanges that were my foreign language staples, to browbeating a six-year-old. We finished our meal in silence.

A few hours later, Ettore came up to my room and presented me with a picture he'd drawn of a little black-and-brown dog with copious amounts of blood gushing out of its head. Little yellow wings fluttered on its back. "Don't worry anymore about it. It's O.K." Ettore said. "Baxter is a happy angel now."

Brilliant. Not only was he projecting his obsession on me, he was telling me to move on as well. Along with my room and board, I was getting the services of a pint-sized analyst.

Nonetheless, I was very moved by his gesture. "Thank you Ettore," I said. "This is so lovely, you've really captured Baxter's true essence here. I'll take this drawing home to remember him and you always." I leaned in to hug him but he pulled back and snatched the drawing out of my hands.

"No!" he cried. "This is mine! Draw your own!"

On my last night in Italy, my host family threw a party for me and invited all the neighbors. Throughout the evening, Ettore was oddly silent. The next day, Marco dropped me off at the train station and gave me a bag of pepper-and-egg sandwiches and almond biscotti that Bianca had made. Though excited to be heading home, I had a heavy heart. On the train, just outside Rome, I opened the bag and found a note:

Love me back soon.
—Ettore

I already did. He had me at *buon giorno*.

❧ ❧ ❧

Marcy Gordon is a contributing editor for the Authentic Italy guidebook series. Her travel humor essays have appeared in several Travelers' Tales anthologies including 30 Days in Italy, The Thong Also Rises, *and* More Sand in My Bra. *She lives in Northern California and writes a blog about wine, food, and travel: http://comeforthewine.com.*

✄ ✄ ✄

Siliguri

Who can you trust when you're traveling sola?

It was 4:20 A.M. when I heard the faint hum in the distance. The noise grew steadily from a barely perceptible hope to a shrieking racket, then slowed to individual *thunk-thunk-thunks* as the train pulled into the station. When it stopped completely, I unfolded myself from atop my backpack and stood. After six immobile hours, my knees creaked and blood rushed to my head. I shivered. Siliguri's daytime heat had long since dissipated and I'd been huddled as much for warmth as for comfort. The family I'd camped near was silently rolling up mats and setting stunned and bleary children on their feet. I hobbled stiffly to the nearest train car, looking for the list that should reveal my name and seat number. There was no list. I looked up the platform and back down again. The line of dusty red cars seemed endless.

Then I heard Mickey's voice behind me, annoyed. "Didn't I tell you that you have to wait down there?" He pointed forcefully along the platform like someone scolding a puppy. "You have to learn to trust people when you're in a foreign country and they're honestly trying to help you!" It was too much. There were too many frustrated tears to hold them all safely inside. I tried to keep my face turned away from him, but he saw anyway.

"Why are you sobbing?" he asked. His voice, caught between annoyance and concern, turned high and shrill. "What's wrong? What happened? Why are you sobbing?"

I wanted to answer him. I wanted to say exactly why I was crying and what he could do with his advice. But I didn't trust myself not to break down completely, to heave and gasp and sob like a child, spewing out snot and incoherent complaints. I couldn't stop the tears, but I could keep my mouth shut tight, wave him away, start walking in the direction he pointed, hoping to find my car, my seat, my ride out of Siliguri.

Mickey walked with me anyway, down the platform to a car that looked just like all the other cars, and he put me in the hands of another man in an MP uniform. I didn't say goodbye as I climbed onto the train. The new MP led me to the ladies' car and pointed at a narrow slice of seat next to the window. The ladies, a blur of jeweled bindis and brightly patterned saris stuffed into the tiny room, stared silently at me, their bright dark eyes roving over my long, black skirt and plain blue hoodie from the GAP. A story about the ladies' car on Indian trains had actually inspired me to travel to India in the first place. A story about how sisterhood reaches across the culture gap, transcending differences and making the ladies' car both a refuge from men and a connection among women. And now my sisters were staring at me as though I were an intruder. I stretched my hood down over my face and cried some more.

Siliguri is a way station. It lies at the foot of the Himalayas and serves as a stopover for those traveling to and from Darjeeling and its tea plantations. Like most towns of convenience, it's not very nice. I had passed through it quickly on my journey from Calcutta up to Darjeeling, but on my way back down, en route to Delhi, I got stuck. There was no train leaving that day. I had to spend the night and the whole next day in Siliguri.

The monsoon had just barely moved south; it was off-season for tourists. Having encountered no other foreigners in the couple of weeks that I'd been in India, I was happy when I met an English girl in Siliguri who was also traveling alone. We spent the afternoon wandering through the market and then ate dinner together. I doubt we would have been friends under other circumstances, but I think we were equally relieved to find each other. I was lonely for someone who saw India as an outsider, someone who understood the pendulum between fear and elation in navigating an almost total unknown.

We sat in a gazebo on the hotel grounds and she told me about the men who'd harassed her everywhere she went. "It's just something that happens here when you have fair hair," she said. She laughed lightly. "Don't worry, you'll be safe." Her hair, which was oily and looked more brown than blond, was scraped back into a thin, straggly ponytail. I doubted that her admirers even noticed it. Her breasts, on the other hand, were visible through her t-shirt. ("I refuse to wear a bra in this heat," she claimed.)

My ethnic heritage, African- and Italian-American, has given me skin the color of delicious things—caramel, cappuccino, toasted almonds. I was the same color as most of the people around me, and my hair was dark, like theirs. *Fair hair.* I took offense on behalf of all of us. When the conversation began to stagger, I escaped the awkwardness by leaving early for the train station.

The hotel manager said it would cost twenty rupees to ride to the train station. The rickshaw man wanted one hundred. I talked him down to fifty, and we set off. He was a small man, and I cringed with guilt when he had to dismount from his bicycle and drag me up a hill on foot. Then he got lost. After a detour around a long line of traffic headed to a puja, or religious festival, he couldn't find his way back to Hill Cart Road. With a sheepish apology, he pedaled me through residential side streets, silent and dark except for distant barking dogs and the occasional splash of yellow light and laughter from one of the small houses we passed. I felt the tiniest bit irritated. Siliguri is not a large town and Hill Cart Road is the biggest street in it, practically a highway. I sat silently, willing the ride to end. The only pleasantry about sitting in a rickshaw was that finally no one was yelling at me: "Hey, rickshaw! Hello, rickshaw! Very good rickshaw!"

And then the ride did end. In a dark grove of trees off a side road, the rickshaw-wallah dismounted from his bike and came to face me. He pointed towards a light at the top of a small hill. "Train station," he announced. I wondered why he didn't just take me around to the front, but I wasn't going to insist. I climbed down and prepared to grab my backpack.

"One hundred rupees," he said.

"Fifty rupees," I said. "We agreed." It didn't yet occur to me to be frightened. I was only annoyed that after all my writhing guilt for this put-upon man, he was now trying to cheat me.

"One hundred rupees."

"No. Fifty rupees."

Then the rickshaw-wallah put a foot up onto the edge of the cart, blocking me from my backpack. He leaned towards me.

"I love you?" he said.

"What?" I squinted at him. What was he talking about? Never mind—I was out of there. I reached past him and swung my pack up and over his leg and out of the rickshaw. I held out six soft, damp ten-rupee notes to him, the amount I had scrunched and readied in my pocket. He wouldn't accept them. He was suddenly angry.

"One hundred rupees!" He said something about the puja that I couldn't understand.

"You knew about the puja. The puja was not a surprise to you. We agreed on fifty rupees." I offered him the money again. Again, he refused it. Other people appeared out of the darkness. Three other cycle-rickshaw-wallahs came from one side and ranged their vehicles in a half-circle. Three men on foot came from the other direction, the direction of the light that I hoped was the train station. They were the only witnesses. Silently they watched.

I backed toward the light, holding out the money at the full extent of my arm. He didn't move. Just as I was finally beginning to feel afraid, he reached out and snatched the bills, and I stepped out of the circle. I turned and half-ran up the hill and followed the wall around to the side that looked the brightest. No one followed.

I exhaled in relief when I saw the pulsing crowd of

people and stepped into the yellow light spilling out of NJP Station. Inside, I picked my way around the families talking, shouting, eating, and sleeping as I tried to get to the information counter. A man wearing a khaki uniform intercepted me and asked if I needed help. He wore a sash that read MILITARY POLICE in big white letters from his right shoulder to his left hip. His black moustache was as shiny as his shoes.

"I need the 10:50 train to Delhi," I said.

"Yes, Platform 3B. I will take you there."

I followed him through the crowd. "But the train is delayed," he said. "It will be coming at 4 A.M." It was 9:05 P.M.

The policeman, Pramod, led me out onto a platform, up a flight of metal stairs to an overpass and down to platform 3B where, conveniently enough, his police booth was located. He commandeered a stool from a nearby chai stand and dragged it over for me to sit on. I sat reluctantly, suspecting that he would try to flirt with me but not knowing how to avoid it. At least he was a policeman. He insisted on buying me a coffee. I tried to refuse, but when the tiny glass was set in front of me anyway, I sipped it. It gave me an excuse to limit my focus on the standard conversation—where are you from? How long have you been in India? Do you like it? Then he veered from the script. "Do you want to go walking to see the scenery?"

Startled, I glanced around. Stray beams of cold white light cut through the darkness at odd angles, slanting across the platform and highlighting the drifts of dust, dirt, and bits of straw on the dark floor. A cockroach the size of a mouse scuttled past. Beyond the stripes of track and platform was blackness.

"No, that's O.K.," I said.

"Your train is delayed. Why don't you take a room to wait in?"

Not even certain that the train was truly delayed, I did not want to be away from the platform at 10:50. And so the conversation dragged on.

"Married or unmarried?" Pramod asked.

"Married," I lied.

"For how long married?"

"Two years."

"And where is your husband?"

I opened my mouth to say "America" but said "Delhi" instead.

"There is a waiting room," Pramod said. "Do you want to wait there?"

I agreed immediately, picturing rows of chairs where I could sit among other passengers and be left alone. He led me back up the stairs to the overpass. We walked over the other platforms, some bright and crowded, others dark and empty, and back down the stairs to the main entrance.

"Here is the waiting room." He pointed up a flight of stairs to a closed door marked OFFICERS ONLY.

I sighed. "You know, I think maybe I should wait on the platform after all."

Then another man came along. Taller and thinner than Pramod, he wore an ordinary button-down shirt and slacks. He claimed to be an officer too. "I am above him," he said, waving a hand in Pramod's face. "I will take you into the waiting room." Pramod looked sulky but did not protest.

"I'd really rather go back to the platform," I said. So Pramod led me away. I didn't know whether his scowl was meant for me or for his superior officer, but it made me nervous. The straps of my backpack dug into my sweaty shoulders as I climbed up to the overpass yet again. Suddenly he brightened. "If you have any problems," he said, "just tell me, and I will solving."

"O.K.," I agreed. I wiped sweat from my forehead with my long, modest sleeve.

He paused on the overpass and pointed down to Platform 6, which must not have been expecting a train, as it was unlit and completely deserted.

"Do you want to go down there?"

"Isn't my train coming to Platform 3?"

He frowned, but began walking to Platform 3 again. I followed, thinking resentfully that his chances with foreign girls might improve if he offered to carry their bags while he led them in circles around the train station.

Back at Platform 3B, I sat on my stool again. There was a small silence.

"Why don't we take a walk?" Pramod suggested, as though we hadn't just returned from a walk with results unsatisfying to us both. He nodded encouragingly. "We can see the scenery."

"That's O.K., I'll just wait here on Platform 3."

"But your train is delayed."

"That's fine, I'll just wait."

I felt relief when the man from the waiting room, the officer who was "above" Pramod, came along and started talking to me.

"You can call me Mickey," he said. "My Indian name is too hard for Westerners to pronounce."

"What is it?"

"Mohan."

I wondered what Westerners he had been speaking with, who couldn't pronounce the name Mohan. But for the purpose of our conversation, the same conversation I had with everyone, it hardly mattered.

"Married or unmarried?" Mickey asked.

"Married."

"I don't believe you! You look like a school-going girl!"

"I'm twenty-four," I said, which was true.

"Well then I must congratulate you on maintaining yourself." That made me laugh, and I felt much better. Until he started telling off-color jokes. Mild ones, of the sort a sixth grader might tell when the substitute teacher had her back turned, but inappropriate nonetheless. I glanced again up and down the platform. The waiting families had begun to quiet, crouched together, the children laid out on straw pallets or pages of newspaper. The MP stand was brightly lit, and my high stool kept me off the floor. "Do you get it?" Mickey prodded. I smiled thinly and stared at anything but him.

When someone called Mickey away, Pramod took another chance. He glanced around before leaning toward me, his teeth white and sharp looking, slick with spit. He whispered, "Sex...enjoy?"

I had no idea how to respond. Should I show my annoyance and disgust, or would I be better off pretending I didn't understand? At that moment Mickey returned, and suddenly he was again the lesser of two evils. So when he invited me to walk further down the platform, closer to where my car would end up when my train finally arrived, I accepted.

"You know," he said as we picked our way around the parcels and bodies scattered along the wide platform, "An Indian girl would not have sat there. I am just trying to help you out, and let you know."

I stared at him. Wasn't it enough that I refused to go "look at the scenery" with Pramod? What was I supposed to say? Sorry, I'd rather sit alone on the filthy platform than sit on a chair and talk to you? I thought I was being polite. Anyway, if sitting on a stool in a brightly-lit area, where everyone could see that I was just talking, meant I wasn't a nice girl (my mind instantly translated "Indian girl" to "nice girl"), then what did that make the one who invited me to sit there? He should've known what's appropriate, even if I didn't. These guys were supposed to be the *police*. Was Mickey going to have an edifying little chat with Pramod, too?

Mickey pointed to a box on the platform. "Sit there. I will bring you some chai, or coffee." I walked away from him, kept walking, ignoring him calling after me about the chai. I found a dozing family of several adults and children and placed my backpack as close as I thought I could without actually joining their party, and sat down upon it, facing away from Mickey and his chai. I pulled my hood over my head and rested my forehead on my knees and wrapped my arms around my legs. I made myself as inconspicuous, as invulnerable, as a stone.

It was not yet 11 P.M. I knew I'd made a dozen mistakes over the course of the evening, but I didn't have the luxury of learning from them because I didn't know what I should have done instead. Perhaps I should have gone into the waiting room after all. Perhaps I should have introduced myself to some women, or a family. But there was one thing, I decided. Regardless of what country I was in, and what social mores it upheld, I did not have to speak to anyone I didn't want to. I had the right to be rude, if I chose. I waited there, slowly turning cold and numb, until the train pulled into the station and sighed to a halt at 4:20 in the morning.

That's when Mickey found me again, and scolded me for not trusting him, and I cried alone in the Ladies' Car, surrounded by staring women. I wished desperately that they would ask me what was wrong, teach me where to sit and whom to ignore, tell me what to say when someone made a crude proposition, or failing that, to at least stop staring at me so that I could recover my dignity in peace. I thought of the English girl and wished I could talk to her again. Maybe the unwanted attention she was getting had nothing to do with her hair, but maybe it had nothing to do with her clothes either. Maybe if I had overlooked the perceived insult, I would have realized how much we had in common.

Some time after the train started moving, a conductor showed me to a bunk. It was an upper, which meant it would not become a communal seat during the day, and it was an end bunk, which meant there was no one across from me. I climbed up gratefully. Lying with my face to the wall and only the blue corridor light illuminating the car, I was as alone as I could be on a crowded, second-class Indian train.

It was a long ride to Delhi at the train's slow, chugging pace. I lay in my bunk for most of the day and into the next night, only climbing down from time to time to buy food or chai at one of the stations, or to pee through a hole in the train's floor onto tracks blurring past beneath me. On the way back to my bunk, I stood in the open doorway at the end of the car, allowing hot, milky chai to soothe my raw throat, the wide vista of green fields and brown ponds to soothe my raw restlessness, and the hot wind to dry the sweat at my hairline. Sometimes children waved, and I waved back. If my empty chai cup was clay instead of plastic, I threw it out the doorway to melt back into the earth.

At around 3 o'clock the next morning, loud chatter and laughter seeped into my sleep, and a tugging at my skirt woke me completely. Half a dozen or so teenage boys were hanging around the passageway near my bunk. They were not speaking English, but it was clear from their staring and gestures that they were discussing me, and that one of them had pulled my skirt. I let my eyes close, but one of them yanked at my skirt again, as though they were daring each other to touch me. I had no choice but to keep my gritty eyelids open. This stopped them from touching me, but it did not stop the jeering laughter and talk. I glared at them with increasing anger. I began to hope one of them would dare approach me again. Touch me and I will kick you right in the face, I thought. I meant it, and I think they realized that.

I was relieved and, surprisingly, slightly disappointed when the train finally slowed at a darkened station and the boys forgot me and hopped off in noisy twos and threes. A few last shreds of their laughter floated in from the darkness and dissipated as the train speeded up again, leaving them behind and carrying me forward, just a few hours away from morning and Delhi.

ॐ ॐ ॐ

Megan Lyles is a native New Yorker who has also lived in San Francisco. Her work has previously appeared in The Thong Also Rises: Funny Women Write from the Road *and in* The Subway Chronicles: Scenes from Life in New York *as well as on Bootsnall.com. She is currently working on a book about her yearlong bus journey from New York City to Buenos Aires.*

❧ ❧ ❧

To Italy, for Family

An heirloom is a powerful catalyst.

Standing in the near-empty master bedroom of my grandmom's condominium, I slid on my great-grandmother's mildewed bridal gown. The mirror no longer hung from the wall, so I couldn't see how I looked. My mother and I had already packed most of grandmom's photos and clothes in boxes, but when I unearthed the dress from a trunk in the bedroom closet, it intrigued me. I could not stop staring at it, touching it. Now I wanted to wear it, feel it on my body.

Donata, my great-grandmother, wore this gown in her wedding to Martino Aquaro, a scoundrel by everyone's estimation, in Martina Franca, Italy, some ninety years ago. The tiny ivory-colored gown barely fit over my own small frame. Specks of mold dotted the wrap-around skirt and the high-necked shirt's cloth-covered buttons appeared moth-eaten. The patient handiwork of the dress's creator was evident—each stitch hand sewn. I imagined Donata walking up the aisle of an unknown church in a tiny Italian town to face Martino, the man who would bring her to the United States.

This was the gown—and theirs was the marriage—that began my family in America. Here in my grandmother's small apartment in Holland, Pennsylvania, the shades were drawn and most of the furniture had already been removed. My grandmother now called an assisted-living facility home, as Alzheimer's prevented her from caring for herself. My mother asked what, if anything, I would like to keep for myself, yet I didn't respond. All I wanted was to comprehend this dress.

My great-grandmother died when I was still in elementary school, but I remember her. She wore her white hair pulled into a loose bun and rose-colored glasses perched on her nose, and we called her "Granny." A blue-and-yellow afghan covered her lap at all times. She didn't speak English, but I knew when she liked things because she would smile and nod, "That's a-nice." I could tell she was kind.

Unraveling myself from the antique bridal gown, I taped shut the final boxes of my grandmother's things and decided I wanted to visit Martina Franca. Decades ago, two relatives traveled there, but they were long deceased and their stories mostly forgotten. No one in my immediate, living family had been there. I wanted to discover what remained of my family before it disappeared altogether. At the very least, I could walk the same streets, sit in the same piazzas, and gaze at the same countryside that my relatives once did—and, perhaps, still do.

Before I left America, I called my grandmother from the airport to remind her of my trip. There was a time, just a few years ago, when she would have wept with joy. A minute after I said where I was headed, she asked, "Do you have plans tonight, honey?"

"Yes, Grandmom, I'm going to Italy tonight," I replied.

"To Italy? You should go to Martina Franca."

We had this conversation six more times before I finally said goodbye. I hung up the phone and cried. She would never comprehend this journey, never know I'd tried.

Visions of poverty, donkeys, and elderly spinster relatives—what I'd been told defined Martina Franca—filled my head when my boyfriend Bob and I landed in the Bari airport and fought our way through the crowds to pick up our rented Nissan Micra. We drove southwest for nearly two hours into the heart of Puglia, passing neatly planted rows of olive trees baking in the hot southern sun and a landscape of hills and valleys speckled with *trullis*, conical stone buildings unique to the region.

Finally we spotted our first sign, then another, and another, until I knew the sprawling clutter of buildings and homes rising from the hill ahead was, without a doubt, Martina Franca. It was enormous, and there wasn't a donkey in sight. Mopeds, cars, and bikes whizzed down the streets as impeccably dressed people strolled past countless shops. We headed away from the newer city toward the town's ancient quarter, crossing beneath an archway into the midst of cluttered homes stacked on top of each other.

The tourist office was little more than a room with a counter, yet four employees looked up expectantly when we entered. One woman handed me two maps and a small English guide and sent me on my way. I stepped away from the counter, ready to exit, but at the last minute I spun back. "My family lives here, the Aquaros, do you know them?"

"Aquaro is a common name, but maybe," the woman replied with little interest.

"Rita and Teresa Aquaro?" I pressed.

This sparked a maelstrom of yelling, hugging and laughing. Of course they knew Rita and Teresa, they said, both women were teachers. Phone books were pulled off shelves and phone calls made, but no luck. No answer.

Then the lone man behind the counter emerged with a torn sheet of paper that read, "Lino," and listed a phone number. "He is their brother," he said.

I had no idea there was a brother; I thought we only had two spinsters. I begged him to call Lino for me, and he complied. His conversation, which I managed to translate from Italian, lasted less than a minute.

"There's an American girl here, she says she's your cousin. Yes. She's at the tourist office. Two minutes? O.K." He hung up the phone. "Lino will be here in two minutes."

I clutched Bob's hand and waited. Everything had happened so fast and easily, it seemed unreal. Within minutes, Lino arrived. And boy, did he make an entrance.

Five foot five with a shock of white hair and tiny, round John Lennon sunglasses, Lino was dressed head to toe in white linen—a man of style and confidence. He blew kisses to the people in the office like a small-time Versace. Spotting me, he swooped me into a bear hug. Babbling introductions, I tried to convince him of my identity, but he paid no attention.

"You are hungry? Great, because we are having lunch." With that, he grabbed my hand, hopped down the tourist office steps, and charged through the piazza.

Lino chattered away with ease, as though he had been expecting my visit. He led us down the Via Vittorio Emmanuale and stopped at a cheese shop to pick up some extra mozzarella. As we walked through the maze of winding streets and whitewashed buildings, he explained that he was the editor of a regional paper, *Il Voce del Popolo*, Voice of the People. His son Angelo (another relative!) was one of four managing editors at *La Repubblica* and widely considered one of the top ten journalists in the country. His other son Pepe (yet another!) was a reporter for *Corriere della Serra*. They were all journalists like me: I wanted to shout, cry, jump up and down.

Soon we rounded a bend and came upon Lino's white-washed house. A woman in a red housedress leaned out an upstairs window and shouted down the street: "Did you get the Americans?" This would be Franca, Lino's artist wife.

They brought Bob and me into their house, hugging and kissing us, insisting we stay in their downstairs apartment, showing us pictures, pouring homemade *limoncello*, and never once questioning my credentials as a relative.

Franca, a spitfire with a penchant for chunky amber necklaces, served lunch, an immense concoction of salad, mozzarella in olive oil, tripe, sausages, cucumber, bread and wine. I tested my rudimentary Italian and learned that while I could speak quite well, I couldn't under-stand much at all. Bob, on the other hand, understood Italian almost perfectly—he just couldn't speak a lick of it. Laughter ensued as Franca joked that I was the mouth, Bob was the ears, and together we functioned as a whole.

Lino occasionally yelled at me to eat more, shoving forkfuls of food into my mouth like my grandfather used to do. So this is where our forced family feedings came from.

We moved onto the rooftop terrace after lunch and Rita and Teresa arrived—only not the spinsters I had been expecting. Sure, they were unmarried and in their fifties, but with college educations, fiery personalities, and fabulous jewelry. Teresa taught preschool; Rita was a professor of classics. Rita smoked long cigarettes and laughed a raspy chuckle, while Teresa stayed quiet but smiled often. Everything I had been told about my family and Martina Franca slowly dissolved.

An early evening tour was planned, and Franca led Bob and me along Martina Franca's web of streets, past palazzos and piazzas, past the theater and the opera and churches filled with elderly women kneeling on pews and saying the rosary. We tried to guess which one Donata married in, but no one knew for sure.

I waited until dinner at the restaurant Il Refugio to broach the subject of my great-grandfather. By the time I did, we had been gorging for two hours on plates of orecchiette with fresh tomato sauce and horsemeat stew, a local delicacy. The *vino* had flowed, and now Lino was enjoying a succession of after-dinner shots of coffee-flavored liqueur.

"Lino, do you know why my great-grandfather left Martina Franca?" I asked.

"No jobs, everyone was very poor at that time, so he had to leave," Lino replied.

But I pressed on. "Could there have been *legal* problems?"

"Oh, legal problems, of course, *si, si,*" he said sheepishly. Details of my great-grandfather's wanton ways remained fuzzy, but it seems he got a girl pregnant— not Donata—under dubious circumstances, landed in jail and was told he must leave Italy. Lino knew nothing more.

And so the mystery of Martino's misdeeds, and the exact details of the family's departure from Italy, would remain a mystery. As for Donata, Lino knew even less, except that she had been an orphan, with little choice but to marry. It appeared the closest I'd get to anything tangible related to their life was that molding wedding gown in Pennsylvania. I told Lino it seemed a shame that anyone would leave Martina Franca.

With that, we left the restaurant and he led us toward the town's main piazza, Plebiscito, and into the back door of a bar, into its back stockroom. I couldn't imagine what Lino had up his sleeve until he pulled me toward some black-and-white photographs hanging on the walls. I stared at a series of drawn, unsmiling faces, men leaning on hoes in the midst of arid fields, wrinkled women crouched over tables and crocheting lace, a shoe cobbler sitting on a broken stone step, a little boy in dirty, tattered shorts alone on a dirt street before a furniture repair shop, glaring at the camera.

"This was the Martina Franca when your great-grandfather lived here," Lino explained. "These photos were taken around 1910, right before he left. This is why he had to leave, why he should go to America."

The next day, Lino and Franca squeezed Bob and me into their car and drove us into the countryside to meet the rest of the Aquaros: Lino's two brothers, Fernando and Pepe, and their families. The entire Aquaro brood totaled more than twenty people. We traveled first to meet Fernando's family, eating mountains of pasta, meats and cheeses, then headed to Pepe's.

Pepe, who barely hit five feet, lived with his wife, children, and their families on a fifty-acre farm in a restored *trulli* compound. They grew all manner of food—olives, nectarines, plums, almonds, walnuts, beans—and fed us an endless stretch of homemade pastries and pies filled with their homegrown fruit. They were amazed I had traveled all the way to their town from America.

"Yesterday, there was nothing and today we have a new family," Franca said. "Thank you."

When I returned to the United States, my grandmother's condo was officially for sale, her boxes and belongings—and Donata's bridal gown—safely stowed at my parent's house. I showed my photos to my parents and told them the stories of Martina Franca and the Aquaros. They hope to go too someday, but until they do, I will continue telling the story—my story—that began with a gown and ended with a family.

ॐ ॐ ॐ

Valerie Conners is a native Philadelphian with a penchant for spontaneous Italy trips, local farmers markets, a good bottle of Nero d'Avalo wine and ogling Independence Hall's Colonial reenactors. She thanks her lucky stars (and any other contributing forces) daily to be living her dream, working as a Senior Producer, Interactive, for The Travel Channel.

SHAUNA SWEENEY

✿ ✿ ✿

The Moustache Brothers of Mandalay

A traveler witnesses a theatrical act of rebellion.

*I*t takes fifteen minutes to confirm I'm being followed. At first I had my doubts, kept second-, triple-, quadruple-guessing. I thought fear was playing tricks on me, making monsters out of shadows. But we've turned too many corners, switched onto too many new streets for coincidence. The car hasn't left my taxi's bumper since we pulled out of the dirt driveway of the Peacock Lodge at the other end of Mandalay. I can't see my pursuers' faces because their high beams are blinding. It doesn't matter. The message is clear. They know where I'm headed.

My taxi, a miniature blue pickup with a cramped tarp-covered bed, splashes through puddles and jolts across potholes on the unlit street. The right side-view mirror catches the reflection of my driver, a sun-weathered

Burmese man with a broad face and thinning black hair. His eyes dart to the reflection of the headlights. My chest constricts with a heady rush of fear. This is riskier than I had thought. Yet, I've come all this way. I have to meet the Moustache Brothers.

I shift on the rain-soaked cushion, grasp one of the steel handholds above to keep from bouncing out the back, and remember the American Vice-Consul's warning that morning in Yangon: "Be careful. Watch what you say. Whatever you do, please don't talk politics. You might be fine, but who you talk to could end up in prison, or worse. And if you happen to end up there yourself, I can't get you out just because you're American. Trust me; you don't want to go there."

I met his suspicious gaze with a wide-eyed, innocent one of my own and nodded *yes, yes of course, no, no never* at all of the appropriate moments. But my itinerary was already mapped out, the tickets purchased hours before. I'd be in Mandalay by mid-afternoon and if all went according to plan, at the Moustache Brothers' doorstep by nine o'clock that evening.

The roots of my trip to Burma (renamed Myanmar by the military junta in 1989) began six months before, in my campus library. As the only daughter of a divorced sea captain, I'd split my childhood between Australia, France, Thailand, and America, depending upon my father's work. But when I enrolled at UC Berkeley, the vibrant and expansive scope of my life shrunk to a cloistered campus and a towering stack of books. From almost the moment I set foot in my dorm room and inhaled the sterile smell of lemon antiseptic, I wanted to escape.

When I stumbled across "The Ghost Road," my dream grew legs. It was the story of a man named Mark

Jenkins who trekked through Burma's off-limit zones on an abandoned World War II road. Jenkins revealed a jungle country that had been on the fast track to modernization before the gears had screeched to a halt and reversed. Burma was a country tightly controlled by a paranoid military junta, where child labor camps, opium smugglers, and slave traders thrived.

Never before had it seemed so clear that my life lacked purpose. I imagined a place lost in time, hidden from the world, waiting to be braved, rediscovered, saved. An epic story was underway and I desperately wanted a role. I withdrew from Berkeley and packed my bags.

The taxi bounces through a deep pothole and my head bangs against the tarp above, splashing tepid rainwater into my face and into my mouth. It tastes of silt and mud and heavy monsoon rain. On the street, a young monk gathers his crimson robe up to his knees as he wades across a flooded alley.

The dusty city of Mandalay has long been considered the beating heart of Burma. The last royal capital boasts a rich history of poetic celebration. Rudyard Kipling, stationed here as a soldier during WWI, paid tribute to the charmed city on the bank of the Irawaddy River in a nostalgic poem called "On the Road to Mandalay," in which he fondly reminisced about the "spicy garlic smells and the sunshine and the palm-trees an' the tinkly temple-bells." But it's hard now to envision any trace of Kipling's Eastern paradise in this drowning, ramshackle city.

It's monsoon season, and thick, viscous sludge coats the roads. The men and women, whose full tawny faces are painted with *thanaka* (a white lime paste that doubles for sunscreen and makeup) stare at me with caution and curiosity from sheet-metal teahouses while a group of skinny children, no older than five or six, run after my taxi in a straggling pack, index fingers and thumbs connected in the Burmese sign for alms. Beside a giant speaker blaring a man's harsh voice in continuous prayer, a baby elephant stands shackled to a heavy iron stake. Nearby, a woman lies supine on the sidewalk. A watermelon-sized tumor bulges from her forehead. Our eyes meet and she tips her head as I pass. A soldier in camouflage fatigues patrols a street corner gripping a glossy black AK-47. All throughout the dark and muddy city, the air holds the threat of imminent violence.

Burma's history is written into the architecture. Crumbling colonial buildings that have been uninhabited since Burma's independence from Britain in 1947 line the streets amidst centuries-old Theravada Buddhist pagodas and stupas. I note with an odd combination of regret and relief the absence of gleaming skyscrapers and bustling financial districts that might have been, if the Tatmadaw (Burmese junta) had embraced capitalism. After all, Burma was once one of the wealthiest countries in Southeast Asia—so rich that Singapore initially modeled itself after the little kite-shaped country dubbed "the rice bowl of the East." But in 1964, when the junta took power, the rice-producing powerhouse retreated into isolation. It was only in 1996, when the military government opened its doors to limited tourism to resuscitate the strangled economy, that the world realized how deeply the country had plummeted. In the short span of three decades, opium fields had replaced rice paddies, shop owners had boarded up their windows, and the formerly bustling ports stood still. Progress had halted.

The truck turns onto a road where dilapidated houses cram together, lining the narrow street. I wipe the sweat accumulated in my palms on my jeans and consider the facts.

Two "Brothers," one joke, six years. This is essentially the story. In 1996, Par Par Lay and Lu Zaw, two famous Burmese comedians, were sentenced to prison for almost six years for telling a joke about a general at a democracy rally in Rangoon. For six years, they lived in a prison cell with a bucket toilet, breaking boulders with iron bars clasped around their ankles.

I think of comedians like Jon Stewart and Stephen Colbert and the incredible license they assume in ridiculing the world's most powerful leaders. In the United States, it is not uncommon for a well-aimed joke about the President to garner admiration and higher ratings. Here, the same leads to torture and incarceration.

I imagine the rush of exhilaration, the fear Par Par Lay and Lu Zaw must have felt as they stepped onto the stage and looked out at their audience, a sea of Burmese pro-democracy activists, waiting in anticipation. The Brothers knew there were military spies in the crowd. What must it have felt like to deliver that joke in the face of oppression? I reach for a comparison, but the thrill of running a red light seems inadequate and I find myself oddly jealous of these men, of the opportunities they've had to live bravely. Of course, I'm aware of the rights I enjoy, and I wouldn't trade places with them. Still, I can't help but wonder, what was it like to tell that joke?

At night the humidity in Mandalay intensifies, and the city turns into a steam bath. Hair plasters my forehead. The smell of wet earth and sour linen rises from my clothes while the mysterious car behind us follows from about five yards away. The taxi headlights illuminate another large, red-and-white sign aggressively painted in both English and Burmese on a crumbling brick building with shattered windows. It's the eighth sign I've seen that day and a different variation of the same message: TATMADAW AND THE PEOPLE COOPERATE, AND CRUSH ALL THOSE HARMING THE UNION.

The taxi slows. The driver veers to the shoulder and stops next to a skinny two-story house with a cheerful neon sign flickering above the door: THE MOUSTACHE BROTHERS. I've arrived.

My tailers slowly roll past us, then stop completely. Through the car window, the dark silhouettes of two men crane their necks to stare back at me. The moment drags on for ten, twenty seconds, pregnant with warning. It occurs to me that no one knows where I am.

When the brake lights fade and the car pulls forward to turn the corner, I release my breath, but can't shake the fear. The driver hops out of the cab, hawking a thick gob of saliva and red betel juice that hits the mud with a splat. He unlatches the tailgate and our eyes meet. His thin lips pull back into a tight smile, revealing kitten-like teeth stained red. He extends his rough calloused hand to help me out and his eyes slide away. Here in Burma, anyone might be a spy. New acquaintances tiptoe around each other, ears pricked for any sign of allegiance.

As I walk in the narrow door, fifteen pairs of eyes, both Western and Burmese, swing my way in the tiny fluorescent-lit garage. I'm late.

It's a tiny garage. A profusion of laminated pictures of Aung San Suu Kyi (the democracy leader whose image the junta has outlawed) crowd every inch of the walls.

A group of middle-aged European tourists armed with camcorders and cameras sit on plastic chairs circling a small wooden-crate stage.

A small, full-moustached man with alert eyes and a thin, wizened face greets me from the stage. With a bright pink headscarf wrapped around his head like a pirate and a blue "Moustache Brothers" t-shirt hanging on his wiry frame, he asks in raspy, rapid English where I'm from as he wiggles his wiry, gray moustache up and down.

"California," I answer.

"Ah, Arnold Schwarzenegger!" the tiny man says. His name is Lu Maw; he is the sole English-speaking brother of the troupe and the one who kept up the shows by himself when Par Par Lay and Lu Zaw were sent to prison. The audience, mostly European, laughs politely.

There is an impish quality to Lu Maw, an element of the ancient and absurd in his dark brown face and zany movements. He wiggles his sooty eyebrows and bugs his eyes as he speaks into a tinny, antique microphone, gesturing with a ringmaster's panache toward center stage.

Lu Zaw beats the rim of a small skin drum while a middle-aged, heavily made-up woman that Lu Maw introduces as his wife cries out a rhythm. She holds a series of traditional Burmese dance positions, kicking the long train of her silk dress behind her, and I begin to see with dawning embarrassment that I haven't come to Mandalay to commune with political renegades. I've bought myself a seat at a campy tourist show.

As Lu Maw's wife dances, I look down at my smooth uncalloused hands and see myself as they must: a naïve American trying to buy a cheap thrill and easy answers.

A Burmese man with warm, wide-set eyes appraises me from the corner. His face is noble and unlined except for the crows feet that fan out from the corners of his eyes—evidence of a lifetime of laughter. A prominent moustache, the telltale mark of the third and final Moustache Brother, sweeps across the top of his congenial smile. With his easy charm and bemusement, Par Par Lay bears some comparison to Mark Twain, if Mark Twain had a Burmese brother. He points to his chest, holds his finger in the air, and mouths, "Brother number one."

They haven't always performed like this, atop wooden crates in their moldy garage. Lu Maw speaks into his tinny microphone, "We performed all over Yangon, Mandalay, Inle Lake, all night on stage." He looks down and his voice softens, "But not anymore." He calls Par Par Lay and Lu Maw to the center of the stage and Lu Maw points to each man as he introduces them, "Lu Zaw, Lu Maw, Par Par Lay. We are comedians, we are blacklisted."

In 2002, after Amnesty International and Aung San Suu Kyi led a campaign for their release, the Brothers were freed on the condition they never perform again. This might have been the end of the story, if the Brothers had learned the intended lesson—to keep their mouths shut and their political opinions to themselves. But when the Brothers returned home to Mandalay from their prison cell, they held several shows in their garage to celebrate their liberation. Inevitably, these shows were reported to the Regional Commander, who demanded the Brothers put an end to the home performances. But the Brothers were both unflinching and clever. They shed their vaudeville costumes, washed off their face paint, and donned plain clothes. Now, the men were merely "demonstrating" a real show and therefore abiding by the Commander's orders. It was a risky, dangerous move but had succeeded so far. And since that night, the Brothers had bravely "demonstrated" performances for foreign visitors every night of the week here in their garage in Mandalay.

Lu Zaw's raspy accent and lightning delivery make him difficult to understand as he speeds through a canned slapstick routine that covers everything from the relative attractiveness of his wife to the quickest way to tie a headscarf. Then I think I hear Lu Maw call the junta the "KGB." I strain to follow his words, but Lu Maw has already switched back to his goofball vaudeville routine. He talks of the friendly rivalry between himself and Par Par Lay: "Par Par Lay, he used to be Brother number one, now Lu Maw Brother number one!" Par Par Lay raises an eyebrow and shakes his head in mock anger, but the mischievous look on Lu Maw's impish face disappears. He speaks gravely: "Par Par Lay spent six years in prison." He pauses, before breaking into a toothy smile, "But, how do you say? Like water off a duck's back!"

It's easy to see why Par Par Lay once held the most famous position in the troupe. There is a magnetic, reassuring quality to him, as if he's tallied the good and evil in life. His voice is strong and even, a silken tenor, and though he speaks in Burmese, his words flow together in a soothing waterfall of singsong syllables as he bows to the audience. He tucks and rolls his nimble body across the small stage then springs up to bow. "My name is Par Par Lay," he says in crisp English, "and I don't even know what I say."

"He don't know what he say! Poppycock, gobbledygook!" Lu Maw exclaims, shooing him off the stage. Lu Maw grabs a scuffed green military helmet—that bowling ball armor worn by all Burmese soldiers—and holds it high for everyone to see. The chuckles subside and the room quiets: "When you see this hat, run away, shoo shoo, very dangerous." Lu Maw puts on the helmet and it slips down with a thunk, covering all but his wiry moustache and red mouth: "Police man, 50,000 kyat. You pay the money in the helmet, you go, you no pay the money, handcuffs." He reaches into his pocket, pulls out a neon green plastic whistle, and holds it high: "Another one that's very dangerous, like atomic bomb." The shrill whistle echoes in the small garage: "Like nuclear. Saddam Hussein, he send it to me, we are friends. He has a moustache, I have a moustache. He is blacklisted, we are blacklisted. It is the Moustache Association!" The comparison is laughable but I know what Lu Maw is risking to portray the regime this way, and what these seemingly minor jokes could cost him. Almost no one in Burma will speak to foreigners about the political situation here for fear of imprisonment or worse.

All three Brothers crowd together in a madcap pose, holding hand-painted red-and-white wooden signs. They're painted identically to the government signs in the streets. Lu Maw holds one that reads, THE MOUSTACHE BROTHERS ARE UNDER SURVEILLANCE, Lu Zaw holds up KGB, and Par Par Lay's sign reads MOST WANTED. They preen in front of the tourists' cameras, tugging and twirling their moustaches. "Tell your friends," Lu Maw says with a flourish of his hand, "Tell your friends about the Moustache Brothers of Mandalay!"

The show ends with the passing of the "donation box," which is the same green military helmet Lu Maw wore earlier. I slip the last of my money into the green helmet and watch as the audience slowly files out the door into the night. I hang back until I'm the only visitor left.

"I admire you very much," I tell Lu Maw. He nods and smiles vaguely, but he gives no sign that he's understood. "You're very brave," I say. Lu Maw nods. His eyes flicker to the door.

His voice is light, but there is an undercurrent of something else, something steely. "Tell your friends about us; tell them to come and see the Moustache Brothers," he says again. I nod, but it's a lie. It'll take something more than these three aging comedians telling jokes in their garage to get the world to pay attention to Burma. It will take a sacrifice of tragic proportions. Suddenly, I'm scared for Lu Maw. No one ever talks about the real cost of courage.

I gather my things to leave when Lu Maw mutters something unintelligible. The only part I catch is "500 children" and "labor camp" but Lu Maw has already grabbed my arm, and is leading me towards an old television at the back of the garage. "Cover the door," he whispers to Par Par Lay and Lu Zaw. They saunter over to the doorway and lean against the sill, idly chatting. It's impossible now for anyone outside to monitor the room. Squinting in the dim light, Lu Maw rifles through a thick pile of white recordable CDs labeled in loopy Burmese before he finds the one he's searching for. For an instant, I feel sorry for this man, and the perilous life he leads, trusting a stranger like me with his safety. Who am I to deserve such trust? I could be anyone.

A grainy image appears on the TV screen and my attention shifts to the picture of Par Par Lay and Lu Zaw on stage in a yellow auditorium. They're both dressed in white from head to toe, in far nicer clothes than the shabby muscle tees they wear tonight. The audio is crackly and the camera zooms in and out at awkward angles. Par Par Lay speaks in fluid, rhythmic cadences.

His hands are animated. Then he crosses his arms and bobs his neck like a rooster: "Par Par Lay and Lu Zaw in Yangon, I couldn't go, I stayed here in Mandalay," Lu Maw says, staring at the screen wistfully.

He fast-forwards through scenes of a large laughing Burmese crowd until he stops upon the elegant face of a smiling older woman with cropped black hair and a long, slender neck. She's simply dressed in a white cotton blouse, her shoulders thrown back like a dancer. It's Aung San Suu Kyi, the leader of the National League for Democracy. I look at Lu Maw. This video is a recording of the Brothers' infamous joke!

Lu Maw's thin face is only inches away from the TV screen. He mouths the words of his brothers. He has memorized them.

On the screen, Aung San Suu Kyi looks amused but tired. There are fine lines beneath her eyes and parentheses around her mouth. The camera switches to the stage, where Par Par Lay pauses, crosses his arms in front of him, and puffs up his chest. He crows something in Burmese and his voice trumpets across the auditorium. When the camera switches back to Aung San Suu Kyi, she shakes her head and suppresses a smile, as a mother might when amused by a mischievous son.

"She couldn't control herself," Lu Maw whispers proudly. "She couldn't stop laughing." A pan of the auditorium shows an audience doubled over in tears.

"What does he say?" I ask Lu Maw, imaging the possibilities.

"He makes a funny song," Lu Maw replies, waving his hand in dismissal. His eyes don't leave the television. I hide my bewilderment. The men spent six years in prison over a joke not worth translating?

Lu Maw pushes the stop button on the DVD player

and the grainy video vanishes, replaced with a dark, blank screen. Lu Maw beams. At the door, Par Par Lay and Lu Zaw grin bashfully. Perhaps the junta didn't imprison the men for the content of their joke, but for the fearlessness they showed in telling it.

Lu Maw slides twenty business cards into my hand as I leave. "Please. Tell your friends to come and see the Moustache Brothers of Mandalay." His voice is solemn and determined. For the first time I see the purple crescents beneath his eyes, hear the fatigue in his voice. But even so, he's smiling.

I came on this trip for adventure, for thrills; for all the wrong reasons. I came to escape the boredom of a privileged life. I suddenly feel embarrassed by my foolish motivations. The disrespect I showed for education, the ingratitude for my rights and freedoms—to speech, to privacy, to laughter—that many only dream of. Yet I will never regret meeting the Moustache Brothers. If every American could see these old men—see them step onto their wooden crate stage in their muscle tees night after night to speak up for a people too terrified of their government to speak for themselves—they would see that heroes exist; that humor, real humor, is a choice. It is the decision to laugh rather than cower. The courage to make light out of darkness.

ॐ ॐ ॐ

A native of the San Francisco Bay Area, Shauna Sweeney lives in Santa Monica and teaches writing at the University of Southern California. She has circumnavigated the globe on a ship, traveled extensively through Southeast Asia, and slept in more airports than she'd care to admit. She is currently finishing her first novel.

/Ω; /Ω; /Ω;

Breaking Frontiers

A writer returns to her war-weary motherland.

*T*he bazaar in Landi Kotal is a gunsmith's paradise: an impressive display of Kalashnikovs, pistols, and hand grenades. I ask one of the merchants if he still has the Stinger missiles that the CIA supplied to the Afghan mujahideen resistance. "They were brave men," he says. "They fight Russians for USA."

A nasty cough ripples from his lungs and then the merchant draws my attention to an authentic Chinese assault rifle. Would I care to see the famous Israeli Uzi submachine gun? He also has some old Enfield .303 rifles.

"From India," he points out. "Indian woman very beautiful. I watch movie on VCR."

I lead him back to the question of Stingers, many of which were unused after the Soviet withdrawal. The U.S. government had spent vast amounts of time and money to recover the surface-to-air missiles, but the covert nature and lack of oversight of arms shipments made it virtually impossible to keep track of what happened once the weapons left American hands and got funneled into Pakistan.

"My friend in Dara," the old merchant says. "He have. Many people buy to fight war in Kashmir."

I turn down his request to see his collection of revolvers. Apparently, he's quite proud of the local knockoffs of the .32 caliber Webley. They're made by a factory in Peshawar, where you can also buy top-quality hashish. He can get me some smuggled stash from yet another friend.

Landi Kotal is an old garrison town, dating back to the days of the Raj. Crumbling watchtowers and insignias of various British regiments still guard this highest point on the Khyber Pass. We drive slowly through the cantonment, past the barracks and the Khyber rifles mess. The driver pulls into what appears to be a spacious guesthouse and salutes a slew of approaching servants. Anwar leads me into a tasteful salon decorated with ethnic handicrafts and black-and-white photographs of former VIP guests. I recognize Prince Charles, Nehru, Jinnah, and the Malaysian Prime Minister Mahatir. After washing up, we settle down to a meal of *daal, chapati, bhindi* and mutton *pulao* strongly flavored with cardamom.

The Pashtun waitstaff hovers around Anwar and me, clearly not accustomed to serving such insignificant company. The two of us sit around a huge teak table that could accommodate at least twenty. Anwar eats quickly and lapses into an awkward silence, eyeing me furtively from time to time. Despite his friendly chatter on the drive, I sense his discomfort in my presence. Underneath his brandy and cigar exterior, he conceals centuries of Rajput blood that has neatly divided the world of men and women into two separate chambers. I am clearly breaching protocol. Nonetheless, Anwar has turned out to be a good host, a friend of a friend whose gracious welcome has given me courage to leave the boring confines of Islamabad, where I've been working over the summer as a research analyst at an international think tank.

It's my first trip back to Pakistan in twenty-one years. I was itching to find out what had become of the place and how it had changed. Media reports painted dire scenarios of terrorist havens and bomb blasts. Pakistan had earned a dubious reputation as a megalopolis of mayhem, the world's most dangerous country. It made me feel ashamed and embarrassed to claim Pakistan as my birthplace and the seat of my childhood. My return is meant to allay the cultural amnesia racked up over two decades during which I never once went back. Like it or not, I had become a stranger to my homeland. But I was haunted by the memories. I had to know, for better or worse, how much of Pakistan was still a part of me, and whether or not I would love it or hate it. I needed to glue back all those pieces from the past in order to make sense of the present.

The drive up the Khyber Pass is nothing short of spectacular. We cruise through what looks like a moonscape of dung-colored hills. For a moment, it feels as if I'm airborne, witnessing sharp angles of earth and sky. The road hugs a series of tight switchbacks. In the back of a Land Rover, I slide from left to right on the seat like a stray hockey puck. Visions of invaders and conquests dance through my head. The Great Alexander, Mahmud of Ghaznavi, Genghis Khan. Men, armor, and horses. They were all here.

During the 1980s, the world's most famous pass was inaccessible to all but journalists and aid workers due to the Soviet occupation of Afghanistan. I learn that the Khyber, which is part of Pakistan's Federally Administered Tribal Areas, is officially closed to foreigners at this time. Since I have a Pakistani passport, a Political Agent has given me permission to travel through.

"He is a very nice man," Anwar says. "We studied at Qaid-e-Azam University together. He also has a master's in International Relations."

A Political Agent, Khyber Pass, and the Tribal Areas. This I couldn't wait to see. Entering Khyber agency at the border outpost of Jamrud, a marble sign acknowledges the infamous Alexander, known to locals as Sikandar. As the SUV climbs up the looping road, a man pedals furiously on a bicycle with three more trailing behind. Anwar points out the cycle smugglers who are paid 200 rupees for each made-in-China bike they transport from the Afghan border into Peshawar, a distance of roughly sixty harrowing miles. It's a thankless job, risking not only flat tires but also head-on collisions and avalanches on an average day's work. Thanks to the poor man's *mazdoori* or labor, those bikes fetch up to 3,000 in the Rawalpindi bazaar.

Anwar is full of interesting tidbits. He talks about the notorious corruption along the Khyber. Imported goods shipped from Singapore, Malaysia, and Japan to Karachi's port are loaded onto trucks for transshipment to Kabul, about a thousand miles away. Upon reaching the Afghan border, the refrigerators, ACs, and TVs are unloaded and smuggled back into Pakistan.

At every checkpoint, bribes substitute for customs duty. Prosperous smugglers and drug barons have built huge villas just outside of Peshawar, complete with manicured gardens, marble entry halls, and a private militia of armed bodyguards. Anwar expounds on his pet theory that the tribal beltway is one of the safer parts of the country. The lack of rigid laws gives less incentive to break laws. Justice is a private concern. For the most part, people are just trying to get by, eking out a living the best way they can, even if that means selling drugs and weapons.

"Afghanistan is waiting!"

I am staring at a tall, dark-skinned man with a mile-wide grin.

"Tayar ho?" He asks if I'm ready to go.

Back at the guesthouse, I finally meet Abdul Ghafoor Shah, the local Political Agent who has given me the green light to travel this far. We sit down for some tea and lemon cookies in the garden. I want to ask Ghafoor about his job, but he keeps teasing me about my low intake of sugar and dumps three heaping spoonfuls into my chai.

"You need to put on some weight," he pronounces definitively. "How can you climb mountains looking like that?"

Ghafoor is probably in his mid-thirties though he looks much older. Clear hazel eyes radiate warmth, making the rest of his heavyset features less foreboding. I like the way he laughs, rocking back and forth and clutching his stomach. His easygoing manner immediately strikes a friendly chord. We carry on a running commentary about our love of mountaineering. Ghafoor recounts his adventures in Chitral. I can almost picture tiny exclamation points dancing in his pupils.

"The Kalash are a very interesting people," Ghafoor says. "They did not convert to Islam so they are considered *kafirs* living in Kafiristan, the land of non-believers. What nonsense! I have many friends there and they are good kind people. And you should see the women. They have long hair up to here," he touches his hips. "And they wear shells in their braids, like your Native American Indians."

"Are you sure about that?" I ask. "I thought they wore feathers. I don't remember any shells."

"Shells, feathers, it's all the same!"

"Yes indeed. So will you take me to Chitral?"

"Well, you'd better fatten up those skinny shoulders first!"

Ghafoor laughs and dumps more sugar in my cold tea.

I try to include Anwar in the conversation, but he sits in a corner and sulks, unable to compete with Ghafoor's easy banter. All of a sudden, my newfound acquaintance gets up and bids me salaam.

"Excuse me, but I have to go extend a ceasefire," Ghafoor announces with a grave expression.

I ask what he'll offer as an incentive.

"Oh you know, the usual carrot-and-stick approach," he replies and hurries off to strike another deal.

Twenty minutes later, Ghafoor is back in the garden. We drive his jeep toward the Afghan border. His three bodyguards trail behind in a separate vehicle, making sure to maintain a respectable distance. More dusty barren streets and gun-filled bazaars come into view. Children in tattered clothes wave gleefully and scatter like frightened rabbits to their mud brick huts in the refugee camps that extend in maze-like contortions. I sneak a glance at a smug-looking Ghafoor through the side-view mirror. Apparently, the ceasefire has gone down well.

Road congestion picks up near the Pakistani/Afghan border at Torkham. We tail a truck decorated with a busy collage of flying partridges, Alpine snow-capped meadows, and Quranic verses to ward off the evil eye. I expect to see caravans of Afghans trickling in from across the gate, but there is scant evidence of human traffic. After the 1979 Soviet invasion of Afghanistan, Pakistan absorbed some 3 million refugees into its northwest province. Along with the poor families and tribes came a culture of guns and drugs, plus the ensuing trafficking, corruption, and violence that have become emblems of all that is wrong with the country. This is not to say that Pakistan had no such problems before the Afghan crisis, but to consider the problems exclusively homegrown is to miss the bigger picture.

When the United States requested Pakistan's help to ward off the Communist threat in neighboring Afghanistan, it nurtured a chummy alliance of self-serving interests. Pakistan offered local recruits, equipped with cash and weapons from Uncle Sam, to fight the infidels next door. General Zia's cooperation with the Americans made him quite a hero in the West. When the Carter administration offered a billion dollars worth of aid to alleviate the Afghan refugee situation, Zia made headlines when he smiled and said, "But that is just peanuts!" Perhaps he ought to have replied with a two-part question that history would answer in due time. *Who was more in need of the other? And who got the short end of the stick?*

We halt near a large concrete customs building and dart inside to enjoy more sweet tea and biscuits in a stuffy room overlooking the border post. I walk up to the open window facing a wall of jagged khaki mountains and wonder what kind of fortitude it must take to cross over them lugging all your possessions in a cloth bundle.

Ghafoor comes up beside me. "What are you thinking?"

"It's such a desolate place. But I feel it has seen many survivors."

He smiles and motions me to join him outside. The three bodyguards spring to life, trailing us at a modest distance, Kalashnikovs in hand, muzzles pointing downward.

"Don't worry about a thing," Ghafoor says reassuringly. *"Yahan, meri hukumat hay!"* (This is my turf.) He sweeps a welcoming hand, pointing out things I should notice, like the WELCOME TO PAKISTAN sign that shares the billboard with Khyber Rifles and Pepsi.

Once again, I find myself the only woman in a sea of men. Camera in hand, I focus on the Pakistan/ Afghanistan border checkpoint and click away at the moving festivity, willing my lens to catch something interesting. A conga line of trucks awaits inspection. Not allowed to step past the gate, I cross a narrow ridge over a gully and sink my feet into Afghan soil.

Ghafoor grins and points to my flimsy sandals. "Is that what you climb mountains in?"

I inscribe our names in Urdu on the gravely earth with the back of my chewed-up Biro.

Just in time for sunset, Ghafoor decides to take us up to a TV tower, sensing my need to prolong the adventure. "There is a fantastic view of Afghanistan from the summit," he says. "But I don't think you are fit enough to climb all the way up!"

I stick out my tongue in retaliation. We pile back into his jeep. I am sandwiched between Ghafoor who drives and Anwar who is chain-smoking Marlboros. Each time Ghafoor shifts gears, his hand digs into my waist and I cry aloud in fake torment that causes him to double over in laughter. The jeep lurches forward, tracing the curve of an unpaved dirt road. I watch the angle of the sky shifting at every turn, just like in an airplane.

The TV tower perches up a steep incline. Fierce winds flap against my chador as I gingerly walk along the edge of a cliff. Honey-colored hills spread out in all directions. Peering toward the horizon, I can only make out ring upon ring of bluish mountain ranges in the disappearing light. From this vantage point, Afghanistan looks serene and beautiful as if newly born and it is difficult to imagine the actual horror and destruction of the war-torn country that lies beyond. It gives me some consolation that no amount of carpet-bombing could obliterate the natural beauty of those mountains, nature's small triumph over man.

Ghafoor's bodyguards squat on their haunches smoking bidis. I walk up to one of them and ask to hold his Kalashnikov. He shrugs and, making sure the trigger is in the locked position, cradles the weapon in my arms like a precious infant that weighs at least twenty pounds. I adjust my headscarf to cover my face and aim towards Kabul, while my onlookers laugh and urge me to find Osama bin Laden.

"You'll be a rich lady if you find Osama," Ghafoor

tells me in a serious tone. "And if we find him together," he adds, "We'll split the proceeds, fifty-fifty."

"Do you know where he's hiding?"

"Only Allah knows," Ghafoor replies and glances at his watch. "Come. Let us pray together."

We spread some jute rugs on the parched brown earth and turn toward Mecca. Maybe not so far away, Osama is praying in some cave. What connection do we possibly have? Granted, we are all Muslims, but certainly not of the same backgrounds and persuasions—a girl from America in search of her roots, a kindly bureaucrat who drinks too much tea, and the world's most wanted criminal—all of us remembering God in the act of *namaz,* united in time by our actions. In our minds, however, we may as well be galaxies apart.

You can tell a lot about a person by the way he or she shakes your hand. Typically, in Pakistan, men and women do not shake hands, except in business settings or in hip young circles. I often made the mistake of extending my hand in greeting to which I received at best a wishy-washy grazing of palms or simply a total lack of acknowledgement. Even among women, pumping hands is more a matter of a loose clasp. So when Ghafoor holds my right hand in a firm grip to say goodbye, I know right away why we hit it off. His handshake is sincere and honest. It seals our friendship. Ghafoor gives me his card inscribed with the quaint job title of *tehsildar,* which roughly translates as village administrator. We exchange email addresses and phone numbers, planning to meet up next time he comes down to Islamabad.

Anwar and I drive back through the Khyber Pass in pitch-blackness, with the headlights of the Land Rover guiding the way ahead. Only the wail of the Pashtun song on the radio keeps my thoughts from drifting. I keep thinking of that exceptionally warm handshake; the kind I had never before received in Pakistan.

જ જ જ

Maliha Masood was born in Pakistan and moved to the United States when she was twelve. She is an award-winning writer in creative nonfiction and author of the book Zaatar Days, Henna Nights. *With a master's in law and diplomacy from Tufts University, she has worked in conflict resolution with the International Crisis Group and is founder of the Seattle-based workshop and seminar group The Diwaan Project. Find her online at www.maliha-masood.com.*

※ ※ ※

Language Lessons

A sister explores her adopted brother's native land.

I awaken with a sweaty forehead to a staticky radio blaring news in a sibilant Northern dialect. This is the first time I've managed to sleep through the pre-dawn patter of chickens and the violent rhythmic sweeping of the betel stain-toothed neighbor that have served as my alarm clock for the last few weeks. Disentangling myself from the mosquito net, I feel for my glasses on the cinder-block floor and dress quickly in the electric-green house pajamas Mai has sewn. Then I step warily into the main room in awkward men's flip-flops, ready to be attacked by a multitude of little arms reaching up for airplane rides.

But the radio is squawking to an empty house. The gilded cat clock with the undulating right arm informs me I've slept through our morning coffee ritual. It's after eight o'clock—which might as well be noon in this part of the world. Sleeping in is a shortcoming in Vietnamese culture, and is especially suspect if one has been out drinking the previous night. Which I have occasionally been known to do.

Since the merciless midday sun discourages reasonable people from venturing too far from the shade, rising before daybreak is directly linked to efficiency in rural parts of this country. In the average Cam Duc family, the children are washed, fed and dressed—chores completed—by 5:30. The dutiful Catholics, many of whom fled here to the central coast from the North after the country was divided in 1954, weave their way through the sandy lanes to daily mass, gathering up their neighbors as they go. Laid-back Buddhists in bare feet bat badminton shuttlecocks to and fro in the street before making their way to school or the market. By nine o'clock, the village women are already home preparing lunch, and the buzzing central market becomes a ghost town. Yesterday I counted one saleswoman for every three stands, halfheartedly fanning herself with a conical hat while her colleagues took turns napping behind the counter.

8:12 A.M. The lateness of the hour has transformed me back into a slothful teenager, guiltily sneaking into the kitchen to forage for whatever's been left behind by the rest of the family, who had their breakfast hours ago. But today the rice cooker is dry, and there are no bananas ripening on the tree near the noisy pigpen. Lan and the girls have, of course, gone to church. The family matriarch thinks it funny that I, a baptized Catholic, don't share her enthusiasm for emerging from bed in the pitch dark in order to submit to ninety minutes of sweltering singsong-prayer-chanting-kneeling-standing-kneeling. Not to mention the staring.

I know that gentle, naïve Lan has had to account for my absence with her neighbors, postulating that I can't

yet understand what's being said in the sermon. And
she's not entirely wrong. But the truth is I can't bear the
countless pairs of inquisitive eyes trained on me during
the service, or the ensuing deconstruction of my outfit.
The glow of celebrity wore off within the first week
here. Now I just wish I looked more Vietnamese. Or
even a little bit Vietnamese.

So it is that Tâm and I have the freshly swept porch
to ourselves. I find him leaning up against the house—
shirtless, smoking, and staring absent-mindedly out at
an ox cart going by, laden with green mangos—the local
cash crop. The cart drivers, an old man and a boy who is
probably his grandson, swivel their whole torsos to stare
at a spectacle that wholly defies their definition of femi-
ninity. Here is a short-haired white woman who is somehow tan (a disagreeable skin tone indicating she has been
born into peasantry or has toiled in the fields), way too
tall and far too old to be unmarried, wearing glasses and
standing around in fluorescent pajamas next to a gaunt
and somewhat severe-looking middle-aged Vietnamese
guy. A dark-skinned Vietnamese guy. Tâm and I share a
complicit laugh, having already been the subjects of this
childlike curiosity on more than one occasion. "I'm his
sister, not his wife!" I float into the ether, in my useless
English. The ox-cart drivers smile shyly and give me a
military salute before slowly moving on.

"Gee Eye!" Tâm says, laughing and drawing out
the syllables. Many locals, the grandfather and the boy
included, suspect that I, with my dark hair, tan skin
and blue eyes, am the fruit of a brief liaison between an
American G.I. and a Vietnamese prostitute. This town-
ship, home to Southeast Asia's deepest natural harbor,
was known to Americans as Cam Ranh Bay—a major
Army, Navy, and Air Force base during the "American

War." Before me, the last foreigner the old man saw may well have been a G.I., hence his assumption that I must be somehow related to the guy. One of the locals' favorite greetings upon meeting me has been "Hello! Number One!"—often accompanied by an enthusiastic thumbs-up sign. Bizarrely, no one on this side of the bridge that once divided North and South seems to hold a grudge. In fact, the natural progression of the "Number One!" salutation has something to do with the Viet Cong being "Number Ten." Which is apparently an undesirable figure.

With a slender, nicotine-stained finger, Tâm silently indicates my coffee, covered with a chipped saucer and waiting for me on the porch step. His son Bao (Storm) has taken to pouring me one every morning before he leaves to play pickup soccer in the sandy field between the mango fields and the cemetery. I slurp the viscous lukewarm liquid readily, savoring the sugar crystals at the bottom. I used to consider myself a tea drinker, but have quickly grown accustomed—fine, addicted—to the stuff, locally grown, roasted in butter, ground, and filtered ever-so-slowly through a tiny aluminum apparatus that sits just on top of a glass half-filled with gooey condensed milk and some superfluous teaspoons of sugar. Tâm prefers the pre-sweetened foil packets of Nescafé instant coffee (made in China) he buys by the dozen at the market. This is the formula, he insists, that gives Italian soccer players their morning boost. I argue that European footballers are more partial to freshly-brewed espresso with their morning pastry. Tâm shakes his head in vigorous disagreement, saying he'd have to go to Italy to confirm my assertion. We both know that's not likely to happen anytime soon.

Tâm coughs his stony smoker's cough and moves

to switch off the radio. As he turns to do so, I catch a stifled smile that deepens the ruts in his face and makes me think he hasn't really been listening to the morning news. The cranked-up radio is one of his wake-up maneuvers—this one intended to save me from the ceaseless questioning that would have undoubtedly ensued if the girls had returned to find me still in bed at this hour: "Is My Nhung sick? How many glasses of rice wine did she drink last night?" And then: "Big sister Nhung *oi!* Do you need *dau xanh* (green medicinal oil)?" This is what Chut, Be Em, and Cot would want to know as soon as they came in to bounce on my mattress and rub my temples with their sticky fingers.

He doesn't need to sketch this scenario for me. My Nhung has learned to cope with complete loss of privacy in this strange new communal world. However, I'm still struggling with the pronunciation of my new moniker, which I've managed to translate as either "beautiful velvet" or "lovely young antler," depending on which borrowed dictionary I've consulted. After a few days of failing to aspirate the crippling line of consonants in "Christine," the family came up with my Vietnamese name by unanimous vote. One way of getting used to my identity change is by referring to myself in the third person, which Vietnamese people do all the time. Speaking this language is kind of like that episode of *Seinfeld* where Elaine meets "the Jimmy," the guy who has removed the word "I" from his vocabulary. He tries to pick Elaine up at the gym with lines such as "Jimmy's been watching you. You're just Jimmy's type," while Elaine swoons, assuming that "Jimmy" is another attractive man she's been eyeing.

Unlike Jerry and George, no one in Cam Duc winces when I put together sentences like "Yes, My Nhung likes eat rice with fish sauce, but My Nhung eat already four bowls, thank you!"—so they must be grammatically correct. I have yet to hear anyone in the village employ the word *toi*, or "I," which I've been told is used only in formal situations. I don't think I've been in a formal situation yet, although I did note the apt use of the word *toi* by a toothsome TV presenter just the other day. It made me feel a little smug thinking of all those backpackers I overheard trying to speak Vietnamese at the internet café in Nha Trang last week, dropping *"toi"*s all over the place.

As the caffeine kicks in, last night's rice wine loosens its grip on my cranium. My mind flits back to the muddy events of the previous evening, which began when the local police chief appeared at the door around dinnertime. This middle-aged man with the beer paunch common to Vietnamese men of his status strode into the main room without taking off his shoes or high-crowned cap. In almost any Asian home, a gesture like this is interpreted as a willful insult.

The chief told Lan he was hungry, point-blank, then shifted his attention to Tâm. The policeman's face was already flushed from too much rice wine; his eyes struggled to find their target. Shuffling a sheaf of papers and carbons that I correctly assumed had something to do with me, he suddenly cleared his throat and spat the resulting yellow gob on the tiled steps just outside the front door. It was not his first visit to the house since my arrival. Although Tâm had already paid the customary bribes that accompanied the official registration process for lodging *nguoi nuoc ngoai*—persons from outside countries—the man in the putrid green uniform wanted more. He seemed to think that a spoiled American heiress like me might just unzip a magic pocket in her gold-lined suitcase and fork over a stack of greenbacks every time he popped in to say *xin chao*. I had considered hauling out the stitched-up, muddy backpack and disintegrating sandals I'd been carting around for more than two years and telling him the embellished version of the woeful Buckleys-from-the-South-Ring-Road-of-Dublin-who-crossed-the-great-ocean-in-steerage-and-made-a-go-of-it-in-New-York-now-isn't-that-lurvely-story, starting somewhere around the potato famine. But recalling that everyone outside the immediate family still miscon-strued my attempts at "hello," I had simply waved goof-ily—a lame attempt to disarm the police captain.

At that point, Tâm's black eyes had banished me to my room. As I walked out, I watched him steel his jaw, turn back to the intruder, and force his lips to form the polite greeting used to invite friends to share a drink or favorite dish. *"Xin moi..."* Through my muslin curtain, I watched him open the locked cabinet where the bottle of imported whiskey and special glasses were kept. Thus began another long evening in which the police chief and his buddies (who trickled in and out over the next few hours) enlightened Tâm on model citizenship while indulging in free smokes, drinks, and salty dried squid. By the time I was summoned again, they had already polished off a case of Saigon beer, a bottle of Johnny Walker Black and had resumed doing shots of *ruou de*, Vietnamese moonshine. "Brother Tâm says you can handle this stuff," the chief had sneered at me. "Let me see that with my own eyes."

Tâm knows where my mind has ventured. He snaps his fingers twice as if to rouse me from this unpleasant reverie, then uses his thumb and index finger to work his mouth into a smile—meaning that I should do the same. The gesture is nothing more than the cheap ploy of a clown plying the party circuit, but it has its intended effect. We sit in comfortable silence on the cool porch tiles for a while, watching the street vendors shoulder their loads of sumptuous breakfast treats: *xoi*, sweet sticky-rice parcels mixed with corn or mung beans, coconut, and peanuts wrapped in banana leaves; *banh bao*, warm chewy pork buns; and *bun*, rice noodles of various widths and shapes served in an alluring assortment of rich broths. To my eager palate, all the options are tempting, but Tâm waves the ladies away with a few 180-degree twists of his wrists. Lan has left us *banh mi* (the Vietnamese interpretation of a French baguette) to dip into our sweet coffee, to be followed by a luncheon feast. Last night, her eyes danced as she recited the list of delicacies she'd be concocting to commemorate the halfway point to *Tet*, Lunar New Year.

So the least we can do is resist the noodle orgy being paraded before our eyes. Tâm can't afford to buy us breakfast, and hierarchy prevents me from offering to do so. I can't help but worry how Lan is going to pay for the upcoming smorgasbord. She won't hear of taking my money for groceries, but I know she is struggling to keep the family fed. The household meals that were so elaborate a month ago—when my brother Phuoc was still here shelling out American dollars to convert into dong—have rapidly decreased in variety and size. Lan has discreetly been instructing her children to direct the choicest morsels into my rice bowl. In turn, I've been surreptitiously sliding chunks of fatty meat back onto the serving plate or into the smaller children's bowls.

Turning away from the vendors, Tâm motions for me to clear the coffee cups out of the way, signaling the beginning of our ad hoc tutorial.

Normally gruff Tâm allows himself to enjoy this game

as much as I do. He doodles in my notebook, enthralled by my Western ballpoint pen. Looping and dotting and squiggling, he takes off on language tangents I am not yet ready to follow. I stop him, remembering that the boy and his grandfather drove by on a new word. I want to know how to say "ox cart," and begin with my latest Vietnamese sentence: *"Cai gi day?"* What's this here? Although the ox cart has long since disappeared from view, I point to the spot where it rolled past.

But Tâm doesn't pick up on my train of thought, telling me, somewhat impatiently, "You know the word for that already. Road, Road."

"No, No," I shake my head, exasperated. I don't know *how* to say "The thing that was here before," or "animal," or even "twenty minutes ago." And I don't have a phrase book. I wasn't planning to stay in this country for more than two weeks.

Tâm pats the notebook, huskily encouraging me. "What? What does *em* [you] want to know?" In Vietnamese, as in many other Asian languages influenced by Confucianism, one never refers to another person as simply "you." There are about a dozen different versions of this simple pronoun, depending on the age and status of the speaker in relation to his interlocutor. In this case, Tâm doesn't really say "What do you want to know?" but rather "What does little sister want to know?" This strikes me as particularly endearing, and I've been basking in his usage of the word *"em,"* while I refer to him as *"anh,"* or older brother, to his wife Lan as *"chi,"* or older sister, and the youngest kids as *"con,"* child. It is this practice, I think, that has sped up my initiation into the family and even the village. In Tâm's mind, *em* is the only pronoun he can apply to me, the American daughter of a couple who adopted his younger brother Phuoc so many years ago.

Tâm has been gradually telling me the story of how that arrangement came about, using water-stained photographs, gestures, and urgent-sounding Vietnamese words that are still mostly unknown to me. Phuoc, he seems to be saying, was too young to remember how or why he took to the South China Sea with his four brothers and dozens of strangers in a rickety wooden boat back in 1978. After Reunification, things got worse instead of better for the Nguyen family. There was nothing to eat, no work or school, and too many children sleeping in their two-room cottage. With their mother dead and their father missing, the older Nguyen brothers sold their remaining possessions and used what little gold they had stashed away to buy passage on a fishing boat. Their seventeen-year-old sister Phi was instructed to stay behind and guard the family home and altar. The next year she was married off to a man she had never met. Three little girls later, her husband succumbed to malaria and left her a widow at the age of twenty-five.

Of the five brothers, only Phuoc and twenty-one-year-old Tri made it safely to America. Tâm, arrested with his seasick youngest brother in his arms after sneaking back home for necessary supplies, was forced to pay for his family's "treason" through years of hard labor imposed by the revolutionary government. Dong—the eldest, the father figure, the Saigon scholar fluent in French and English, who would have kept them all together—drowned a week later, attempting to save their boat from certain starvation. Or something like that. Tâm is frustrated with my low level of comprehension: *"Em co hieu khong?"* Do you understand? He yells impatiently at top volume. *"Tai sao khong hieu?"* Why not?

"Because, you asshole, I-AM-NOT-VIETNAMESE!" I yell back. He laughs for no reason except perhaps that he recognizes the word "Vietnamese." I'm finding it immensely liberating, this blurting out of expletives at top volume. Biking home from the beach near the sugar factory the other day, I inexplicably found myself screeching "Uterus!" at the post-pubescent soldiers who had snuck down to watch and snicker while I attempted to teach frail, uncoordinated little Chut how to swim in the tepid sea. The soldiers left us alone after that.

I have been in Vietnam for almost two months now. A spontaneous little detour from my solo round-the-world journey—sparked by a last-minute email from Phuoc inviting me to meet him in Saigon and then drive up north to surprise his family—has turned into all of this. Although Tâm is criticizing me for not understanding enough, the police are concerned that the opposite is true. According to one of Tâm's friends, who heard it from a neighbor, their latest theory is that I am a C.I.A. agent infiltrating the community and spying on military operations in the deep-water harbor.

State suspicions aside, as My Nhung, I find it impossible to feel estranged from the neighbors. No matter how hard they stare and cover their mouths at my otherness, they still must address me in their language as their "daughter," "niece," or "older sister." In turn, with every conversation, these strangers become my "aunt," "uncle," "grandmother," or "younger sibling." Even the young waitresses at the local noodle stand are affectionately referred to as *"be,"* another way of addressing the youngest child in a family, kind of like calling them "baby."

Not yet ready to give up on the word "ox cart," I call over the dusty black dog, Minot. "O.K.," I start.

Tâm snorts. It's hard to translate the infinite uses of "O.K.," but he's finally grown accustomed to the word's constant presence in my speech.

"O.K. So I know this is a dog. This is small... But what is big?"

Tâm looks at me hard. If we focus, we know we might achieve mutual comprehension. I probably didn't get the pronunciation right. Fuck.

But no; he repeats what I've just said: "The dog is small and what is big?"

I smile in affirmation, and he thinks some more. I trot out to the lane with the dog following me, and stand right in the ruts the ox cart left in the sand. "What is big...?" I want to say "was just here," or "left a little while ago," but I have no idea how to say either, so instead I settle for "go now."

"What is big go now?!"

The villagers are beginning to trickle back from church, some heading down the street past Tâm and Lan's house to the market. One of them pushed me on to the communal rice scale last week in order to confirm that I did, in fact, weigh 63 kilos (140 pounds), an unspeakable heft. As they pass, they take in the details of the scene so they can retell it later: "We just saw the lady giant—yes, it's true, she really does weigh 63 kilos!—in those strange glasses and men's sandals, hopping around ranting 'What is big go NOW!' Did you hear that she's twenty-eight and still hasn't found a husband?" (Insert tongue clicking.)

Minot helps me ignore the kibitzers, backing up my mantra with some energetic barking. At this point, a few of the neighborhood kids pop over and add their voices to the sideshow: "What is big go now…What is big go now!" we chant. Tâm exhales the smoke through his teeth and nods his head coolly. He gets it, I think.

He beckons me back to my notebook, lying open on the cool porch tiles. A couple of the kids follow and stretch themselves across my legs, fingering the pen and flipping the pages of the pad with intense interest. Tâm scatters the group of them like a flock of frightened chicks with one forbidding glance and a flick of his cigarette.

Last week the neighborhood children experienced the wonders of Frisbee, so they now expect me to show them something new and exciting every time they pass by. Unfortunately for them, my student's notebook is nonsensical to anyone but me, since it has no real system of organization and is scrawled in dozens of different scripts, depending on who has taught me each particular word or phrase. Its pages randomly chart my unsteady progress with the language over the past weeks—a program of total immersion involving no contact with English speakers and haphazard memorization of the word for every object physically encountered. Nouns are the most important, I've discovered. Verbs can be acted out, and adjectives just add nuance. I've been getting by fine with only two of them—*dep* (beautiful) and *ngon* (tasty).

Tâm turns to a clean page and draws the face of a dog. Next to it he writes *"con cho."* A cartoon cat quickly takes shape on the page, next to which he scrawls, almost illegibly, *"con meo."* The second word is new to me, probably because I have yet to see a cat in Cam Duc. I have only learned the words for things that have crossed my path—or have appeared in karaoke videos—since I arrived. Here in what locals still call "South Vietnam," dogs are both domestic pets and the occasional snack food. But Southerners tend to reproach their mysterious Northern cousins for eating cat meat. The word *con meo* rhymes with the term *xui xeo*, unlucky: a bad omen, for sure.

Although I'm trying to be patient, I begin to doubt that Tâm has remembered the ox cart, because he then draws a monkey in a tree and scrawls *con khi*. So far, no ox. But *there* is a bloated duck, *con vit,* which dances off the page with a few quacking sounds from Tâm that make the younger kids giggle. They cover their gap-toothed mouths with tiny hands, having been taught how impolite it is to smile or laugh without hiding it, in the same way that Westerners mask their yawns. I already know the word *vit,* since on several occasions I've watched Lan slit the throats of these unfortunate creatures, mixing their still-warm blood with herbs and peanuts to concoct a dipping sauce for rice crackers. Suddenly I realize the pattern: the use of *con* before a word must indicate an animal.

Gratification comes at last when Tâm sketches some kind of bovine and writes *con bo* underneath. The diacritical marks and circumflexes and curly things he includes on some of these words are crucial, I now know. At first I treated them as mere ornamentation. Without its tonal indicators, Vietnamese at first looks easy to those accustomed to the Roman alphabet. But until one masters those six tones, it's virtually impossible to communicate. Tâm looks up and gives the fleshy part of my arm a pinch to make sure I'm paying attention before pronouncing the names of all the animals again. Slowly, he waits for me to repeat the words, correcting me each time, before turning over the page and beginning the next lesson.

But suddenly I'm impatient to set aside the choppy, simple talk and have an in-depth conversation with this man, my brother's enigmatic older brother. I want to find out what it was like to be a reluctant young soldier and have to kill people you might even know and hide out in the forests eating bugs while living on a bowl of rice a day if you were lucky and picking up your friends' bodies not knowing if it would ever end and later spend months in a re-education work camp only to be arrested again by your own government for being on the wrong side and realize there *was* no good side and so sorry, so sorry, knowing there is nothing to do but get out, any way you can, but even at that you fail and the rest of the family or what is left of it makes it to America and Australia and other places you'll never see where they drive fast red cars on superhighways and mail you shiny snapshots of those cars and mention mortgages and schemes to make more money and you don't really understand these relatives anymore so you just fold into yourself and struggle to feed your family and send at least half of your children to school and ask yourself why they prevent you from doing any legitimate work purely because your father was a lieutenant in the losing side's army and everyone who ever mattered to you is *chet roi,* dead, dead, and those who are *not* might as well be dead anyway and there is nothing to do and so you drink cheap homemade moonshine poured from greasy plastic water bottles and maybe eat dog meat if anyone can afford it that month and get drunk and more angry and bitter while your wife cries and you hate her for it and your five daughters and one son shrink from you in terror and that's all you have—their fear is the only form of respect you've ever known.

This is what I need to hear. This is what I want to know. Yet this is what no language lesson could ever yield.

❧ ❧ ❧

Christine Buckley's travels have taught her to shear sheep, cultivate rice, sail without a GPS, and edit a state-run newspaper with a straight face. Her LA Weekly *cover story on human rights activist Aaron Cohen was a 2008 LA Press Club and Maggie Award finalist and led to the book* Slave Hunter: One Man's Global Quest to Free Victims of Human Trafficking, *co-written with Cohen. Christine has contributed to National Public Radio and* The New York Times. *Her reporting has also won her an Associated Press award. Born in New York and based in Paris, she is working on a second book. Find her online at www.christinebuckley.com.*

DEBORAH MILSTEIN

𝒮𝒮 𝒮𝒮 𝒮𝒮

Holy in the Land

A seeker finds truth in nonsense.

*I*n college, I unofficially minored in New-Agery, spending more hours poking through the shelves of metaphysical bookstores than I did in the stacks of the campus library. I scoffed at organized religion, especially my own: Judaism. I attended exactly one Jewish event at Wellesley, devoting my time instead to vegetarian dinners with Hare Krishnas, Hindu prayer services, yoga, astrology, tarot cards, and a wide range of alternative healing methods: shiatsu, massage, tai chi, the Rosen Method of bodywork, bioenergetics, past life therapy, acupuncture (both Chinese and Japanese), and a brand of energy healing that entailed lying on the living room floor of a witchy woman's house as she clapped her hands over me and spoke in tongues.

My favorite New-Age activity, however, was channeling, not coincidentally because Shiva, the magical man intoning spirits, was divine—as in, delicious. His slow, deep voice resonated not only in my spirit, but other earthly parts. Handsome Shiva and his ex-wife Auralia (they were happily divorced) led spiritual trips to sacred sites around the world: India, Egypt, Hawaii, Brazil, and now Israel. Auralia channeled the spirit of the Egyptian goddess Isis, who had invited us to the Holy Land to bring peace to the world. After a tarot-reading class Shiva handed out a Xeroxed invitation:

Goddess energy is back in her full glory, clearing and healing. You reading this message are one of her light workers!

> *The Date: October 2–17, 2000*
> *The Place: Israel*
> *The Mission: Global Karmic Clearing*
> *The Sacred Number: 22 souls*

Dear Hearts,

One thousand, nine hundred, sixty-six years ago, you were present at the crucifixion of the seed of unconditional love.

You've cried and asked, "Why?" You've mourned the loss. Come now, my dears, and celebrate the anchoring once more of the unconditional love of Mother Goddess, bringing with it forgiveness and closure to all the challenges that humanity has chosen for the past 2000 years.

Join me to connect physically and spiritually once again and fulfill our mission of Divine Choice.

My Love and Blessings to you all. See you in the Sacred Land,

Ra Ba Ra

Isis

So many holy coincidences: twenty-two people on the trip! Twenty-two cards in the major arcana of the tarot deck! Twenty-two letters in the Hebrew alphabet! *I* was twenty-two! This trip was destined! (Expensive destiny: $2222.) I wasn't sure about being a light worker, or clearing karma, or Isis calling, and what was Ra Ba Ra? But all the magic of twenty-two and my urgent, unconfessed crush on Shiva—these were calling. I needed this trip, a sacred journey to fill me with divinity.

In October, I met up with my fellow New-Agers in a glossy four-star hotel in Jerusalem. There was Serena, who'd taken every trip Shiva and Auralia had led; belligerent-faced Krista, whose scowl lifted during channeling sessions; Steven Cloud, who was just as grounded as you'd expect.

"Rebecca?" a young woman named Lisa asked me. "Or is it Rachel?" We'd met briefly, months before, and she seemed to remember only that I was Jewish.

"It's Deborah," I said, but she seemed pleased by her mistake, confusing me with the matriarchs.

Carrie and I grinned at each other when Auralia told us we'd be roommates. A friend from tarot class, chirping, cheerful Carrie bubbled around our room, blond curls bouncing. She unpacked her bags, grabbing a bathrobe, sunscreen, a hot pink bathing suit, a hundred pairs of shorts. "So excited to be here! In *Israel*! I can't believe it!"

In the morning ("Christ, my eyes are dry") she snatched a bottle and inattentively decanted not eye drops but contact lens solution into her eye, having picked the wrong bottle. "Christ, that *burns*!" she yelped, pressing a wet towel to her eyes. I murmured sympathetically. There was a lot of cursing and splashing of water and "Christ" and "I can't believe," until she said finally, pondering her blurred vision, "I wonder what I didn't want to let myself see."

After a hotel breakfast of melon, mediocre bagels with cream cheese and lox, and the ubiquitous Israeli salad of chopped cukes and tomatoes, we hopped on our tour bus—so many holy sites to see!—and headed towards the Old City of Jerusalem. The bus driver idled by the sidewalk, unable to find a parking space, and we ventured into the ancient city, where everybody saw Isis but me.

I'd traveled to Israel before, a bratty eight-year-old with my family. As a child, I bawled over the hundreds of stray cats, injured and skinny and mewling through Jerusalem, missing eyes and limbs and fur. Now I was twenty-two and the cats were still scrounging around, but I was unmoved. They were filthy and loud, the feline equivalent of pigeons, but Serena crowed when she spotted a stray.

"Isis!" she cried, pointing.

Everyone *ooh*-ed and gasped delightedly at a sign we belonged here—the cat being the animal embodiment of the goddess.

"The goddess welcomes you to Israel," Auralia announced with a big smile. "Isis is glad you accepted her invitation to the Holy Land."

And that's when I realized maybe I wasn't so glad.

Cats, eyedrops, Isis, Rachel, Rebecca: everything a metaphor, larger than itself, significant and symbolic; everyone someone else, given a new name. I didn't want to be the jerk on the trip, pooh-poohing while everyone else salivated with excitement, but these sites and this history were nothing new to me, familiar from previous travels and years of Jewish education. Already I'd approached the Wailing Wall, tucking a blessing between its gold stones. Already I'd walked the Via Dolorosa, the path Jesus took through Jerusalem on his way to the crucifixion at Golgotha, because it's just another street in the complex of the Old City, busy with scurrying people carrying parcels, selling pita out of storefronts, hushing babies in strollers stalled on cobblestones.

Now, with this group, I tried to walk the Via Dolorosa in a new way, thoughtful and deliberate. A few steps ahead of us, alone and hooded under a blue shawl, Martha resembled a modern Mary, singing to herself. Lisa, who'd taken out a loan to come on this trip, threw herself to the ground, cried, coughed, choked, fell to the cobblestones spitting white, overcome by His pain. Startled by the spectacle, strangers clustered around us on the path until we shooed them off as Lisa, weeping and wailing and sputtering, stood again and shuffled on.

In the afternoon, we visited the Shrine of the Book at the Israel Museum to see the Dead Sea Scrolls. The scrolls are some of the oldest surviving Biblical writing, about two thousand years old, discovered by a shepherd searching for a lost kid in the caves of Qumran. We wandered around the dimly-lit exhibit among glass cases draped with faded parchment. I squinted, making out fragments of Hebrew and Aramaic. Carrie, who couldn't read a word of it, sighed. "I wonder what happened to me then," she said. "You know, at the time of the scrolls?"

I tried not to hear. I was becoming wary of all our past lives, tentacles through history.

"My stomach kind of hurts," she said, then gasped, wide-eyed. "I must have been stabbed then—stabbed in the stomach!"

Or maybe she was just hungry—it was two o'clock and we hadn't eaten for hours.

"Maybe," I shrugged. "Want to go find some lunch?"

Auralia told us we were to be reborn at the Dead Sea. Rebirthing—one alternative treatment I'd never tried— uses breathing techniques to relive the birth experience, which many people, apparently, found traumatic. I felt just fine about being born, but it didn't seem worth making a fuss.

The Dead Sea is 1,300 feet below sea level, its shores the lowest point of dry land on Earth. In Hebrew it's called the Salt Sea, but "Dead Sea" is accurate too— nothing can live in such salty water, so thick and oily you can float on it.

The last time I'd been there, the salt stung my skin and made me feel I had to pee, so Mom took me to a bathroom where a beggar asked at the door for two shekels before she let us in. Now it seemed much more civilized, with a gift shop selling Ahava mud cosmetics.

We slogged our way from the shore to the water. The salty sand was solid on top, a hard thin layer above deep mud mushy underneath, like a bowl of frosting left out on the counter. Try to walk and you fall right in. We laughed, toppled off-balance, and coated our bodies with mud, then lay down to bake in the sun, purifying our- selves for the rebirthing ceremony. Then into the sea, the water like grease. We wiped off our coats of mud. Salt stung the razor nicks on my leg. We needed partners for rebirthing, and Karen chose me. She fairly leapt on me, actually, explaining I was the youngest in the group and she was the oldest, which, she said, would make the rebirthing more meaningful. She tied her long white hair into a bun and I lay down on the water, her hands holding my shoulders gently. I could hear my pulse in my ears, felt the sun heavy as mud on my eyelids. I wasn't sure what to do, what I was supposed to feel; I tuned out sound, ears underwater, just breathing.

Suddenly, yards across the sea, someone splashed and hollered. My eyes snapped open and I turned to see Krista, crying and kicking up waves—reliving a traumatic birth, perhaps. Auralia's voice came soothing and sure, talking her down, but although the water seemed peaceful before, the day now seemed ominous.

When it was Karen's turn to lie down on the water, I panicked. Usually the sea stands still, but now came wind, waves, water lapping at the side of her face. I put my hands by her ears to keep it out of her eyes. It didn't work. She began to float away and I sloshed through the water to stay by her side, wobbling on my tiptoes. She grimaced as the saltwater splashed against her cheek, her closed lips, disrupting her reverie.

What have I done? I lamented silently, knowing I failed as a partner. What past-life process, what rebirthing had I interrupted? Karen sighed as we came shining out of the sea. Were we changed in those waters? I wondered. What newness within us was born? What within us had died?

Our next destination, more life and death: Yad Vashem, "Hand and Name," the Israeli Holocaust memorial museum. My family had dragged me to the museum as a child; even on vacation, Jews seem unceasingly drawn to the phenomenon of the Holocaust. It was dark. I was hungry. I wept and my mother ushered me outside into the sun.

But at my Jewish day school at home, I couldn't escape the Holocaust. We'd lingered on the Shoah, as it's called

in Hebrew. On Yom ha-Shoah, the day of the Shoah, a
few months before our eighth-grade graduation, my class
stood onstage wearing white shirts, black bottoms, and
somber expressions. We took turns naming each concen-
tration camp and how many of our people were exter-
minated there: Buchenwald, 56,000. Majdanek, 360,000.
Treblinka, 870,000. Auschwitz-Birkenau, 1,100,000. We
sang a Hebrew song; in English it goes like this:

> *Oh Lord, my God,*
> *I pray that these things never end,*
> *The sand and the sea,*
> *The rush of the waters,*
> *The crash of the heavens,*
> *The prayer of the heart.*

The song sings itself again and again forever, a child's
round.

Our music teacher played the piano, upon which
stood a vase of six yellow flowers. Six, one for each million dead. Yellow, for the badges Jews wore as prisoners.
I remember tulips—Dutch, like Anne Frank—but my
mother tells me they were daffodils, their petals star-
shaped, like the star-shaped badges forced on prisoners' chests. We'd seen the Holocaust pictures in class:
"Jude"—Jew—written on the loud yellow stars pinned
to the chests of gaunt, shocked, frozen people, clad in
shabby striped pajamas, shoeless on the gray streets of
Europe, terrified every day of shattered windows, train
rides and cattle cars to oblivion, camps, emaciation, starvation, those striped uniforms, showers of gas, smoke.

The song, the yellow flowers, the dim auditorium
were haunting, familiar, always the same: I'd seen this
presentation every year at school. But when I was in

eighth grade, my turn to stand onstage, it was different; the school had invited an audience of kids from
the public junior high next door. We were educators,
the ambassadors of our people. Except I didn't want to
represent this people. I didn't want to be stuck in this
group, persecuted, damaged, still unconquered but constantly under attack, the scum of the earth, the villain
in *The Merchant of Venice*, hairy, stingy, cheating, filthy,
despised, cornered, fugitive, fleeing enemies all over the
world, losing so many along the way. I didn't want to be
on stage. I didn't want to wear the yellow star.

I know better now, but in eighth grade there was
always an out: keep your prayer book shut, keep your
mouth shut, steal yourself out of the club, convert. My
teachers promised I'd discover the hate the world carries
for Jews, and, overwhelmed, I set out to extricate myself
from the equation.

"I want to convert," I told Mrs. Levy, my social studies
teacher, in the hallway outside the art room.

She made a thoughtful face. "Why?" She had such a
loud voice you could usually hear her all the way down
the hall, but I'd surprised her into speaking softly.

"I don't like Judaism."

"No?" she asked. I shook my head, quite sure of
myself. "What do you want to convert to?"

I hadn't thought of this. "What do you mean?"

"Well, you have to convert *to* something. That's the
point of it."

I'd missed the point, as always. I didn't want to be
Jewish but even if I'd converted, I'd still be a member of
the tribe. This is an ethnicity as well as a religion, and
even if I could discard part of this identity, I'd still be
stuck with my genes, this blood, murdered along with
the rest in the death marches.

Now, at age twenty-two among the self-professed New-Age light workers, I was the only Jewish Jew. Auralia was Israeli and on that level Jewish, but by embracing Christ and Isis, Kwan-Yin and Mother Mary, crystals and aliens and channeled spirits—so many tasty religious bits—she had thinned her blood.

It's hard to be clear and thoughtful and ask questions and at the same time go with the flow and belong. Of course I didn't belong, already disappointed to see through some of the spiritual glitter. And here at Yad Vashem, as a Jew (no matter how conflicted), I did not belong.

I remembered the museum not for its exhibits but for its tone: dark, somber, solemn. The New-Agers did fine in this setting. Everyone was good at being serious, holding a sacred space and thoughtful facial expressions, sensitive to the soul fragments hovering in the atmosphere, eyes dripping, appalled at the suffering.

Crying: this made me bristle. These were *my* people, mine to cry over. Seeing these clueless tourists cry over my history, take it upon themselves, take it for themselves, twisted in new nonsensical ways, infuriated me. Lisa, bearing her own cross on Via Dolorosa; Martha, handing out roses because Mother Mary told her to, trying to out-holy everyone else; Steven, who sincerely believed in aliens and people who lived under the surface of the earth: all this was odd, but inoffensive. The light bearers were sometimes silly, sometimes disturbing, always convinced of their truth, but usually harmless. Jesus isn't mine, and I don't believe in aliens. But Jews are mine, and too many of us are dead.

In the museum lobby, Shiva spoke sadly. "We all must take responsibility for our own actions now"—he said slowly with meaningful pauses—"and in our past lives."

We were here now, he reminded us, in Israel, to collect soul fragments. We needed, he said, to be open to our own roles in these tragedies, no matter how horrific.

"I," he confessed, red hair shimmering, voice wavering in shame, "was a Nazi in a previous life."

Oh, no.

"I killed people," he continued. "It was brutal. Heartless."

My heart.

"I participated"—he was indignant—"in atrocities. There is no way to forgive what I did." He knew, he told us, that all of it, murder, was unforgettable, unforgivable. "My acts as that person were unforgivable, but I have forgiven myself, as myself, in my soul. I am no longer that person."

What to make of this? No matter how foolish I thought the New-Agers were by now, Shiva was special to me, and it hurt to see him in this unkind light. I loved him, in a puppyish way, so I forgave him, dazed, as he orated with such conviction, even picturing him handsome in uniform, the swastika armband blurred out of my fantasy.

We squinted from the dark museum into the sunlight and through the names engraved along the walkway, names of the lost and names of the saviors, those who took my people in, hid them in attics and basements and who knows where. "Wladyslaw and Stanislawa Szepolowski, Poland": I copied names into my notebook, hoping, in a sidelong way, I'd been connected to them in a previous life, that I'd had a previous life.

A bus ride back to the hotel. Dinner. We were all exhausted. I was dehydrated. Climbing the stairs back from the vending machine—another bottle of water—I ran into Jude.

Jude, yes. That was her name, just like the yellow stars. I'm not clever enough to have made this up.

Jude had smiled softly at me when I met her that first day in the hotel lobby, and I felt friendly towards her. She had a sweet face, kind and doughy, and long brown hair she wore in a ponytail. She was in her mid-fifties, I think, but if she had any gray it wasn't much. She wore a lot of purple. She moved at her own unhurried pace. In that dreamy atmosphere of wild willingness to believe, because we were all knitting up fantasies of past lives, Jude and I had decided she'd been my mother in another life. She didn't have any children in this lifetime, and here I was, ready made.

In the stairwell, Jude lost it, weeping, clutching me to her, seizing upon me for salvation. "I just can't believe it," she cried, "what happened—and not long ago—and so many people, and nobody helped!" Her face was blotchy and soft and ripe with tears. "I don't know—maybe I did this—maybe I was a Nazi, too"—choking, she stopped to breathe and gather apologies for being a Nazi, but she isn't a Nazi, but maybe she was once, or she hated Jews or she hated someone, and if she didn't other people did, and it's unforgivable, just like Shiva said, unforgivable, and she didn't stop anyone, she didn't help.

Jude, my false mother, is a sobbing, hiccupping child. She asks my forgiveness. I represent the Jewish people all of a sudden. I forgive. There is in me, somewhere, a mother, so I hush her. I soothe her. I rub her shoulders and find a tissue in my pocket, both of us damp in that echoing gray stairwell. She snuffles into it and I tell her again I forgive her, I exempt her from responsibility, on behalf of my family and my people and myself.

She smiles, relieved, and I walk up the stairs alone.

She was never my mother, and I want to go home.

Deborah Milstein lives in Brookline, Massachusetts, within walking distance of six synagogues. She holds an MFA in creative writing from Lesley University and won the 2009 nonfiction prize in Columbia: A Journal of Literature and Art. *Find her online at deborahmilstein.com.*

ॐ ॐ ॐ

White Lady Scrubbing

Cleanliness is next to godliness, indeed.

*B*efore I even step inside the lunch hall, the children
zero in on me. "Sara! Sara! *Ciaoooh*, Sara!" A pack
of them, all boys, rush at me as though the circus has
come to town. They pluck at my clothes and play tug-
of-war with my hands, fighting over who gets to hold a
thumb or two fingers. A wrist. They try to drag me this
way and that. They are delighted by my unexpected visit.
Aggressively delighted. Raucously and jealously delighted,
as if there might not be enough of me to go round. Too
bad there is only one of me and a couple dozen dusty little
boys. Their shouts and laughter echo through the hall like
a flock of hungry seagulls, birds as distant and unknown
to these children as any ocean.

Going to Africa had not been the plan. Going to rural
Ethiopia certainly had not been the plan. Several months
ago, when I learned that my volunteer organization

had an assignment for me in Dilla, a small town half-way between Addis Ababa and the Kenyan border, I nearly turned it down. I was secretly hoping to return to London, where I'd been an exchange student in college several years earlier. Adventure with little risk. But the Great Rift Valley? I could hardly find it on a map.

The evening after receiving the email with my new assignment, I stared at myself in the bathroom mirror, at my pale and freckled face, my blue eyes, my light brown hair. I was scared. Truly scared. If I didn't go to Ethiopia, it would be because fear had stopped me. Nothing more and nothing else. I would never forgive myself such cowardice. And so I looked in the mirror and double-dog dared myself to do it. Go to Africa, alone, without knowing a single word of the language. Live with Roman Catholic nuns. Teach English. Do this for six months. I accepted the assignment and began imagining a land that had only just entered my imagination.

Here in the lunch hall, I can't step in any direction without risking a set of bare toes. I'm hemmed in by boys like the last bit of dry sand at high tide. Small fingers find all my buttons and pockets. One youngster squats down to feel the buckles on my sandals while another gives my elbow a vigorous yank. I turn. *"Ante! Ie!"* But Amharic from my mouth invariably provokes fits of giggling from groups of children. These boys laugh heartily with open mouths.

I scan the hall quickly for Beatricia but she is nowhere to be seen. "Beatricia?" I ask the boys hopefully.

"Iza!" they shout with enthusiasm and point through the hall toward the water pump outside. And more words I cannot understand tumble from their mouths like marbles down a staircase.

White lady tug-of-war continues until the white lady is tugged out. *"Becha! Becha!"* I cry uncle. Enough. An older boy, perhaps ten years old and six inches taller than the rest, strokes my arm in cheerful sympathy as if to say, we like you but we don't know why and we're awfully sorry you're too dim to understand what we're so obviously telling you. Now do some other silly thing to make us laugh. He looks familiar, but I don't know his name. He wears a red, white, and blue-striped shirt with a bright red collar that looks impossibly clean and pressed. What buttons remain, he keeps fastened up to his chin. Before I can remember his name, I will come to know him by that shirt, just as I will come to know his friend by the giant soccer ball on the front of his blue t-shirt with the words "Jamestown Soccer."

Beatricia, the Italian doctor who runs the lunch program, comes to my rescue and scatters boys in every direction with a few sharp words. Red Collar and Jamestown Soccer stay by my side, self-appointed bodyguards for the newcomer to Table of the Poor, the Salesian Fathers' feeding program for Dilla's malnourished children. *"Ciao,* Sara," Beatricia says. "Welcome."

The large open-air hall is filled with long, child-sized tables and benches, now swarming with hungry children still wound up from the excitement of my arrival. As brightly colored plastic bowls are distributed among them, however, their fascination with me greatly diminishes. Beatricia introduces me to a small knot of women who cook and help run the feeding program and we squeeze out seats at the end of a table. One hundred and twelve children arrive everyday to eat a lunch of vegetable and bean stew. Meat when they have it. Twice a week they drink milk. These children are not orphans, she explains, but many have lost their mothers or have fathers who cannot provide. The children have started eating, but the decibel level in the hall remains near deafening, just like elementary school cafeterias at home.

"Where does the food come from?" I ask, as a gap-tooth youngster proudly shows me her bowl full of beans.

"From the Fathers," Beatricia replies. "What they cannot grow they buy in town." A stray dog skulks into the hall, hoping for a lost bit of meat. A cheerful roar rises from 112 food-filled mouths as the cooks give chase. Beatricia smiles indulgently and shouts over the din, "Can you come again on Saturday?"

"Sure. What's on Saturday?"

"Bath day."

On Saturday afternoon, English teaching obligations done for the day, I sneak away while the girls are busy with Bible lessons. Sister Sundari is off on some holy business and has left me in charge again. In charge of what, exactly, is unclear. In charge of being the only white lady on the playground? In charge of not being able to communicate with the girls beyond the volley-ball score? In charge of my sunburn? Meaza, Tesfansh, and Mihret manage better without me. So while all the brown noses are deep in little books with stories of Mary and Jesus, I follow my peeling pink one down the path past the clinic to the lunch hall.

Along the way, I join a procession of marching children, most with younger siblings in tow. "Sara, Sara! *Ciao!*" Two little hands slip into mine, one on either side, like kisses blown through the dust. A small flock of pilgrims in search of soap and water, we continue on our way. Before we reach the hall, we hear it. The racket of

bath day puts the raucous lunch hour to shame. "*Enhid,
Sara!*" My companions hear the shouts of their friends
and pull me along in eager anticipation, unwilling to
give up the prize of my hands.

"*Yeat no?*" I ask, feigning ignorance just to carry on
the conversation. Where?

The little boy on my left points ahead with his free
hand. "*Wuha!*" he shouts with a grin. Water! My little
companion, equal parts dust and enthusiasm, escorts me
into the hall.

"Sara, Sara! *Ciao!*" A small crowd of children rush to
my side as though I had a load of sugar cane strapped
to my back. They bounce and bounce in a semi-circle in
front of me.

"*Ciao, ciao. Dehna nachu?*"

It is bath day indeed. Heaps of soggy once-white towels cover the lunch tables. A long line of loud, unruly
children in various stages of undress snakes along the
back wall. The children pinch and poke one another,
play games, slap hands, and prop up younger brothers
and sisters on hips and shoulders. They sing and shout,
holler and cry, and swing discarded pants and shirts in
wide arcs like threadbare helicopter blades. Yellow sunshine cuts through the shadow and warms the concrete
floor. It is then that I notice the concrete floor, rough and
uneven. Perfect for the scraping of knees and stubbing
of toes. It is then that I see the hundred sets of bare toes.
The hundred pairs of knobby knees. At the front of the
line is a massive concrete sink with two giant basins and
the ends of two rusty pipes spouting cold water in fits
and starts.

I feel a tug. "Beatricia *alle*," my escort points out
proudly, as if the white folks would never be able to spot
one another without his eagle eye. Beatricia squats in

front of a little girl with dripping braids and a pained but brave look on her face.

"Sara, *brava*, *ciao!*" she shouts, looking up from the girl's foot squeezed firmly between her knees. She pushes back a sweaty lock of hair with her forearm, a pair of tweezers in her hand. "*Vieni.* Come." I chart a path between towel-covered tables and half-dressed children and make my way to Beatricia.

She is tweezing jiggers out from between the little girl's toes. I wince inwardly. That soft tender skin is a mouth-watering feast to flesh-obsessed insects, who fill their bug bellies to the brim. One night out of the shower, I will spot my own small whitish eruption between the toes on my right foot. I will run to the sisters' house before dinner. "Sister Rebecca, look!" Sister Rebecca will tweeze out my little burrower and instead of disgust I will feel pleased. Triumphant. It is a rite of passage and a story I will tell with a self-satisfied air of accomplishment.

Outside the hall, the older children crowd around the water pump reserved for dishwashing during the week, squirting slivers of slippery soap, splashing each other, and squealing as though frolicking around a backyard sprinkler.

"What can I do?" I ask Beatricia, hollering above the din. She points to the giant concrete sink at the front of the line.

"Wash," she grins.

I take a deep breath, roll up my sleeves, and begin scrubbing children. My first customer goes easy on me, an enthusiastic bather of five or six who can't get enough sink time. He soaps and rinses vigorously until the dirt-smeared mob behind him begins to get restless. "*Ishi, ante. Becha.*" Out you go, bath hog. He climbs out of the sink, pushing water off his wiry arms and legs. I throw the cleanest towel I can find over his head and he yanks it down to his chin, smiling.

When I turn around, a little girl of three or four is standing in the sink. *"Kochebaye,"* I tell her and she sits down on the concrete. I hand her a bit of soap and she begins to wash, but she is less than thorough. *"Izi,"* I say, pointing to her feet. She soaps up her toes. *"Iza, iza."* I gently poke both her cheeks and she rubs her face obediently. I fill one of the plastic lunch bowls with water and pour it over her head. It runs brown down the drain from her week's worth of dust. I fill up the bowl a second and third time until the water runs clean. *"Ishi, gobez."* She climbs out of the sink and drips her way to a towel.

Next in line is an older boy of eight or nine, patiently disentangling himself from the arms of his screeching baby sister. She is perhaps just a year old, eighteen months at the most. This howling protest, I see from his stoic boyish face, is routine. Today, perhaps everyday, she is his responsibility and he will see her washed. He will see her clean for another week. But his baby sister is equally determined to keep her dirt and she clings to his shirt with all the fierceness she can muster. Brother carries her to the edge of the sink and I try to pry open her little fists. Suddenly she lets go and stretches out her arms to me, certain I'll save her from her cruel babysitter and the big scary sink. My heart skips with joy and I pull her close, feeling her little hands grip my neck.

Double-dog dare. There are no dusty baby girls and bowls full of beans in London.

For a moment I hold her and her sobbing eases. But there is a long line of half-clothed little boys and girls pinching and hopping and poking and hollering behind

me, each dustier and more impatient than the last.
"Sorry, sweetie," I whisper before plopping her bare
behind down in the sink. Her big brown eyes go wide
with my betrayal and she begins to howl. Crocodile tears
roll down her cheeks and I turn on the tap before she
cracks my washerwoman resolve with her heartache.
"Woynea, woynea. Muskee." I try to soothe her with
familiar words but she'll have none of it. She screeches
and wails. I scrub. She pushes at my hands. I soap and
rinse. She rubs her face and sobs in dismay. I bundle her
up in a towel and hand her off to her brother.

Together in twos and threes, children troop back
into the bush. Until lunch tomorrow. Clean for another
week or two or three or whenever their big brothers and
sisters cart them off, kicking and screaming, for another
cold dunk in the sink and a white lady scrubbing.

☙ ☙ ☙

*In addition to living with nuns in Ethiopia, Sara Bathum has
visited cocoa farms in Ghana, skied down a volcano in New
Zealand, had her heart broken in Taipei, and nearly been abandoned at the border in Honduras. She now lives in Seattle with her
husband and son, having begun her latest adventure—parenthood.
This story is for Fulvia.*

❧ ❧ ❧

An Ode to B-Cups

Love is sort of in the air.

L ife is about the choices we make. It's also about taking responsibility for those choices. Even the bad ones. Like working for a low-cost airline called Sun Jet International that's based in Dallas and never flies overseas. But that's another story. This one is about ramifications.

Enter Passenger 22B. I'm working a morning flight from Los Angeles to New York, but somehow I missed him during the boarding process. That's insane, considering that he's the kind of guy who makes heads spin like Linda Blair in *The Exorcist*. Tall. Tanned. Decked out in a dark pressed suit with black wing-tip shoes. It's not until my coworker and I push our 150-pound cart six rows back and I place a napkin on his tray table that I finally see him. "Would you care for something to—"

As soon as we lock eyes, I can no longer speak. I forget where I am. Who I am. Why I am. I can only swallow and, after the shock wears off, blink.

"Hello," he says. The Dutch accent just about kills me.

"I'm sorry. Let me try that again," I say with a nervous laugh. "Would you care for something to drink?"

He flashes a movie star smile. "Please, Coke Light," he says, only it sounds more like Co-kah Light. *Adorable!*

That's when I do what any single girl in her mid-twenties would do: freeze. I stand there in the aisle wearing navy blue polyester, staring him down like an idiot. Then I do what my mother would: check for a ring. Nope: no wedding band, not even a tan line. Yet he's so far out of my league, it's not even funny. Trust me, I know my man equivalent, and he's not it.

I shake myself out of it and smile my first- and business-class smile. I try to think of something to say, something witty but with an edge, something that could lead to an interesting conversation, like one about dating.

"Co-kah Light?"

He nods, which is my cue to shove the plastic scoop into the drawer of ice. I glance across the cart at my overly Botoxed coworker. His dropped jaw and wide eyes scream "Gurrrrl! Oh…My…God."

Oh my God is right: my gay competition is now drooling all over his pinstriped apron. I shoot him the evil eye. *He's mine,* I mouth.

Whatever, he mouths back, pursing his lips and striking a pose. Even though I have no shot—zero—I'm feeling defensive. What is Botox doing, standing there licking his lips? He's practically humping the cart. "Do you have any Diet Coke on your side?" I ask.

"Of course, doll, anything for him," he purrs, handing me a silver can. Then he leans over the Styrofoam cups and whispers: "Make sure to give him extra pretzels."

Which is exactly what I do. I place a can of soda and four bags of pretzels on his tray table without saying a word. Then I do what any single girl who is also a flight attendant would do: move on to the next passenger.

I've seen enough TV to know that doctors date nurses, lawyers date court reporters, and the one in the corner office with the amazing view dates the one pouring the coffee. So what's the big deal if I date passengers? Where else am I going to meet men—lots and lots of men—who don't ask me to smile when I don't feel like smiling because I'd rather slap them across the face for feeding me the same line they gave the girl at the bar?

Here at 30,000 feet, that doesn't happen. I get the chance to know men, really *know* men, and they are completely unaware of it. Because I am in control of their comfort and safety, I see them at their most vulnerable, and some men can't do vulnerable without being a jerk. I wouldn't date a jerk on land, so I don't extend any more than professional courtesy when a jerk is in my airspace.

I'm an equal opportunity dater: first class, business class, coach. I don't care where he's sitting, as long as he *is* sitting and his seat belt is fastened, even when the sign is not on. They say you can tell a lot about a man by the way he treats his mother. Turns out, you can tell even more by the way he treats a woman in uniform. Does he make eye contact? Does he say please and thank you? Is he polite when I run out of the beverage of his choice? Does he move his newspaper out of the way when I place a drink on his tray? Does he remove his earphones when I ask a question? Does he show respect to those who serve him? Does he show respect to the passengers seated around him? If the answer is yes, he's a winner.

"Major boyfriend potential," I say to Botox about Co-kah Light. We're sitting side by side on the jump seat, where we spend 50 percent of our time on long-haul flights. There are only so many magazines a flight attendant can read, and who wants to balance a checkbook this far off the ground? Invariably, we talk, and what we usually talk about are relationships—or, in my case, lack thereof.

Botox stands and pours himself a glass of water. "Whenever a passenger flirts with me, I just assume they want something for free: alcohol, headsets, whatever!"

"Maybe they just want you?" I suggest.

"It would be nice to find a future ex-husband who could keep me in the lifestyle I'm unaccustomed to." When I laugh, Botox snaps his sassy fingers. "Gurrrl, I may be blonde but I've got dark roots!"

I point to my own dark roots. "I hear ya!"

"I'm not judging, sweetie."

That's when it happens. I'm sitting there with Botox, discussing which hair salon does the best highlights in Queens, when Co-kah Light stands and starts walking to the rear of the aircraft. I jump up, my ironing board seat slamming against the wall, and run into the galley.

"Give it to me!" I demand, playing tug of war with Botox over the preferred soda of our desire. "Give it to me and I'll do the entire second service alone!"

When Co-kah Light steps into the galley, I do not scold him for committing a passenger faux pas by crossing the carpet-to-linoleum line. Instead, I release my grip on the Coke can right when Botox does. With a loud thud, it hits the ground and rolls toward a pair of shoes so new, they must have come straight out of a box.

"Umm… Hi," Co-kah Light picks it up and places it on the counter. "I was wondering…I hope this doesn't sound weird, but—could I get your number or email?"

"Of course!" squeals Botox.

Why are all the good ones gay?

"Not you," Co-kah Light laughs. "Her!" Her? Who the hell is Her? I turn around, but there is no one. Just a couple of carts and me. Me!

"Sure," I say coolly, then wait until he returns to his seat before giving Botox a high five. Score!

Weeks go by, emails are exchanged, and just when I think it won't go anywhere, Co-kah Light invites me to visit him at his home in Zandvoort, a seaside resort in the Netherlands.

"Go for it!" half of my friends exclaim. The other half thinks I'm crazy. But my mother says what I need to hear: "As long as there's an airport nearby, you can always leave."

That's the great perk of being a flight attendant: you can hop on a flight whenever you want, as long as a seat is available. I log online to check out the resort town. There is, in fact, an airport near by, but there's also a naturist beach. As in, nudist. Oh dear. You might find this hard to believe, but I'm, well, I'm sort of a prude. I just don't do naked well, especially not in the middle of the afternoon surrounded by strangers. I don't even feel comfortable being nude in the privacy of my own bedroom. Plenty of people don't mind letting it all hang out, but I really don't need any reminders of what I don't have. Maybe if I had a voluptuous body, I'd feel differently, but I barely fill my B-cups. And I'm forever pushing up those B-cups as high as they will go. I learned how to do this from the pros during a brief waitressing stint at Hooters the summer between my freshman and sophomore years of college. They showed me how to slip two shoulder pads inside each bra cup. My tips didn't just double afterward—they quadrupled.

These days, I prefer the water bra, a technological leap up and out from the science of stuffing. I, alone, keep Victoria's Secret in business. This probably explains why the men in my life either stick around for three dates or three years. I am a woman of extremes, starting with my cup size.

Sunlight wakens me in Zandvoort. There are no blinds. No curtains. Just me and my jet lag in an unfamiliar room painted a bright shade of yellow. I throw back the covers, stumble out of bed, and pull on a pair of shorts and a t-shirt. Although we made out like teenagers all night and my lips are now chapped red, there are no other exciting details to report. Except that he's the best kisser ever. Oh, and I was able to position my body in such a way as to offer his hungry mouth and hands my slightly larger breast. Besides that, we just had fun. I'm pacing myself, one B-cup at a time.

I drag my tired body to the kitchen. Coffee. I need coffee. Strong coffee.

"Morning," I mumble to Cok-ah Light, looking divine at the breakfast table. I scan the room for a coffeemaker. There isn't one. He offers a very small cup of tea. "Thank you," I say, trying not to blush.

"I've got a big surprise for you," he says with a grin.

I smile back, but it recedes when he divulges his plan for the day: sunning at the naturist beach. I can't believe he's suggesting it so soon. I mean, I just got here last night. If it were up to me, we'd get to know each other a little better before getting naked on the sand.

"Is it O.K. to wear a bikini?" There is no way I'm going if it's not.

"Of course! Bikinis are all the rage in Europe right now," he lies through his perfect white teeth.

I shoot him a look and he sighs. "Most women go topless, but you can do whatever you want."

What I want is not to go. But I put on a string bikini and tie a long fringy sarong around my waist. We stroll through a neighborhood street to a beach two blocks away. The sun is blazing, but a cool breeze whips the air. Enormous, Skittle-colored beach umbrellas dot the white sand, and naked children dart about, splashing in the waves and squealing. We find a quiet spot and spread our towels side by side on the sand. Co-kah Light is right: most, if not all, of the women are topless, while the majority of men sport banana hammocks. Mortified, I quickly lie down, pull my shades over my eyes, and gawk at everyone who passes.

The only women I've ever seen naked (in real life) before today are the ones at my gym in Los Angeles. They spend nearly as much time standing naked by the locker room mirrors, rubbing lotion into their unnaturally tanned skin, as they do on the treadmill. Their bodies look as if two giant medicine balls got stuck on a Q-tip. No wonder I have such a complex!

The women on this beach, however, are a far cry from a California silicone beauty. They're perfectly normal, which—to my twisted mind—seems bizarre. In fact, they look like me. There are fat boobs, flat boobs, long boobs, short boobs, even a few sideways boobs swinging in the breeze. And the nipples! Who knew there were so many different kinds? Bologna skins, pepperoni slices, clam heads, pinecones, ink stains—all in different shades of pink, red, and brown. For the first time in my life, I feel pretty darn good about my perky B-cups, no matter how small or uneven they are.

The rest of the day, I'm sorry to report, is a bit of a disaster. A woman with banana-shaped breasts and long pink nipples saunters by, and guess who starts to flirt with her? He even invites her to join us for lunch. Unable to follow their conversation—which is in Dutch—I gather my things and strut my cups down to the water, where I spend the rest of the afternoon alone. As disappointed as I am, I refuse to let Co-kah Lite squash my airline philosophy about how a man who can treat a woman in uniform with respect is a keeper. Nothing is perfect: I know I'm not. But what I've got is fine with me. The following morning, I catch the first flight back to New York City.

Three days later, I'm wearing scuffed-up Mary Jane's and standing behind a rolling beverage cart. That's right, I'm back on an airplane, only this time, my breasts are tucked in an *un*padded bra under a form-fitting uniform dress. And I'm feeling good. Natural. Beautiful.

"So, what did you do over the weekend?" Botox asks when I hand him a can of Co-kah Light.

"Not much," I say with a smile. Then I turn my B-cups to a row of passengers and place napkins on their tray tables. "Something to drink?"

♫ ♫ ♫

Heather Poole has worked for a major U.S. carrier for fourteen years, spending most of that time flying back and forth between New York (where she works) and Los Angeles (where she lives).

She met her husband on a flight over Illinois seven years ago and now they have a three-year-old son who travels so often, he calls his belt a seat belt and prefers to keep it buckled at all times. Though Heather loves pushing and pulling 300-pound carts, she also writes a column, "Galley Gossip," on Gadling.com, and is writing a book of essays about her life at 30,000 feet, scheduled to be released in 2011.

✆ ✆ ✆

Bali Birth

Nature's own love drug intoxicates a writer.

*I*f you want to fall in love with the world, really fall in love with it, watch a birth. Better yet, move to a developing country, volunteer at a birth center for poor families, and then watch a baby born into water.

I was walking home after an evening out when I got a text message from Robin. She is a Filipino-American midwife who helped start the birthing center in Bali where I work as a grant writer. Occasionally, she is summoned with desperate calls on borrowed mobile phones to deliver babies in tin shacks with dirt floors for women so poor they cannot afford to pay the local untrained birth attendants two dollars to help. The family lacks transport. The women have never received prenatal check-ups. When Robin gets a call for a birth like this, she tucks several large rupiah notes into her tunic pocket to buy food for the postpartum woman and any other children she may have. She knows from experience that the new mother may not have eaten for days.

Apparently, a woman from just such a family was having a baby and had already arrived at the center in a *bemo*, one of the small, public buses that ply Bali's roads. The twenty-cent fare was contributed by the entire family. "If you want to see a quiet, gentle birth," read Robin's electronic summons, "come now."

Robin was adamant that I watch a birth, so I could see the work I was helping support. Yet, I was leery of watching a stranger's birth. Wouldn't I be intruding? Reluctantly, I altered my walk home to head to the birth center, leaving behind the hum of Ubud—with its shops and sidewalks and restaurants full of overweight tourists sweating profusely in the tropical air—and strolling through the quiet lanes of Nyuh Kuning, a village of woodcarvers. The night was redolent with the smells of incense, smoke from burning garbage fires, and night-blooming jasmine. Street dogs stirred at my approach and sniffed the air for my scent, one loping along behind me silently. It was just after 11 P.M.

Robin met me outside the birth room. "This will be a good birth for your first time," she said. "She's a second-time mom, and fully dilated. The baby will be out soon."

She took me into the room with her and handed me a clipboard and a pen. "I've told her that you are helping record the details of the birth," she said. She briefly ran over the method of charting fetal heart rates. "This won't take long," she said.

"Will she mind that I'm here?" I asked.

"Right now, you could be Richard Nixon, and she wouldn't care," said Robin.

The woman was on a bed, half-sitting, half-laying,

moaning. She was naked. Her skin was dark for a Balinese, sun-darkened by outdoor work. She had huge, globe-like breasts that hung pendulously across her great moon belly. A pregnancy band, a band of darker pigment, stretched across her belly. Her hair was long, matted to her neck with sweat in the hot, still air of the birth room. A lone fan turning lazily high up on the ceiling did little to dispel the tropical heat.

Another midwife stood nearby while Robin sat on the bed with the laboring woman. The woman's husband squatted behind her shoulders, supporting her as she leaned against him. He was clad in jeans and a khaki fatigue top, marked with sweat stains. With eyes wide and fearful, he watched every move of the midwives, uncertain as to his role. The birth center was atypical in that the midwives expected husbands to be present at the birth and help support their wives. This had been the tradition in the Bali of their grandparent's generation, but was passing out of fashion now. Some husbands managed better than others, coaxing, coaching, reassuring their wives, while others looked around them with all the composure of a rabbit caught in the headlights of a car. This one was of the rabbit variety.

A nurse moved quickly, expertly, in and out of the room, bringing a receiving blanket for the baby, water with spirulina for the mother, and towels for the blood. I watched and waited. A half hour passed. Then an hour. From time to time, Robin leaned toward the woman and spoke to her softly in Indonesian. After a while, she spoke, frowning, to the second midwife.

She looked at me. "This is taking too long," she said.

"Is there a problem?" I asked.

"No, the baby's fine. Two good pushes and he'll be

out," she said. "But every time she starts to push, she stops and pulls the baby back in."

The woman was growing increasingly agitated. Her moaning was turning to a kind of guttural screaming, which made something in the lower vicinity of my gut tremble. The woman was thrashing on the bed, knocking her husband as he tried to stroke her arms to comfort her. Robin was looking very solemn. Every time she spoke to the laboring woman, the woman would cry and moan louder. She was covered in a sheen of sweat that glistened in the glare of the overhead light. There was a strong smell in the room, like a mixture of every type of odor the body could emit, earthy and musky, combined with the antiseptic tang of amniotic fluid. This was the smell of birth, the second midwife explained.

Robin and the other midwife tried to help the woman position her legs apart, but the woman kept pulling them back together again. Robin spoke to the husband, and he nodded. He shifted his position forward so he could hold one of his wife's legs apart. The second midwife held the other, also open. Yet the woman fought them, wrestling her legs back together, her fists pounding the bed. One of the fists knocked the husband. He retreated to the head of the bed, trying to hold her shoulders still.

Robin turned and looked at me. "I just don't get it," she said. "This is the second baby. She's given birth before. She doesn't want to push. She says she's scared to push."

The woman was screaming and yelling now, hitting out at the walls and the bed. She twisted on the bed, her huge breasts rocking side to side. However, Robin's reaction was unexpected: she was getting visibly annoyed.

Suddenly, Robin spoke sharply to the woman and,

standing up, gestured for everyone, including the husband, to leave the room. I didn't move, not understanding. Robin waved impatiently at me. "Everyone out.
She's behaving like this because she has an audience. I've
never seen anything like this. The baby wants to come
out and she's keeping it in," she said.

The staff and I left the room. Through the open
window to the birth room, I heard Robin talking in
Indonesian in a firm voice. The woman was crying and
even I could understand her. "No, please," she kept
saying.

Robin walked out of the room and closed the door.

"Is this normal?" I asked.

"No," said Robin, "I think she might be developmen-
tally disabled and doesn't understand what is happening.
But I don't get it. She's had a baby before. I told her two
pushes, the baby will be out, and this will all be over."

The woman was screaming and pounding on the
walls. I looked at the clock. Almost 1:30 in the morning.
So much for a quick, gentle birth. The odd thing was
that I didn't care. I was happy, almost uplifted. I felt like
I could wait for hours.

"I feel so bad that this is your first birth," Robin said.
"I was sure that it would be no longer than a half hour."
She paused. "But then, I should have learned by now
that every birth is different."

She was apologizing to me, but I felt that it should be
me apologizing to her, to the parents, for intruding on
something as personal, as intimate, as birth.

"I don't mind," I said. Actually, I felt energized,
almost a bit high. My fatigue had vanished. "I feel like I
could go all night."

She smiled. "That's the oxytocin," she said. "The love

drug of birth. The room is full of it. Sometimes, after a long birth, it's the only thing that's keeping me going."

During birth, oxytocin is released by a laboring woman in large amounts after the cervix and vagina stretch and distend for birth. Oxytocin helps make the uterus contract for birth, causing the milk to "come down" into a woman's breasts so she can start to nurse after the baby is born. It increases trust, and reduces fear. Oxytocin binds mother and child at birth and triggers "maternal behavior," that is, it binds mother to child. But oxytocin also works on those around a laboring woman. Women present at a birth have been known to start their periods immediately afterward, or crave sex. Hence, it's called the "love drug."

Bali's Hindu Dharma culture once had rituals that left mother and baby alone to bond in isolation for a period of weeks after the birth, with the mother doing no activity other than nursing and sleeping. Both culture and religion recognized the essential nature of mother-baby bonding, and that something special happened when women were alone with their babies. The culture also treated the placenta as the twin of the child, giving it special rites, and prescribing that it be buried in a certain part of the family compound. Women "married out" in Balinese culture because, it was believed, they could stand the separation from their twin, from the compound where their mother's placenta was buried, better than men could. Still, they always carried with them a small box of dirt taken from the spot where their placenta "twin" was buried. Sadly, Bali's westernized medical programs and the hard sell of infant formula companies have disrupted these rituals.

"What happens now?" I asked Robin.

"I'm going to have to be tough with her. This is the hard part about being a midwife. If she won't push this baby out, she will have to go to the hospital for a Cesarean. The Health Department has strict guidelines we have to follow. If she can't get the baby out on her own soon, we'll have to transport her."

I knew that a hospital birth, and a likely Cesarean, was not a financial option for the family. They wouldn't have the money to pay for it. They'd barely been able to scrape together the *bemo* fare to bring the mother to the birth center.

Robin returned to the room. I heard her speaking firmly. The woman's screams subsided; now she was sobbing. She was asking Robin something over and over. Robin stepped back out of the room and stood, waiting. The woman continued to cry and call out Robin's name.

"She's begging me not to take her to the hospital," said Robin. "She says she would rather die here with the baby than go. But I told her if she won't push the baby out, we will have to take her. She's being stubborn. She could do this, but she won't."

We all stood outside the room and waited. I looked at the clock again. It was after two. I still didn't feel tired. I felt somehow bonded with this stubborn woman who refused to push out her baby. I felt a sort of glow. Everyone else seemed to have it too, a sort of flush in the cheeks, an animation in their faces and voices, despite the late hour. Finally, the woman's shouts subsided; she was crying softly. Robin returned to the room alone. I heard her talking quietly again. Then, Robin opened the door and gestured the staff back in.

"We're going to try a water birth. That should help relax her," she said.

The birth tub was an old spa bath, liberated by Robin from a friend who never used it. It sat, hulking, in a corner of the room. The nurse filled it with water from the small gas heater on the wall, then bobbed a thermometer in the tub to check the temperature. Robin and the second midwife helped the woman sit up on the bed, then stand awkwardly. With a midwife supporting each arm, and her husband trailing in her wake, the woman shuffled ungainly across the floor, her chest heaving, her breasts flopping. The staff lowered the woman into the water. She sat up with a start and exclaimed something in Indonesian. The second midwife and the nurse talked reassuringly to the woman and she relaxed into the tub. Robin turned to me, explaining. "This is the first time she's ever been in warm water. Usually, she has a cold water *mandi*, or bathes in a river."

The staff directed the husband to sit at the edge of the tub, behind his wife. His legs dangled awkwardly into the tub. Finally, he squatted on the edge, looking uncomfortable, holding his wife's shoulders tentatively. The laboring woman sank back into the tub, into the water. Her body seemed to lose some of its tension. The second midwife began to scoop warm water over the woman's breast and belly with a blue plastic pail. Robin talked steadily with the woman, keeping one hand on the woman's knee. Soon, the woman was nodding. She was visibly relaxing. Suddenly, a spasm passed over her, she leaned forward and cried out, one hand going to her belly. Robin leaned forward, peering into the space between the woman's legs. She spoke more urgently as the woman made short, high sounds through her nose. Another spasm gripped the woman and again she cried out, leaning forward. Robin parted her legs, and her right hand seemed to be cupping something between the woman's legs. The staff began to intone a low chant, a Hindu song for welcoming new life into the world. Unaccounted tears sprang into my eyes.

"The baby's crowning," said Robin, looking up at me quickly, then looking back into the tub. "Make a note of the time."

The woman cried out again, and now I could see a whitish-slime-covered bulge between her legs. The chant grew louder. The woman was panting and crying out in short, sharp breaths. Robin inserted her other hand, and suddenly a tiny, white body slid into them, with a long white cord snaking back into the mother's body. The baby was half in the water, half in the air. The chant reached a crescendo, then fell away. Robin lifted the baby and placed him onto his mother's belly. "It's a boy," she announced.

Suddenly, everyone around the tub sprang into action. Hands held out a small, cotton blanket and wrapped the baby. Other hands stretched a tiny cotton hat onto his head. The baby was breathing now, a great suck of air, then his thready cry filled the room. The mother was crying, her chest heaving. She strained her neck to look at the child. The father was also smiling and crying.

Tears were running down my cheeks too. I never expected this. I had always wanted children, but—due to reasons of physiology and possibly hormones—never had any. In my technologized, sanitized Western world, I had only seen medical births on film, with all the participants and attendants gowned, masked, and capped. I hadn't expected birth to be so visceral, so sweaty and full of sound. I hadn't expected this feeling of being in a holy place, watching an age-old rite, that somehow was unique to this woman.

People bustled in and out of the room. The woman was helped out of the bath, dried, wrapped in a sarong, and then walked slowly back to the bed, her great moon belly reduced to almost a third its size. As the mother lay down, the midwife placed the baby to her breast. Within minutes, the boy was nursing.

I was watching new life, and it was amazing. I knew this child was born into poverty, that his life was uncertain. I also knew that because of Robin's efforts, this birth didn't place the family in crushing debt to a hospital or force them to use a midwife who would sell the child to cover the bills, which happens in Indonesia.

The mother kept repeating the same sentence to Robin. I waited in a corner of the room until Robin was finished with the mother, and walked over to me. "She was thanking me for not hitting her," she explained. "That's what they did to her in the hospital with her first baby. They hit her to make her be quiet in labor. That's why she was terrified of pushing. She was scared that the pain would be too much and she would cry out." Suddenly, Robin looked tired. "Luckily, her fear of going back to the hospital was greater than her fear of the pain and she pushed the baby out."

I crept over to the bed to look at the baby. His face was still red and wrinkled. His mother was touching him softly, as if she couldn't yet believe he was real. The father kept grinning as he patted his wife. The woman looked up at me, directly at me, and smiled. It was a smile that defied the reality of her hardscrabble life—a smile full of pride, of joy. Tonight, she wasn't one of Bali's poor, who toiled in the rice fields and never quite had enough to eat. Tonight, she was a victorious heroine who had overcome a great struggle. Tonight, she was beautiful. Hair still disheveled, with a damp, rayon sarong wrapped around her, she glowed, radiating contentment, satisfaction, and accomplishment. The part of me that was white and Western and felt pity for her shriveled in the heat of her smile. I smiled back at her, and her smile grew wider. She beckoned me to come closer, drawing back the blanket covering the baby. Look, her smile said, I have created life and it is wonderful. She took my hand and held it out to touch the baby. (Later, I would learn that she was hoping some of my luck, the luck of being white and privileged, would rub off on her new son.) I felt his tiny heart beating. He was mewing like a kitten. Something melted open inside me. New life.

૪૱ ૪૱ ૪૱

Liz Sinclair is a writer with a degree in anthropology and restless feet. She divides her time between Melbourne, Australia, and Bali, where she watches births as often as she can.

෫ ෫ ෫

Tea in Kabul

An activist witnesses a nation's struggle for peace.

"Those are the Hindu Kush Mountains, the killer of Hindus," said the Afghan man seated beside me, pointing. We were on a flight from Dubai to Kabul and, through the window, could see the flat desert of Iran and southern Afghanistan suddenly give way to barren blue-and-gray ridgebacks, like waves of a stormy sea. I wondered how stormy the political situation would be during my visit to this war-weary land. Twenty-four hours ago, as I prepared to leave for the San Francisco airport, a neighbor had called to say that another bomb had just exploded in Kabul. "Should you delay your departure?" she asked.

It was 2002, one year after the World Trade Center bombing and the subsequent fall of the Taliban. I was traveling to Afghanistan as part of a human rights delegation sponsored by the San Francisco-based organization Global Exchange. There were eleven of us, mainly young Afghan-Americans and me, a recently retired college professor. Our mission was to assess the state of Afghan culture and the arts and set up projects both immediate and long-term. Having worked for women's rights all my life, I planned to focus on that area.

Yet, I had never visited a war-zone and couldn't help feeling anxious. Small villages of stone and mud dwellings grew visible as we angled in toward Kabul Airport. Voices and nervous laughter grew louder as excitement mounted among the passengers. Many were Afghans returning home after absences of fifteen and even twenty years.

"I left when I was three," one man said, while another confided: "I'm afraid to get off. Everything will be so changed."

Our plane swept past bunkers and a graveyard of smashed planes and cadavers of military aircraft. We were entering a land of lawlessness, anarchy, warlords, and twenty-three years of conflict—a part of the world where civil war and foreign invasions were more "normal" than peace.

We stepped off the plane into the "Country of Light," as Afghanistan has been called. A young Afghan-American traveling with us said: "I thought I wouldn't remember anything, since I moved to the States when I was five, but now that I feel the air, I know I am home." Inside the terminal, young men in ragged brown garments who looked straight out of the Middle Ages pleaded to help me with my luggage to earn 10,000 Afghanis, about twenty-five cents.

A van awaited us outside. "Don't worry that there are no seat belts," said the driver. "I drive slowly." Then he floored it, racing up the wrong side of the divided street against the oncoming traffic. Indeed, there seemed to be no traffic rules or stop lights in Kabul. Traffic moved like spilled milk—anywhere space allowed.

Through the open window of our van, I bought the autumn 2002 *Survival Guide to Kabul* from a street child. "There's a lot to see, even if most of it is wrecked," it noted. On the way to our hotel, we passed bombed-out houses, stores, and even palaces. Near the center of the city, burned skeletons of buses were stacked on top of each other around the devastated former public transportation center. Women in blue burqa and street children begged at the windows of our van. Men with no legs, victims of mines, negotiated along on a sort of skateboard amidst the traffic, pleading for baksheesh, or money.

As we approached our hotel, I noticed the top floor had no roof, only jagged remnants left behind by a past shelling or bombing. Affecting nonchalance, I joked to the driver that I sure hoped our rooms would be on a lower floor.

Our guide suggested we visit the Darulaman Palace and the Kabul Museum first. We climbed into a minivan and bounced along through the dust on the remnants of a formerly paved street. From a distance, the palace looked appropriately majestic high upon a hill. Photos I had seen from the 1920s depicted an impressive three-story turreted edifice, but as we drew near, we realized that the palace walls were now pocked with cavernous holes. Security guards yawned as they waved us through the gate. At the front entrance, we came upon a young guard sleeping on the ground, atop a red woven rug. A Kalashnikov lay beside him.

"Salaam," we said, hoping to sound friendly. Staring up at us, he rose slowly to his feet, rubbing his dark brown eyes and running his fingers through his curly hair. In his late teens or early twenties, he would have been a heartthrob in any American high school. Our guide explained that we wished to visit the palace. The guard waved us in, and soon we were wandering through rooms that had once been grandiose, but now lay in ruins. The large chunks of missing wall permitted panoramic views of the countryside: parched rolling hills backed by hazy blue mountains.

Noticing some fresh graffiti on one wall, I stopped and peered through a doorway. The smaller adjacent room was newly plastered and painted. Noticing my curiosity, the young guard motioned for me to follow him into the bathroom next door. It featured a sparkling new white porcelain bathtub. In hesitant English, he said: "A few weeks ago, bin Laden stayed here. They prepared these rooms for him." This couldn't be true—could it? Regardless, the notion that I might be staring at the world's number one terrorist's recently-used bathtub made my temples pound. I hoped that he wouldn't be bathing here today.

I was about to rejoin the others when the guard held out his Kalashnikov and pointed at the camera hanging around my neck. Curious to hold one of these infamous Russian weapons, I accepted his offer, cradling it carefully with my fingers far from the trigger. He snapped my photo with his weapon in my hands.

From there, we drove back down the hill to the equally battered Kabul Museum. The director met us at the front door, above which hung a sign that read: A NATION IS ALIVE WHEN ITS CULTURE IS ALIVE. "Welcome," he smiled. "Please allow me to show you through as best I can. We have no electricity, but I have a flashlight."

Until 1992, this museum housed one of the finest collections of Asian art and artifacts in the world. Ten years later, there was little to see but rubble. We shivered in the musty chilled air as the director pointed his flashlight at piles upon piles of shattered ancient treasures. Most were either destroyed by the Taliban—who believed that any portrayal of a human form was sacrilege—or by bombs. Somehow, the director seemed optimistic about its recovery. "With international assistance, we are sure we can restore most of this," he said.

Our final visit of the day was to the Allahoddin Orphanage, home to hundreds of girls and boys on the outskirts of Kabul. Immediately upon entering the gray cement façade, we were surrounded by shouting crowds of children, from tiny toddlers to teenagers. Little hands pulled on my jacket and grasped to hold my hand, eager for human contact. Although initially unnerved by their sticky fingers and unwashed faces, I was soon reaching out and hugging everyone within my reach.

"We only have that one pump for water," announced the director, a middle-aged bespectacled man with a short gray-streaked beard. "And our plumbing rarely works," he added, pointing at the small water pump standing in the courtyard. "The children make a game out of pumping the water and filling buckets." Sure enough, the kids were jumping around the pump, energetically taking turns at keeping the water flowing into receptacles.

Inside the girls' quarters, I noticed a tiny child sitting alone quietly. Through the chill and dank air, her dark eyes stared with an expression beyond sadness and hope.

One thin arm extended from the baggy sleeve of her oversized tan-and-yellow dress as she repeatedly crayoned the same simple pattern on a piece of paper.

The director gathered a group of children, aged four to fourteen, for us to photograph. A fifth-grade class of girls sang to us in Dari, the language of Northern Afghanistan: "My mother is gone away. Afghanistan, you are now my mother, and I must take care of you."

Afterward, the director took us aside to explain the direness of the situation here. "When the Taliban took over Kabul in 1996, they came here and threw all the girls out in the street, taking some of the older ones with them. We don't know where they are now. Please help us in any way you can. Money would be best."

We distributed the pillows and wool mittens that we'd purchased in town for this purpose. These gifts seemed like a paltry contribution, but it was all we could do at the moment. As we drove off, I tried to envision life for women in this nation. Western news coverage of Afghanistan generally consists of illiterate warlords and draped women. However, up until the mid-1990s, Afghanistan was a progressive society. Women's equal rights were guaranteed by the constitution. In pre-Taliban Afghanistan, urban women were educated and active participants in society, comprising 50 percent of civil administration, 70 percent of teachers, and 40 percent of physicians. Women made up roughly 15 percent of the highest legislative body in Afghanistan—a much larger number than the U.S. Congress.

The Taliban, of course, changed everything. Suddenly, these modern women were confined to their houses, with all their windows painted black, permitted outside only when accompanied by a male relative. They got beaten for showing even a bit of wrist or ankle. They were denied an education or access to earning a livelihood, and deprived of medical care. They were even forbidden from visiting the public bath on occasion, even if they had no running water at home.

Somehow the Afghan people's resiliency persisted, bolstered by their sense of humor. The Afghan women I befriended during this visit and subsequent trips mocked the Taliban-imposed restrictions. They cracked jokes about many things, including the blue burqas they had been forced to wear. One evening at an all-women's party, our hostess pretended to address a large crowd, asking: "Will the woman in the blue burqa please stand up?" Everyone giggled. Continuing the joke, another woman waved her arm as if signaling to an imaginary coat check girl: "Mine's the blue one."

At first, I was surprised at these jokes, yet their laughter was infectious. Soon, we were doubled up in laughter, rolling amidst the cushions on the floor, trying to avoid the plates of kebabs and fruit.

Having worked with Afghan women, who were living in exile, I was accustomed to their hospitality, courage, and wit. But because of our stereotype of the Afghan man as a misogynist warrior, I did not know what to expect during my interactions with men. Yet, even in the dusty chaos of Kabul's perpetual traffic gridlock, I never saw any men get angry. My driver used the traffic jams to shout messages to other drivers and passengers: "Tell my cousin to ask his friend Hamid about the tire he is fixing for me." Even when cars crashed into each other, the drivers didn't seem very upset. Once, one of my drivers knocked a man off his bicycle. They chatted about it for a few minutes, then laughed and drove on.

ॐ ॐ ॐ

On one of my last days in Kabul, Tarek, a university student, and I hiked up the side of a mountain near the city's ancient walls, which date from the fifth century. Some twenty feet high and twelve feet thick, these walls ascend almost perpendicularly from the Kabul River. As we clambered up the loose shale on the steep hillside, security helicopters buzzed above, while far below, women washed clothes in the trickle of river remaining after five years of drought.

On that day, most people were heading toward the Ghazi Sports Stadium. This was the infamous stadium where the Taliban performed public executions and stonings every Friday until they were routed by U.S. and Northern Alliance forces earlier this year. Today's event was a commemoration in honor of Ahmad Shah Massoud, the great Afghan freedom fighter who was assassinated on September 9, 2001, two days before the attack on the Twin Towers in New York City. Al Qaeda is believed to have orchestrated the killing in order to deprive the United States of Afghanistan's most capable ally commander.

Up in the mountains, the hum of the city softened and the air grew slightly less choked with dust. Most people in Kabul have a hacking cough or bronchitis and I did too—a worrisome condition, given that air particles are believed to contain depleted uranium from Soviet and U.S. bombings. Children waved at us from doorways of mud-brick houses cantilevered into the slope, so that one end of each roof was at ground level. A woman yelled something to Tarek. He translated: "She said that I should assist you more, as the hillside is slippery."

At the next house up the slope, a one-legged man on

crutches waved and shouted, too, beckoning us over with a smile. "He's inviting us to come in and have tea with him and his family," Tarek explained.

As we approached, I could see that he had the movie-star good looks of many Afghan men: gorgeous symmetrical features, muscular build, dark hair and beard, and expressive dark eyes. Afghan eyes really look into you, and their gaze is not pained or demanding or threatening in any way. It is dispassionate and composed, perhaps the result of millennia of survival.

"English, American?" the man asked. "Don't you have hills like this? Stay here awhile and you'll get stronger legs. See what it's done for me!" He pointed to his stump and laughed. His four children peeked out from behind him as he ushered us into the living room. There was no electricity but windows cut through the mud brick let in daylight. Unlit oil lamps sat in one corner.

Introducing himself as Ashraf, our host lowered himself on to a pillow on the dirt floor and indicated that we do the same. His wife, a beautiful woman with golden-green eyes, nodded hospitably as she brought in a teapot, cups, and bowls of nuts and raisins.

"I'm the mayor of this section of the city," he said, a broad smile on his face. "I've fought against the Soviets and the Taliban to protect my family and little community here." A mine had blown off one of his legs, he explained, and he showed me various holes in his chest and back from mortar fire. He'd even been friends with Massoud, serving with him in both wars against the Soviet Union as well as the Afghan civil wars against the Taliban.

Yet, despite his personal tragedy, Ashraf was one of the most jovial people I'd ever met, cracking jokes and grinning. As we talked, I realized that his knowledge of world affairs would put many Americans to shame. Where did he learn so much?

"I've never had time to go to school but I listen to the BBC in Dari," he explained.

"My husband is a very good man," his wife chimed in.

Given the amount of affection he showed toward their children and to her, this seemed sincere. Still, I wanted to probe more deeply. What did he think of the cruel treatment his country had inflicted upon its women? Didn't he want his daughters to receive an education and find a good job?

He gave this some thought, then responded: "I'm an Islamist. I believe that women should have full rights to have careers, to go to the university, but still they should wear the hijab. We are Muslims, we want to respect our women wearing the cover. It is not the burqa which is the point but the freedom to move about in their lives, to live full lives, that is important."

"But it's uncomfortable inside the burqa and difficult to see and to walk," I persisted. "I tried one and it gave me a headache. Do you think I'm a bad woman because I'm wearing trousers and a sweater with only a scarf around my neck? Look how nice it is for us to discuss life and everything together!"

He laughed and nodded in agreement.

We sipped tea with Ashraf for nearly two hours, sharing stories about our families, our travels, our lives as we pushed bowls of raisins back and forth. Finally, I said: "Here you are, after twenty plus years of war. You've lost a leg, your body has been shot again and again, yet you are so cheerful. How is that?"

"Diane," he said, leaning forward from where he sat and gesturing toward me, "Now we have peace," he said. "And peace is everything."

න් න් න්

Diane LeBow, award-winning travel writer, photojournalist, and president of the Bay Area Travel Writers, is based in San Francisco. She writes about such adventures as horse trekking on the Mongolian steppes, diving with Red Sea sharks, and exploring Parisian cafés. She is currently working on a book about her search for the best of all possible worlds. Check out more of her work at www.dianelebow.com.

A. KENDRA GREENE

జ్ఞ జ్ఞ జ్ఞ

I Regret Eating
the Caterpillars

Where is Miss Manners when you need her?

*W*e were on our way out, completing a lazy loop round the small stretch of field where a team dressed in red competed with a team dressed in blue, passing along a scattering of stands and clusters of folding chairs filled with older people chatting in soft voices. We had come because my host felt obliged we attend this annual community festival, that I might learn from it, the same way she felt I should visit the local bamboo museum, try my hand at traditional archery, and attend the funerals of people I'd never met.

The day was gray and cool, the festivities fit in the elementary school's courtyard, and, having finished with them, we were headed toward the car when she asked if I'd ever tried caterpillars. She waved one hand toward a narrow booth as she asked, never shifting her gaze or breaking her stride. I glanced at the booth, the top half glowing warm through wide windows, and said no, I hadn't. In a single motion, she turned on her heel and placed an order.

Mrs. Tak gave no indication that she in any way enjoyed our outings, yet she arranged them with diligence. I suspect there was a schedule to them, but unless they required me to wear a special dress—a blue and white *hanbok* with delicate flowers painted at the cuffs, haggled for and acquired on one of our first surprise outings—I couldn't expect to know our plans until we were already on our way to see a ballet based on traditional folklore or eat a particular kind of squid on the coast or climb a famous mountain in the interior. And ever since the morning she announced curtly, "I don't like English. I don't want to practice anymore," I was reticent to ask.

I could, however, count on a certain amount of conversation. At the end of every excursion, my host asked what I thought. At this prompting, I was to summarize my thoughts and reactions, give a kind of cultural book report on the day's events. I understood that good Korean manners forbade me from saying anything remotely negative. Modesty and moderation were also virtues, so the upper ranges of enthusiasm were to be tempered with decorum. Which meant, as far as I could tell, the acceptable expression of sentiment started at good and only got better—all of human emotion compacted to fit between a smile and a laugh.

It wasn't just a matter of conversion though, no simple translation from one scale to another, like slipping from degrees Fahrenheit to degrees Celsius. This convention of civility, the narrowed range of presentable opinion I

felt allowed to use only heightened the importance of
choosing the right words: words to operate both at face
value and simultaneously convey or conceal subtexts
never explicitly expressed. It seems in no way unreason-
able that I was expected to communicate personal experience in a socially acceptable form, yet in attempting to
do so, I felt locked into an emotional inflation of expression that made ambivalence read as distaste, distaste as
loathing. Good, then, was hardly good enough.

The thing is, I liked being in Korea. It was taxing, to
be sure, it was hard and confusing and brutal at times,
but I was very aware just how much there was to be
thankful for. I had no difficulties enjoying my year in
Korea, but I labored the whole time to communicate
my enjoyment believably. A vocabulary of Janus words
serves its purpose of buffering the friction of disagreement and disappointment, yet such a two-sided lexicon
tends to undercut or authenticate the good intention of
a kind word by hinting at what it so carefully omits. A
purely positive sentiment, then, has no critical assur-
ance and becomes a flimsy thing with no backing, no
currency.

It did not seem to help that I myself was living under
a certain heightened emotion, charmed as I was by every
new utensil, delighting in the triumphs of mailing a letter or laundering a shirt. Mrs. Tak and I lived under the
same roof and taught the same subject to the same students at the same school, and yet, no matter how many
cultural excursions she orchestrated for us to share, we
struggled to find things in common. She shook her
head at me. Who could get so animated over coat hooks
and kimchi refrigerators? How could I not want more
bread? What was the point of attending a play when
I didn't know the language? No wonder she seemed

uncertain whether to question the honesty of my reports or her interpretation of them.

The broad-faced man behind the counter acknowledged her order with a nod, stepped back, and rocked forward again, now with a paper cone in his hand. Striped in red and white, it looked like any other container of fair food. It might have been fried dough or roasted nuts or, turned around, the handle to a spindle of cotton candy.

I reached for it. The contents settled in my hand like shells, like weights. Like bodies, I thought as I looked at them, the roasted exoskeletons of caterpillar pupae tan as pecans, defined as breastplates, pleasantly warm and starting to stain light circles of grease on the paper against my palm.

I wanted to like it. I wanted to be a person with an open mind. I wanted to express my appreciation to Mrs. Tak for her interest in me, all the trouble she went to on my behalf. I was trying to be the cultural ambassador eight weeks of orientation had trained me for, and as far as I could tell, that meant enjoying everything and smiling through whatever challenges might arise. Pleasantries first, establish a rapport, let everyone save face. That was enough to carry me past the smell, an odor with the bite of bitter and burn and rot. It allowed me to ignore the legs. And it might have gotten me past the bodily crunch and texture of limbs falling apart—if I could have kept them in my mouth.

"I don't like them, either," she said.

᧞ ᧞ ᧞

A. Kendra Greene has brought porcupine quills and flamingo feathers through customs without incident, but was recently detained by airport security for trying to carry a bag of corn masa onto a domestic flight. Weddings and writing have taken her recently to four continents, but for the moment she is happy to be home, making tortillas and chapbooks, in Iowa City.

ട്ട ട്ട ട്ട

Desert Queen

A teacher on holiday becomes a prisoner of love.

I first saw the Bedouin's gun when he stripped off his short-sleeved, khaki-green jacket. It was nestled in the back of his matching khaki-green, sharp-creased trousers.

His hands reached up and untwisted the red-and-white checked kaffiyeh that draped around his head and flowed down the back of his neck. He tossed it onto the cracked wooden dresser, along with the skullcap worn beneath. Then he reached behind, pulled the gun from its roost, and placed it beside the kaffiyeh. Unbuckling his brown belt, he unsheathed a large hunting knife from a brown leather case and tossed it next to the gun.

Blood rushed to my temples as I watched him undress. Was this man my protector, or my enemy? I had no idea. I didn't really know him at all. I could be his guest or his captive.

*** *** ***

We met three months before, in the Wadi Rum Desert of Jordan, where two teacher friends and I were spending a holiday from our English language school back in Istanbul. Our tour guide had arranged an overnight stay at a big, black Bedouin tent run by a man named Sheik Abdul. Rebhi—as I later learned his name—was spending the night there too, along with his own group of Japanese tourists.

I was dancing in my usual New York jazz-meets-Turkish-belly-dance fusion to the music playing on someone's battery-operated cassette player. Rebhi was poking the fire with a stick, his eyes swinging between the flames and me. At the end of the song, he patted the spot on the cushion beside him and said: "Please sit. I must ask you something."

I did. He sat cross-legged upon the pillow like an Arab prince, a traditional brown robe draped around him. Maybe thirty-two years old, his black eyes etched with sun-creased crow's feet, he looked straight out of *Lawrence of Arabia*. Solemn and brooding, he was clearly thinking deeply about something. He glanced at me several times but kept averting his eyes shyly. Finally, he tossed his stick into the fire, turned to me, and said, "Do you think there is anyone in the world who has everything he wants?"

"No," I said. "I doubt even the richest man in the world thinks he has *everything*."

"Yes," he said, continuing to stare into the fire. "I agree. But I didn't know what I was missing until I saw you dancing across the fire. Then I knew what it was. It was you."

I didn't believe him for a second, but a man capable of an opener like that clearly deserved additional time.

"Come," he said. "Let's look at the moon on the desert."

I rose to my feet. He pulled aside the coarse wool flap of the goat-hair tent and we stepped into the moonlit desert. He knelt ever so slightly and I found myself being lifted into his arms and carried like a baby across the sands. Conflicting emotions arose. Of course, it was thrilling, but as a 105-pound female, I have issues with empowerment. All my life, men have been lifting me up, while I've fought to stand on my own two feet. Yet I abandoned myself to romance, allowing this desert prince to carry me.

Rebhi was built like a satyr: slightly swayed back with a melon ass and powerfully muscled arms and chest. Satyrs had never been my type, but poets—alas—were my weakness. He quoted Rumi and then the Persian poet, Iqbal: "The moment you recognize what is beautiful in this world, you cease to be a slave." Then he added: "It's true. I see your beauty and I become as an eagle and soar beyond the mountains to the stars."

We shared a few slippery kisses that night, but I put a halt to anything more. I didn't want to spoil the sensuality of the evening with the possibility of bad sex. Another Bedu in the tent had tried to impress me earlier saying: "We Bedouin treat our women, camels, and donkeys with great care." Rebhi, meanwhile, had been raised by a father with three wives. Would he have any idea of the kind of intimate, mutually-gratifying sex an experienced Western woman would expect?

The next morning, Rebhi arranged a ride to the sea of Aqaba for us with a Bedu driving that way. He walked me to the car, asked for my mobile phone number, and I complied. What harm could there be?

"Come back to me," he whispered, his eyes growing moist.

I felt like the heroine of a trashy supermarket romance novel.

The first text message arrived that night:

LOOK...
the moon is calling you!
SEE...
the stars are shining for you!
LISTEN...
the birds are singing to you!
HEAR...
my heart says,
I LOVE YOU.

The next one arrived while I was eating lunch with my girlfriends back in Istanbul:

> *My heart is a small bird sitting in your hand singing to you "I love you."*

I gasped and nearly dropped the phone.
"What is it?" my friends asked.
Speechless, I handed over the phone.
"Wow!" was their open-mouthed reply.
Rebhi was good. And he was capturing my imagination. What did I have to lose? I was a fifty-five-year-old, twice-divorced, American teaching English in Turkey. My two children were fully grown and living their own lives back in the States. And I had a five-day vacation

coming up in June. Why not fly back to Jordan for a visit?

"When you arrive at the airport, I will shower you with 2,000 kisses so that all of Jordan will know how much I love you," he whispered during a phone call two days before my departure. Cardamom and desert sage wafted through the receiver.

I hardly recognized him. His flowing desert robe had been replaced with a khaki-green, short-sleeved suit. He looked awkward and ill at ease out of the desert. He extended his hand in a business-like manner when I walked out of passport control into the hub of the Amman airport.

"Where are my 2,000 kisses?" I asked. My lower lip pushed forward and I could feel my face pouting like a disappointed five-year-old.

"What?" he asked incredulously. "Here? In the airport?"

"Yes. You said you would shower me with 2,000 kisses."

He planted one rooster-like peck on my cheek. "I am too shy. It is not possible," he whispered. "Wait till we get to the room."

How many times had I fantasized our meeting? How he would drench me in kisses, pick me up in his strong, robe-draped arms, carry me to the cab of his 4X4, drive off into the tawny sand desert, and make desert love to me beneath the starlit sky....

"There's a sandstorm," he said. "We can't go to the desert today."

He started his spiffy new four-wheel-drive vehicle and headed out of the airport.

"Where are we going then?" I asked.

"My brother's in Amman."

His "brother's in Amman" turned out to be a dingy hotel room strewn with dirty clothes, remnants of take-out food, and crumpled bed sheets. The dresser was missing two of its drawers, the gaps as empty as promises. The sole window faced a construction site.

I whispered, "slowly slowly," but he stripped in thirty seconds flat and started tugging at my clothes. With his gun and hunting knife in clear view, I really had no other options, yet I had fantasized about making love to him for three months. Desert or no desert, I had to find out if sex with Rebhi would be as poetic as his words.

Outside, the roar of the construction jarred my brain as he pulled me up onto him. With my legs straddling his waist and his hands cupping my ass, he carried me to the mirror where he watched as he bounced my rump up and down like a trampoline act in time to the jack-hammer beat outside our window.

So much for romantic delusions.

The following morning, as he emerged from the disheveled bed sheets, he announced that we were going to the desert. Finally, I thought, we'll be alone in the desert. The desert will restore Rebhi to his poetic self. Alone under the desert sky, we can recapture the magic of our first meeting.

From the hotel, Rebhi's submissive little brother, Iman, followed us to the car, carrying our bags like a porter. Rebhi indicated that I should get in the passenger seat in front, while Iman climbed in the back. Apparently, he was coming with us.

At twenty-one, Iman was Rebhi's youngest brother from his father's third wife. Their relationship seemed like one of owner and slave: Rebhi barked out orders, while Iman silently carried them out. Iman rarely said

anything, looking sadly out at the world from his perpetually lowered head. I squirmed as Rebhi growled
at him, sent him on errands, and treated him like a
servant.

We drove to a restaurant, where we loaded up on
falafel, hummus, and *fuul*, then hit the road. Within a
half hour, Rebhi had picked up two more Bedu who
were hitchhiking along the road. One was a tall skinny
black-skinned man; the other, a pock-faced, gap-toothed
fellow. Both were in their mid-thirties. The blacker
man grinned wildly and rattled on in Arabic for a few
minutes before falling silent. The cassette player whined
Arabic songs. *"Ha bibi, ha bibi..."* The scenery changed
from urban to desolate. My mood changed from hopeful
to fearful.

Rebhi growled something to the three men in the
back of the cab and their hands shot up in the air and
started twirling about.

"What did you say to them?"

"Diane loves music and dancing: dance, or I'll shoot
you!"

Rebhi placed my hand atop the knob of the stick
shift and etched delicate patterns across my skin with
his thumb as he drove. The car in front of us was driving too slowly for his taste, so he flicked a switch on his
dashboard. A police siren blared out. The car promptly
moved to the side of the road and Rebhi sped past.
Apparently, Rebhi had fitted his car with police and
ambulance sirens. He issued another order to the back
of the vehicle. Iman mixed whiskey and Coke in plastic
cups and handed one to Rebhi and to me, then made
drinks for the other two Bedu. Considering the situation, I decided a little alcohol could only help. Rebhi lit
one cigarette and handed it to me, then lit another for

himself. It seemed a good time to take up smoking, too. With the cassette player blasting *"Ha bibi, Ha bibi,"* I circled my arms through the air, rolled my shoulders, sipped my drink, and blew smoke out the window as Rebhi sped south along the Kings Highway.

Behind us, a siren sounded. This time, it was a real police car. Cursing, Rebhi pulled over. Two policemen peered inside the car and Rebhi told them he was a guide taking me to the Wadi Rum. They demanded his driver's license and then refused to return it.

"Fucking police!" he said when he got back inside the car. "Now I have to go to court in Amman. Fuck them! Fuck the government! Fuck the fuckers!" He urged the back-seaters to join his protest. They obligingly raised their fists: "Fuck the police."

He drove to the nearest town, parked on a side street, rummaged through the back of the car, and emerged with a new license plate. Adeptly, he replaced the old one and slipped a new driver's license into his wallet. The two hitchhikers got out, thanked Rebhi for the ride, and we continued on.

Finally the desert appeared. Rebhi drove along the sand-strewn road, then stopped. I walked into the sand and felt my heart lighten. There was something so mystical about the orange sands and craggy ancient cliffs: a sense of something lost being recaptured. I understood why T. E. Lawrence had been so captivated by this place.

I turned to see Rebhi ferreting about in the back of his car. He emerged with his revolver and strode straight toward me.

There was only the passive little brother, the sands, the cliffs, and me. Nobody else. No other vehicles. The silent desert stretched before us. He was going to kill me.

Take my passport, my bankcard, and my credit card, cast me into the ditch, and leave me for the vultures.

"Shoot it," he said, handing me the gun.

"I've never shot a gun," I said, forcing sound through my parched lips. I was both startled and relieved.

"Just pull the trigger."

I took the amazingly heavy gun, pointed it at the wide-open nothingness, and attempted to press the trigger. But try as I might, I lacked the finger strength to fire. Reluctantly, I handed the gun back to Rebhi. He placed it back into my hand, covered my hand with his, and squeezed the trigger. The shot rang out into the desert.

We climbed back into the vehicle, my head swimming in fog. I was still alive: that was what mattered. We drove further into the Wadi Rum, into air heavy with pink-orange haze from the recently subsided sandstorm. Finally the huge tent of Sheik Abdul appeared like an apparition. We stopped.

Rebhi and Iman pulled out some bedding, lay down in the shade of the tent, and fell asleep. Filled with manic energy, I bounded across the sand to the cliffs. Each footstep that sank into the amorphous sand brought me joy. I spread my arms and twirled like a drunken madwoman, then scaled the rocky plateau for a 360-degree view of desert and craggy mountains. In the distance, a camel caravan of two families trod over a dune. For the longest time, my heartbeat and the whoosh of the wind were the only sounds audible. Then came a muffled drone of car alarms. It slowly dawned on me that it was Rebhi's car. I tried to sashay down the mountain like a goat, but the going was slow. Back on the sands, I crested the ridge and—to my horror—saw nothing. Rebhi's car was gone. There was not a human in sight.

I kept turning in circles, as if a previously empty spot would suddenly reveal something new. I couldn't absorb this situation. How could he possibly have abandoned me in the middle of the desert? I ran in one direction and then the other. Everywhere the truth was the same. No car. No Rebhi.

I sat down on the sand, my heart pounding in my temples. With no other options presenting themselves, I decided to go inside the tent, try to rest, and pray that Rebhi would return.

Temporarily blinded by the darkness of the tent after the harsh light of the sun, my eyes took a minute to acclimate. Slowly I distinguished the shape of someone lying on one of the rough settees that circled the inside of the tent. I tiptoed toward the sleeping body. As I approached, it suddenly sat up. I nearly fainted, then realized it was Iman.

"Oh," he said in his quiet voice, his Arabic accent as thick as cardamom-flavored coffee. "You are back."

"Where is Rebhi? Where is the car? Where did he go?"

"Other brother stuck in sand with tourists. Rebhi, he go pull out of sand. We wait here. You need something, you tell me. I do it. O.K.?" His eyes peeked up from his lowered head and a smile tugged at the corners of his mouth.

Rebhi didn't return that night, but Sheik Abdul— King of the Bedouin—and several Bedouin boys did. They cooked a dinner of tough chicken, vegetables, and pita, and shared it with us. I was relieved to see food, but trepidation remained my overriding emotion. I had read stories about intrepid European women who ventured into the desert, only to be forced to share their bodies with their hosts. What fate awaited me?

When night fell, Iman shyly took my hand and led me to a settee where I was to sleep. Sheik Abdul brought me blankets and bid me goodnight. I slept fitfully as the winds surged. The wooden tent poles shook, and the sides of the tent flapped about like a hoochie-koochie dancer. It made such a racket, I decided to try sleeping outside. Big mistake: although wrapped in a heavy blanket, I was suddenly besieged by mosquitoes. What they were doing in the desert, so far from any water, was a mystery, but they attacked in full force. As I scurried back inside the tent, some slipped under the flap with me.

Morning finally arrived, and Iman explained what happened.

"Wind push them from Sea of Aqaba. Only happen one time in year."

And I just happened to be here for it.

The boys brought in platters of eggs and potatoes, pita and jam, and a pot of sickeningly sweet tea. As I ate alongside Iman, an approaching vehicle grew audible. I rushed outside to see a bus filled with tourists arrive and park.

"Oh, isn't this quaint?"

"Like something out of *National Geographic*."

"I've heard camels are nasty beasts."

"Yes, I hope ours will be well-trained."

"Can't trust these people though, you know."

As the tourists spilled out of the bus, their words spilled onto the sands. They'd come for a short camel ride and would then return to Wadi Musa, the city that had sprung up outside Petra to accommodate tourists.

I followed the driver into the tent.

"I want to return to Wadi Musa with you," I said.

He looked up at me, then turned to the Bedouin boys in the tent. Though I didn't understand a word of

Arabic, it was clear that he was asking about me. One of the boys said Rebhi's name.

Without looking at me, the driver snapped: "No, not possible."

"Why?"

He refused to answer.

Iman glanced from me to the bus driver and then carefully wiped the sand from the toes of his city shoes.

"Why?" I persisted, hoping for a human response. He only glanced at me sideways, his head tilted. Then he resumed his conversation with the Bedu.

It was a male conspiracy. I was now the property of Rebhi and had lost my freedom of movement. It was like some awful film where the heroine gets herself in a bad situation and you think, "Stupid woman! How could you?" Only *I* was that stupid woman: a prisoner who had blithely stepped into a trap.

Still, my prison guards were accommodating—as long as I didn't try to escape. My friends back in Istanbul knew what I was doing. One had even spent the night in Sheik Abdul's tent. I was only being held temporarily, until Rebhi returned. I sure didn't like it, however.

"You want see special place?" Iman asked. "Not far."

With nothing better to do, I accepted his offer.

He gently took my hand. "Come," he said and led me into the dunes.

We walked hand in hand across the sand. An only child, I felt like I had acquired a sweet little brother. Ascending and descending dunes, we at last arrived at a hidden cove surrounded by burnt sienna cliffs.

"Lie down," he instructed.

My heart beat wildly as I realized my vulnerable situation. Had I misunderstood Iman's intentions? He looked up at me with such innocence, I chided my mistrust and sat down beside him. He lay down on his back and motioned to do the same. Above us the cliffs almost touched, forming a pinnacle with points of light angling down onto the shaded sand. As we lay on our backs gazing up, Iman took my hand again, and for an hour we lay side-by-side, holding hands and gazing up towards the apex.

His ringing phone shot me back to reality: "Rebhi want speak to you."

"My brother is coming to pick you up," Rebhi crooned over the receiver. "There was another sandstorm, my darling, and I couldn't come to you. How I've missed you, but we will soon be together."

We drove away in the new brother's jeep. Orange sand seeped through every crack and crevice in the car, coating our faces. The brother rubbed his sleeve across the windshield, then dabbed his eyes with a rag. As we sped away from Sheik Abdul's, the winds grew fiercer. The jeep swayed like a toy.

We finally reached the highway, then stopped. I could see a robed figure emerge from a vehicle on the other side of the road. Rebhi. He opened the door of the jeep and I stepped out. Bending over, he picked me up into his arms and strode across the highway, bearing me like the Queen of Sheba to his vehicle.

"Oh my darling, how I've missed you," he whispered.

I got in the front seat. Iman hopped in back and we slowly made our way back to Amman.

At the airport, Rebhi stood awkwardly, studying his boots. "I pray that you will return to me. Let me show you the glory of life in the desert. Together we can live beneath the stars. You are my Desert Queen."

As I turned toward the glass doors of the airport, Rebhi put his hand on my arm.

"I never asked you for anything, did I? I paid for everything, didn't I? You were my guest. Is that not so?"

I nodded.

"But now we are together. You will return to me and we will live the beauty of the desert. There is just one thing I ask of you."

"What is it?"

"Please, my darling. Give me your bank card." His eyes held mine for a split second before he resumed studying his boots.

An involuntary laugh escaped. "Why would I give you my bank card? Do you think I'm crazy?" I pulled my wallet from my backpack and slid out the few remaining Jordanian bills. "Here, I can't use these. They'll help cover the cost of my food."

"But my darling, it is normal for a woman to share everything with her man, is it not?"

"I am not your woman," I said. Then I turned to Iman. He looked up at me and I lightly kissed both of his cheeks. "Take care of yourself," I said.

With that, I entered the airport, where music bellowed from the sound system: *"Ha bibi, Ha bibi..."*

That night I wrote my final message to Rebhi:

> *My heart is a small bird sitting in your hand*
> *singing to you:*
> *"You will never get my bank card."*

ᣣ ᣣ ᣣ

Stifling her sobs and dabbing her eyes, Diane Caldwell boarded a plane to Greece in 2003 and hasn't returned home to the United

States since. She currently lives in Istanbul, where she dances with gypsies and washes her hair in the welcome rain of August thunderstorms. She won the Solas Awards Gold Medal for Best Travel Memoir in 2009 and is a featured author in the anthology Tales of the Expat Harem, *a collection of stories written by women living in Turkey.*

KELLEN ZALE

Madonna and Mr. Hu

Desperately seeking sanity at a banquet of the Chinese Communist Party.

The disembodied chicken foot hovered before me, its caramelized claws hooked between a pair of ebony chopsticks. "Touched for the very first time?" Mr. Hu, the portly Chinese man on the other end of the chopsticks, shook with laughter as I squirmed in my seat and declined.

Undeterred, Mr. Hu turned to Stephen, the other American guest at the banquet. Stephen taught with me in Foshan, a grimy industrial city a few hours and a million amenities away from the Great Wall-Terracotta Soldiers-Yangtze River Cruise tourist route. Three months into our yearlong stint as high school ESL teachers, we had been invited on a weekend excursion to the only slightly less grimy countryside by Mr. Hu, a provincial Communist official.

Stephen reached across the table with his chopsticks. *"Wo yao!"* He finished off the chicken foot in two crunchy bites as Mr. Hu raised his glass of rice wine in a toast.

"I will always cherish you!"

Like a Prayer, Madonna, 1988. After dinner had reached its second hour and we had only completed the third of ten courses, I began playing a mental game, pairing Mr. Hu's toasts with the album and year of the song from which they derived. But Mr. Hu put my pop music knowledge to shame: as a result of what must have been years of intensive karaoke training, his entire English vocabulary consisted solely of Madonna lyrics. I had assumed he would run out of conversation-appropriate lyrics after a few hours. But I had underestimated both Madonna and Mr. Hu: one a prolific songwriter for over two decades, the other a Communist Party savant determined to impress the two foreign teachers in his district.

Being Mr. Hu's guest was supposed to be an honor. Not all 1.3 billion people in China are members of the Communist Party. Only a select 70 million or so are invited to join. And only an even more select few thousand are nominated for official Party positions. To be invited to the home of a Party official, then, was an intimidating proposition. Before tonight, I had worried about my almost complete ignorance of Chinese history and about being drawn into debates on free speech and pollution and AIDS. But Mr. Hu was only interested in two things: converting me into a carnivore and convincing me to have sex with Stephen. And Madonna was his co-conspirator.

Early the next morning, Mei, the translator the Party had supplied to accompany us for the weekend, crept into my bedroom. Given the rain streaming down the windows, I had envisioned a day of bubble baths, microwave popcorn, and satellite television. I assumed my host would want me to enjoy these comforts of his Western-style home that were lacking in my dormitory cell at the government-run high school.

My host did not. "Mr. Hu wants to visit the famous waterfall in the Reiming Valley. You will be ready, yes?"

This wasn't actually a question. In my three months in China, I'd learned guests were expected to accept every invitation. If Mr. Hu invited me to hike to a middling-sized waterfall sure to be obscured by the overcast weather and throngs of Chinese tourists in yellow ponchos, that's what I was doing today.

When I emerged into the living room a few minutes later, Stephen was lounging on the faux-leather sofa, leafing through a contraband copy of *Playboy*. "Good morning, sleepy. You missed breakfast. Highly delicious pork and onion soup."

Stephen wasn't being ironic. He loved Chinese cuisine; the more unidentifiable animal parts, the better.

"Getting up at eight to go on a walk in the rain is just how I wanted to start the day."

"Don't be so cheerful. *Zuo shehui cha shi jin fangfa you dui xueshi.*" He translated: "The only way to have correct knowledge is to make social investigations." Stephen had also taken to memorizing sayings from Mao's *Little Red Book* and reciting them in Chinese to impress people. And in English to remind me how little Chinese I had managed to learn so far.

Mei and Mr. Hu entered the room. "We shall go now?" Mei smiled her non-question.

Outside, the rain poured like dirty ink from the colorless sky. Perhaps, I suggested, we could wait until the weather cleared? Mei spoke quickly in Chinese to Mr. Hu, who shook his head and turned to me with a manic glimmer in his eyes. "Let your body go with the flow, you know you can do it." He put his arms around Stephen and me and pushed us toward the door together.

"Did you pay him to do that?" I hissed at Stephen.

"You flatter yourself." He followed Mr. Hu and Mei out the door, adding, "It's you who's hard up, not me."

Unfortunately, he was right. Stephen was the only male fluent in English and over 5' 5" within a 100-mile radius of our school. However, since he was also a conceited, pretentious know-it-all, I'd resigned myself to a year of celibacy. Unperturbed by my lack of interest, Stephen basked in the constant attention of beautiful Chinese women. It was yet another benefit of being a male Caucasian: Stephen was an ersatz Brad Pitt, while I was a 5' 9", brown-haired, blue-eyed freak that Chinese people couldn't stop staring at.

Luckily, during our walk to the famous waterfall, no one could distinguish my freakishness thanks to the sheets of rain, which obscured both my face and the famous waterfall. For the next two hours, we sloshed through puddles and evaded vendors hawking dried fish to screaming schoolchildren. Even Stephen looked less cheerful than usual when we returned to Mr. Hu's Mercedes.

As we waited in the car with the driver, Mr. Hu and Mei stood under an umbrella, presumably discussing what cultural activity to impose upon us next. After a few moments, Mei slid into the backseat, forcing me into the middle next to Stephen.

"When the clouds come in and try to darken our days, I'll always want you to stay, stay darling." Mr. Hu said something in Chinese to Mei, who blushed and giggled as Stephen pinched my thigh and winked at Mr. Hu.

As the driver navigated the potholes, rickshaws, and the assortment of pigs, goats, and elderly villagers that crowded the road, the *Evita* soundtrack, with Mr. Hu in the starring role, serenaded us.

"All through my wild days, my mad existence, I kept my promise, don't keep your distance." Mr. Hu reached into the back seat and pulled my hands together with Stephen's as he improvised a crescendoing chorus. "Don't cry for me, Steee-pheee-eeen, the truth is I never left you."

When we finally arrived back at the house, I hurried toward my bedroom to take a hot shower and nap before what was likely to be a marathon dining experience. It was a national holiday and we'd been invited to a banquet honoring local Party leaders. But before I was halfway up the stairs, Mei stopped me.

"Mr. Hu has another distinguished guest tonight. This visitor needs to stay in your room." Mei looked at me guiltily. "Stephen's room has two beds. You can stay with him."

My eyes almost rolled out of my head. "There's no other room?" Mr. Hu's McMansion dwarfed the two-room apartments most Chinese families shared. I couldn't believe there was nowhere else in the house for me to sleep. Mei turned to Mr. Hu and asked him again. He brought his hands together and bowed, but when he raised his head, a not quite apologetic smile quivered on his lips. "Last night I dreamt of Reiming, where a girl loves a boy, and a boy loves a girl."

I should have forgiven Mr. Hu for assuming that

Stephen and I would shack up. After all, we were two foreigners who were the same age, spoke the same language, and were marooned in the same remote region of China. Like a meddling grandmother trying to fix up her granddaughter with the neighbor's son, Mr. Hu was playing matchmaker. Except grandmothers don't usually encourage their granddaughters with chants of "In the midnight hour, I can feel your power" and "Come on, shine your heavenly body tonight."

"Mr. Hu apologizes for any inconvenience," Mei shrugged. Inconvenience, my ass. Mr. Hu knew exactly what he was doing: stuck in this provincial backwoods, with no fun other than field trips to trickling waterfalls and late nights drinking rice wine with his comrades, he'd decided to use the foreign visitors to provide some much-needed entertainment.

My bags were waiting for me in Stephen's room, together with Stephen, sprawled out in his boxers on the only bed I saw in the room.

"I hear we're to be bunkmates tonight." He glanced up from the Chinese soap opera screeching on the television.

"Bunkmates implies bunks. Mei said there were two beds in here?"

Stephen reached over the side of the bed and kicked something with his foot. A less than twin-sized trundle bed fell out from under him. "I believe that dodgy contraption is what she was referring to." He stretched his other arm across the remainder of the queen-size bed. "Although if you behave yourself, I could be convinced to share."

"That would put a damper on your bringing home the next lucky local lady," I said as I walked into the bathroom and shut the door.

Suddenly, I was in paradise: an enormous jacuzzi bathtub gleamed in one corner, while the other held a multi-head steam shower and sauna, and, most luxurious of all, a Western-style, glowingly clean toilet. If sharing a bed with Stephen was the price I had to pay for a night of sanitized bathroom facilities, it might be worth it. During my first few weeks in China, enraptured by living in a foreign culture, I forgave my dormitory's "Western-style" bathroom, an all-in-one shower/sink/toilet, which reeked of sewage whenever it rained (or I suffered from dysentery, which was about as often). I didn't even mind the stall-less holes in the ground that passed as public toilets. But after three months, the novelty had worn off.

Ninety minutes later, I emerged to an empty bedroom; Stephen was probably scheming with Mr. Hu about how to incorporate pork lo mein into foreplay. I pulled on a once black, now gray, pair of underwear and a stretched-out bra. The school's Soviet-era washing machines somehow washed away color and shape, while retaining all the dirt. As I rummaged in my bag for appropriate attire for a Communist banquet—*Vogue* has yet to publish an article on that fashion dilemma—the door edged open. Grabbing my yellow poncho, I clumsily attempted to cover up.

Stephen stood frozen in the doorway. "Sorry. Completely unintentional." He gave me a quick once-over as I pulled the yellow plastic around my butt. "Though Mr. Hu might be right—not a bad little body."

He turned around, blocking Mr. Hu's view, and escorted him away. "Um, Mr. Hu, *dui bu qi, xianzai bu xing.*"

Fully clothed, I reluctantly joined the others in the living room a few minutes later. Mr. Hu eyed me and pointed at Stephen. "Open your heart to he, baby, he hold the lock and you hold the key."

"Stephen, what did you tell him?" I hissed.

"Just that you couldn't keep your clothes on around me," he smiled smugly. "And that you have a great ass."

"Please don't encourage him," I pleaded. "Aren't you tired of this yet?"

Stephen shook his head. "The fun's just starting."

A middle-aged Chinese man in a slate gray Mao suit joined us, presumably the distinguished guest who'd usurped my bedroom. Mei introduced him as General Lizong and informed me that I would also be bumped from the Mercedes so that the men could talk business. Despite his lack of knowledge of the "business" at hand, Stephen's penis apparently qualified him for a seat in the Mercedes. Mei and I were demoted to a 1985 Toyota taxi smelling not so faintly of fish sauce and rotting vegetables.

The banquet hall was a squat, gray, and properly Communist structure imposed on an otherwise timeless landscape of rice paddies and fields of palms. Inside, giant banners emblazoned with gold and black Chinese letters hung from the stage. Mr. Hu look-alikes filled the room, milling about and shaking hands with each other. Peppered amongst them, a handful of young, beautiful Chinese women tottered around in four-inch heels and low-cut cocktail dresses.

Mei leaned over to Stephen and me. "These women are not their wives. They are escorts for Party officials."

"Excellent," Stephen grinned at me. "If things don't work out with you, I can ask Mr. Hu for an official favor."

Mr. Hu, General Lizong, and one of the escorts, a barely legal woman wearing a skin-tight green dress and a push-up bra corralling up and out what little flesh hung on her emaciated frame, waited for us at our table. Mr. Hu pulled out a chair next to Stephen and indicated I should sit there.

"Cherish the thought of always having her here by your side," Mr. Hu winked at Stephen, then sat across the table from us for an optimal view of the amusement he had planned for the night.

I'd already attended one Chinese banquet and knew that I'd likely emerge four hours later famished. Banquets were an opportunity to offer guests high-priced meat dishes; vegetables were considered the food of the poor. Since only an insane person would want to eat like a peasant, most Chinese understood "vegetarian" to mean not "without meat," but "with vegetables." So I poked suspiciously at the "eggplant specialty" that the waiter brought me, and after a bite, realized that the "specialty" was the unidentifiable chunks of meat dumped into the mix. I made a few polite stabs with my chopsticks and let Stephen eat the rest.

When he saw us sharing food, Mr. Hu cackled and made an obscene gesture with his chopsticks. "So if you want it right now, make him show you how."

It's just a few hours, I told myself. The jacuzzi will be worth it. I summoned a serene smile for Mr. Hu and resumed drinking my beer. Another mysterious meat dish was brought to the table as a parade of men in ill-fitting suits stood at the podium and spoke about other men in ill-fitting suits.

By the time the last speaker finished, we were on the fifth course. Mr. Hu raised his glass for a toast as Stephen replenished my supply of watery Chinese beer. "Let your body take a ride, feel the beat and step inside." Mr. Hu winked at me as he drained his glass.

"You know I will never be drunk enough to fulfill Mr. Hu's dreams for us." I toasted with Stephen and sipped my beer.

"You say that now. There's still three courses to go, which means three more meals you won't eat and three more drinks that will go straight to your head."

Stephen was right. For self-protection reasons, I needed to eat. So when a bowl of congee was brought out as the next course, I gave a silent prayer of thanks. Congee is a kind of watery oatmeal, bland and harmless. I eagerly started lapping up giant spoonfuls. Halfway through my bowl, I paused: a glistening gray chunk of something hovered ominously on the surface of the white, viscous paste.

"What is this?" I elbowed Stephen.

"She geng," General Lizong held his spoon up, his own glimmering mass of gray floating on it.

Mei looked across the table at me, and then at Mr. Hu. "You give her snake congee?"

The beer and the snake soup washed all lingering traces of politeness away. I shrieked as my spoon and the chunk of snake splattered onto the table. Mumbling a garbled "Excuse me" in Mandarin, I stood up and ran out of the room, past red-faced Party officials and their giggling escorts. Hoping the dim hallway would lead to a bathroom, I kept walking until I eventually stumbled through a door leading outside.

The blackness of the rural night enveloped me, and for a moment, it was as if everything—the banquet, the weekend trip, the very idea of me living in China—was a murky dream. But my overflowing bladder was a painful reminder of reality. As my eyes adjusted to the darkness, I saw a small shed with two adjoining doors and realized that I had found the bathroom after all. I eased open the outhouse door and was instantly struck by an olfactory tsunami: wave after noxious wave poured forth from a hole in the ground overflowing with human excrement. Slamming the door shut, I threw up the liquid and reptilian contents of my dinner.

Then I started crying, with complete and unrestrained self-pity. Why was China like this? Where were the elegant palaces and Buddhist tea ceremonies? Why didn't I live in Beijing where expats could get *The New York Times* and frozen yogurt? Why did I have to ride everyday on a minibus overstuffed with undiapered babies, spitting old men, and chickens exploding out of their cages? How did I get stuck in a jail-like dormitory infested with cockroaches the size of hamsters and shrieking Cantonese neighbors? Why was I living in a place so polluted that I couldn't run outside, so crowded that I couldn't have a square foot to myself in the street, so different that I had nothing in common with anyone?

As I sat in the barnyard outside the banquet hall, wallowing in self-pity and vomit, Stephen appeared from around the corner. He handed me a bottle of water. "Here. You're a mess."

Wiping my eyes, I tried to stop sobbing, but the tears kept coming: three months of loneliness, frustration, and confusion streamed down my cheeks.

"Let's go." Stephen put his arm around my back and helped me stand.

"I can't go back inside, I've been so rude, I—"

"I told them you were ill and I was taking you home."

An hour and another taxi ride later, I lay in the pink tiled bathtub, trying to soak the vomit and manure and self-pity away. When I returned to the bedroom, the lights were off and all of Stephen's six feet four inches were mashed into an unnatural-looking fetal position on the trundle bed.

"Stephen, you can sleep in the bed, I'm fine."

"No, you're not." He didn't open his eyes. "Now get in the bed before I change my mind."

So I did. And in the morning, I awoke, unmolested and completely embarrassed. Embarrassed that Stephen saw me behave so poorly, embarrassed that I'd disrupted the banquet, embarrassed that I hadn't been appreciative of Mr. Hu's generosity. More than anything, embarrassed that I wasn't the brave foreign traveler I thought.

Stephen stepped out of the bathroom. "You were pretty hammered last night."

I grimaced. "Thanks for taking me home and sparing me from doing anything else stupid."

"It could have happened to anyone. That is, anyone who is a non-Chinese speaking, vegetarian, attractive female." He sat on the edge of the bed.

For such a pompous ass, he was trying hard to be nice. Maybe I just needed to give him another chance. "I owe you one."

"There is a little thing you could do." He stood up and fidgeted with the door handle. "Mr. Hu saw me this morning, and, of course, he wanted to know how our evening went last night. And I didn't want to disappoint him. He seems to have his heart set on, you know, the whole Madonna thing and all."

"What did you tell him, Stephen?"

He looked at me sheepishly. "That you were the best sex I ever had."

"You didn't," I groaned.

"Afraid I did. What would he think, me having you in here all night, and not even making out? Not even sleeping in the same bed? No, I couldn't do that to him."

"Or to your pride." I got out of bed and rummaged in my bag for clean clothes. "What do you want me to do?"

He took the bag out of my hands and put his hands on my shoulders. "Stay just like that. You look nice and rumpled. Convenient that a hangover and sex have the same effect."

"And just let him think you scored?"

"That's the idea."

And so, a few minutes later, after making sure my hair was appropriately tousled and my bra straps misaligned, I walked into the living room where Mei, Stephen, and Mr. Hu awaited.

"Are you feeling better?" Mei eyed me curiously.

"Yes, thank you. Please tell Mr. Hu I am very sorry for being rude and leaving the banquet early. I didn't feel well and wasn't thinking clearly."

Mei translated and Mr. Hu nodded. "Mr. Hu says he understands, you needed Stephen to take you to bed." Mr. Hu's gold molars glimmered from the depths of his mouth as his grin stretched to his earlobes.

Outside, the sun hovered listlessly in the gray sky, as if uncertain whether it was worth the effort to shine through the smog.

"Mr. Hu wants to know if you enjoyed your weekend in Reiming?" Mei translated for Mr. Hu, who lingered by the side of the driveway to see us off.

"*Xie-xie wan fen,*" Stephen nodded and winked at Mr. Hu.

I gazed out my window. The compound of sherbet-colored McMansions with BMWs and Cadillacs lining the driveways loomed on one side of the road. On the other side, a farmer covered in mud and sweat pushed an oxcart through an overgrown field. He stopped every few minutes to dislodge a wheel from a rut or to wait for his animal to graze in the weedy marsh. This was the China I lived in. Not the romanticized China of colonial England or the sanitized China of expat diplomats in Beijing and Shanghai. I lived in the China of snake soup, the China of barefoot men selling live chickens and dead dogs, the China of all-night karaoke sessions with drunken Communists.

I leaned forward and slid my arms around Stephen's neck as I locked eyes with Mr. Hu. "Wanting, needing, waiting. For him to justify my love." If this was my China, I might as well speak the local language.

⁂ ⁂ ⁂

Kellen Zale is a freelance writer and editor who is currently working on a collection of short stories based on her unintentionally intrepid travels on six continents. She lives in Los Angeles, California.

LAURIE WEED

🎵 🎵 🎵

Riding the Rails with Mother Theresa

A travel companion lives up to her name.

"Madame, Ordinary Class is very full, you see," the ticket seller waggled his head in a discouraging manner. He was the last of several head-wagglers to try and herd me into First Class, where foreigners in Burma officially belong. I wasn't resisting because of the price difference so much as my desire to travel among regular people rather than be exiled with the "wealthy."

"In First Class, one person, one seat," he continued. "But in Ordinary Class..." he paused and rolled his eyes toward the other ticket seller. The poor fellow was pinned to his desk by a disorderly flock of flapping, cawing women. "Many people. You see?"

When I left San Francisco last fall, I knew I wanted this winter to be different. Yet I had gotten a little more than I bargained for: a bout of tropical maladies in Laos, a hellish typhoid episode in Bangkok, a prolonged breakup on a desert island, and a riverboat mishap that was a really, really close call. After five ridiculously unlucky months on the road, the end of this trip was rushing toward me like a rogue wave and I longed to slow it down. I was tired of disasters, of airports, of tourist destinations, and tourists; I was tired of racing around and not getting anywhere. I was out of money and nearly out of time. I had to go home, but first, I longed to spend a few days traveling alone, in slow motion. I wanted to remember what drew me to Asia in the first place, and I wanted a proper goodbye.

Even in the high season, tourists rarely visit Burma's arid, neglected Shan State, and it is utterly devoid of them in April. However, it is a peak travel time for locals trying to escape the pre-monsoon heat of the plains. In the hill station of Pyin U Lwin, formerly British Maymyo, time has literally stood still since the British left. The shining hands of the clock tower that looms over the town's crumbling colonial buildings and tattered rose gardens haven't moved for decades. I decided to slow time down even further by riding a Burmese train. It doesn't get much slower than that, even here in the Forgotten Land. So, that morning I'd hailed a brightly painted horse cart to carry me to the red brick station at the edge of town, where I repeated my Ordinary Class ticket request to various officials until I found myself talking to this gloomy, head-waggling man. Just one more bureaucratic hoop and I'd be on a slow train to Hsipaw, temporarily frozen in time.

"Ordinary Class will be just fine," I said firmly. "One Ordinary-Class ticket, please." He gave one more resigned head waggle, got out his pen, and painstakingly scratched my name into his book.

"Madame is in Coach 2, Seat 23," he said, handing me the ticket. As I walked away, I heard him sigh, "Godspeed, madame."

I was still snickering when an elderly Indian lady sidled up to me.

"Ordinary Class?" she clucked, trying to peer over my elbow and read the ticket in my hand. "How much you pay?"

"I paid two thousand kyat," I said reluctantly, knowing exactly where this line of questioning would lead. Getting the best price is a national pastime in this country, and I played the game poorly.

"Two thousand!" she snorted. "Look, I pay only five hundred—and we are on the same car, Coach 2. See?" Gloating, she held up her ticket stub for my inspection.

"Foreigners have to pay more—what can I do? I tell them I'm half Burmese, but they never believe me." I shrugged and drew an imaginary line across the top of my head to illustrate my height: I'm an average-sized woman in the West but a giant in Asia.

This made her laugh, and she took me under her scrawny wing. "My name is Theresa," she said. "In our country, we call old ladies 'Mother'—this is polite. So you can call me Mother Theresa!" Hooting at her own joke, she badgered me into buying her a cup of tea. Her children had bought her train ticket, she explained, but they refused to give her any tea money. "*Peh*, so cheap!"

Squatting across from Mother Theresa at a table sized for Lilliputians and humming with flies, I learned that this short, slightly hunched woman was a seventy-two-year-old retired schoolteacher of South Indian descent, and a widow of nearly two decades. Two of her four sons had moved to the Chinese trading post of Lashio, at the end of the Burma Road, and she was on her way to visit them. Shaped like a gourd with long, twiggy arms, Theresa was swathed in a faded cotton *longyi* and a knit sweater, even though the air was at least 85 degrees Fahrenheit. Thick, round glasses enhanced her inquisitive expression. Her English was a little rusty and she shouted whenever she spoke, as her hearing had faded. She sported one tooth, elephantine ankles, and a goatee that would make any college boy proud. I was charmed.

Ticket or not, I would never have gotten into Ordinary Class without her, because when the train pulled up to the platform, there was a frenzy. All at once, the milling crowd surged forward, pushing and shouting, hurling children and cargo into every available inch of space. I plodded after Theresa to Coach 2, but there I was stymied: the narrow wooden benches, already overflowing with people and goods, were numbered only in Burmese.

"Come, come!" Theresa commanded. She forged a path through the tangled swarm of bodies and I bumbled after her, taking care not to brush anyone off the train with my backpack. When I caught up to her, she was engaged in a shouting match with a scowling Chinese matron and a young Burmese lady who kept rattling her small son's arm for emphasis. Their voices escalated until abruptly, a seat was cleared. Theresa beamed at me; the other women glowered and looked away.

"Sit!" Theresa motioned to me. "Quickly, this your seat—you don't give up!" She shook a gnarled finger at the Burmese mother, who was making a pouty face. "That one there, she a cheeky one! She try to take your seat!"

"Oh…well, thank you very much," I said, slightly embarrassed.

"I tell them: You my daughter! And if they try to steal your seat, I coming back!" Theresa swept her threatening digit around the group one last time, then marched off to claim her own seat at the rear of the car.

Conscious of being scrutinized by my fellow passengers, I stuffed my big backpack into the overhead rack and sat down on the hard bench, cradling my smaller bags in my lap. The Chinese lady who'd been arguing with Theresa settled on the opposite bench, pointedly ignoring me, and the woman who'd been ousted from my seat began cajoling me in Burmese, nudging her reluctant child forward. I smiled, patted the bench and scooted into the wall so they could both squeeze in, although it seemed likely that ticketed passengers would soon claim the coveted seats. Every other bench was packed and so were the aisles. Most travelers clutched at least one large bag or small child on their laps, and the floor was piled high. Shopping bags bulged, baskets and boxes overflowed with fruit, flowers, and miscellaneous foodstuffs to be eaten, delivered to relatives, or sold at some point down the line. In fact, the other passengers looked prepared for a voyage of several days, which worried me since we were only ninety kilometers from the end of the line. Exactly how long did they expect this trip to last?

Just when I thought we might get underway, the missing ticket holders of our seat showed up and another shouting match ensued. The squatter and her son were shooed away again by a bustling young family that had hauled aboard two enormous grain sacks filled with green mangoes, which they clearly intended to park in the space that would normally accommodate our legs. My grumpy Chinese seatmate tapped my knees impatiently with her fan, signaling me to move my feet. Envisioning how I would feel after a whole day spent in a yoga position, knees hooked over my ears, I decided to hold my ground. What little space remained would have to be shared fairly, if not comfortably. Taking a cue from Theresa, I negotiated in pantomime: I would make room for the mangoes, but only if the Chinese lady repositioned her five-gallon basket of limes—currently wedged against my shins—so I could extend my legs occasionally. When she began to object, I merely twitched an eyebrow toward the rear of the coach where my adoptive "mother" was holding court. Like magic, my opponent subsided. Perhaps the most useful thing to take on a long Burmese train journey is an irascible Indian mother. The shuffling of bodies and baggage continued, and when the train was positively bursting with people and goods, it lurched gently forward.

With my feet propped on the mangoes and my knees tucked just below my chin, I could extend my legs, one at a time, whenever they began to fall asleep. A sticky toddler camped beneath the awning I made with my legs, snacking nonstop throughout the journey and happily making use of my pants as a hand towel. Her older brother, a whining, fractious child, shrieked whenever his mouth was empty and threw garbage at people for amusement. Everyone else just grimaced and ignored him, but on the heels of Hurricane Theresa and the Great Mango Standoff, I felt obliged to show some goodwill. Rummaging through my bag, I found some paper and a few colored pencils to distract him.

The ticket clerk had not exaggerated the popularity of Ordinary Class. We were stacked wall-to-wall and eight deep in Coach 2, with bodies wedged between and draped astride a colorful strata of agricultural and domestic cargo. Immigration to this area had surged during the relatively flush years of British occupation, and the northeastern quadrant of Burma's geographic "kite" is now home to ethnic Burmans, Chinese, Nepalese, South Indian Tamils, Shan, Karen, and too many other hill tribes to name, creating a cultural mix as rich and dense as a heap of green tea-leaf salad. There were no other foreigners in sight and, other than Theresa, no one in our overcrowded car seemed to speak English. It was perfect.

As the train chugged lethargically up the valley, Coach 2 swayed and lurched like a small vessel in rough seas. The view was mostly an endless scroll of parched hills with a few tiny villages huddled under ragged patches of trees. Inside the train, it was lively chaos: the children cracked out on sugar and the excitement of a journey; the chattering women dressed in their best clothes, their cheeks swirled with fresh *thanaka* designs. The train stopped every twenty minutes or so to allow a few more vendors to crawl in through the windows and scramble around on our shoulders, sing-songing the attributes of their wares. I hadn't packed anything to eat, so the mother of the naughty little boy kindly offered me a packet of sour pickled plums.

There was no potable water on the train, but that was all right, because there was no toilet, either. Toddlers and babies were unceremoniously stripped of their pants, if they had any, and dangled out the window to answer nature's call. Bigger folks who needed facilities would hurry outside during one of our frequent stops and sprint to the opposite track, squatting down in full view of the entire train. It's a reasonable system if you're wearing a baggy *longyi*, but I could not imagine attempting it in blue jeans. Fortunately, I didn't feel thirsty. I also had little appetite for food; I was eating quite a lot of dust and the occasional chunk of coal through the open windows. The other passengers gorged their way merrily up the line, dropping their fruit peelings, plastic bags and soiled paper wrappings to the floor.

About halfway through the trip, the population in our coach dipped below maximum capacity and Theresa came over to join me.

"Every-ting O.K.?" she cooed, patting my arm as she threw the Chinese matron a stern glare.

"Oh yes," I assured her quickly. "Just fine. We're all getting along famously."

Still staring at my seatmate, Theresa announced loudly, "She's very fat! Isn't she fat?" Although I knew the woman didn't understand English—and didn't like me anyway—I felt mortified on her behalf. Again, I dug into my bag of tricks in search of a distraction, and this time emerged with one of my printed name cards. In most of Asia, you haven't really made a friend until you've handed out your name card, and so, with a little flourish, I handed mine to Theresa. Delighted, she exclaimed over it for several minutes and then passed it around the coach for everyone to admire. Up and down the car went my photo and contact details. Nearly every passenger took a turn to hold it up, flip it over, and either spell or sound out my name aloud. While I continued to chat with Theresa and she translated for the immediate neighbors, I had the disconcerting experience of hearing my name echo up and down the aisles of Coach 2, over the rumble of the train:

"Laurie Weed...Laurie Weed...?"

"El, Ay, Yoo."

"ARuh. Ayee. EEE."

"Wuh. EEE. Duh."

Whenever I glanced in the direction of the voices, eighty faces in every shade of South Asia would look back, beaming and nodding as if the card confirmed my existence and granted me a genteel introduction to Ordinary Class. *So much for traveling incognito.*

As we neared Hsipaw station, Theresa leaned over and nudged me.

"Give me one dollar!" she demanded, gumming up at me slyly. This caught me completely off guard. I was not expecting her to ask for money, and while I didn't mind giving her some, I had a limited supply of U.S. currency and no small bills. There are no banks in Burma; you have to plan carefully and bring whatever cash you need. Instead of a dollar, I handed her a thousand-kyat note (about 95 cents). I had a whole stack of those.

"T'ank you!" she chirped.

"You're welcome," I said.

Theresa inspected the banknote, snapped it once, and tucked it into the folds of her *longyi*. "I write you one letter!" she crowed. "I need one dollar to send to America. My children, they no give money for letter...*peh*, so cheap! If they ask me where I get these money, I tell them, 'my American daughter, my *good* daughter, she give me!' Ha-ha!" She slapped her thigh, chortling at the thought of outsmarting her miserly sons.

With another coy glance she asked, "O.K.? You O.K. I write you one letter? You like?"

I grinned. "Mother Theresa, I would *love* for you to write me a letter."

"O.K.! I writing you! No joke!"

"Excellent."

The iron wheels shrieked as the old train heaved into Hsipaw and I gathered my belongings to disembark. Theresa showered me with hugs and kisses, promising to write soon. Bidding her a fond farewell, I waved to the rest of Coach 2 and attempted to wade through their compost heap of food wrappers and scraps to get to the door. The other passengers smiled and waved back, even the fat Chinese lady. We had come a long way together in Ordinary Class. "Bye-bye," someone murmured shyly, and all around the car, heads began nodding and waggling in unison.

"Bye-bye!" Another anonymous voice piped up. The car was still jammed and I could not quite reach the door without risking injuries. "Bye-bye!" Another voice joined in, then another, and as I clambered over a mountain of green mangoes to launch myself out the window, wearing my bags, all the riders of Coach 2 were flapping their hands and chorusing, "Bye-bye!"

"Laurie Weed, Bye-bye!"

"Bye-bye, Laurie Weed, bye-bye!"

As the steam engine puffed away to Lashio without me, I stood on the tracks waving and grinning, content that at last I'd had my proper goodbye.

☙ ☙ ☙

Laurie Weed is a freelance writer who divides her time between Northern California and the Southern Hemisphere. Her work has been anthologized in Best Women's Travel Writing 2007 *and throughout the* To Asia With Love *guidebook series.*

෯෨ ෯෨ ෯෨

Wanderlust

A vagabond feeds her desire.

I met my first love on an airplane. He was seventeen and off to England with his rugby team, a posse of blond boys in blue-striped jerseys sitting near the back of our jet. I was sixteen, on a school trip to Europe. We talked sitting shoulder to shoulder on the floor, feigning a more sophisticated knowledge of our upcoming itineraries than we actually possessed. He called a couple of weeks after I returned home and, a few months later, invited me to his graduation ball.

As I entered my senior year of high school, he scrimped and saved, working two jobs while living with his dad, and bought himself a ticket to see the world. It wasn't until he left, and began sending notes from afar, that I really began to fall for him. There was no email back then, and I wonder if they would have seemed as alluring as his light-as-dust aerograms, written in a dense ballpoint scrawl. Once he mailed a photograph of himself, now with longer hair and darker skin, accompanied by a letter saying he was living in a trailer and picking fruit. Later he mailed a small bag of pebbles collected on a Grecian beach, with instructions to put them in water so that they would shine like they had when he found them. From my circumscribed life of homework and curfews and college applications, I was so captivated by his voyage—by the fact that you could just *do* that, go off into the world and let it carry you along—that after a while, I couldn't be sure where wanting him stopped and wanting to be him began.

Our paths long ago diverged. But two decades on, the most recurrent features of my love life remain airplanes and letters. I've met people who can't separate love and lust; for me the tricky distinction is between love and wanderlust. They're both about wanting and seeking and hoping to be swept away, so lost in the moment that the rest of the world recedes from view.

Some people spend their lives looking for anchors. For years, I cut ties as fast as I formed them, always struggling to be free. I had known for a long time that I was inordinately peripatetic, but it wasn't until I was in my hometown, Vancouver, a couple of years ago, trying to get to know a friend of a friend, that I realized how unusual my path had become. I asked Jen to tell me about her work and her fiancé, the two compass points, I figured, of her existence. She told me a little—she worked for her family's engineering firm, she would get married in Hawaii—and then asked where I had been living all these years. I started to answer, but I had lived in a lot of different places, and the whole circuitous route was too convoluted to explain. What period of time counted as "living" somewhere, anyway? What about extended periods on the road? I did a quick calculation.

"I haven't lived in Vancouver for more than sixteen years," I said. As the words came out of my mouth, the figure struck me as stark, made all the more so by my utter lack of a concrete life.

Then Jen asked, "Don't you like it here?"

Her question made me realize the width of the gulf between us. As someone with wanderlust and someone without, we were foreigners to each other. "No, it's lovely, it's beautiful," I said. And on some level I meant it. If Vancouver's residents are a touch smug, it's because they feel lucky to have wound up in a Shangri-La of dramatic scenery and socialized medicine. To me, though, those qualities are beside the point, because wanderlust, like adultery, is not about what is being left. It's about the person who is leaving. I felt like Jen was my pretty, perfect spouse asking: "How could you?" And I was the cad saying I just couldn't say no to my urges.

"Wanderlust," the irresistible impulse to travel, is a perfect word, adopted untouched from the German, presumably because it couldn't be improved. Workarounds like the French *"passion du voyage"* don't quite capture the same meaning. Wanderlust is not a passion for travel exactly, it's something more animal and more fickle—more like lust. We don't lust after very many things in life. We don't need words like "worklust" or "homemakinglust." But travel? The essayist Anatole Broyard put it perfectly: "Travel is like adultery: one is always tempted to be unfaithful to one's own country. To have imagination is inevitably to be dissatisfied with where you live…in our wanderlust, we are lovers looking for consummation."

In my chronic chasing of that consummation, wanderlust has taken me both into romantic entanglements and out of them.

I met Stu when I was a senior in college in Seattle. That romance, too, started on an itinerant note. We bonded talking about the time we had spent abroad—in my case studying in Egypt; in his, learning sculpture in Bali. I was planning to spend the summer in Pakistan; shortly after I left, he volunteered to join me, and did. Someone who could regard this as so natural a course of action was surely someone for me. Not long after we returned to Seattle, I embroiled myself in the heavy weight of domesticity. We moved in together, got engaged, and bought the mother of all fixer-uppers.

Overwhelmed by love, my wanderlust had gone into abeyance like a briefly dormant volcano. But there was so much of the world I hadn't seen yet. There were lives—so many—that I hadn't experimented with. What if I was meant to be a spy or an aid worker or a scuba-diving instructor? What if I was meant to be a writer in New York? And forget even what I was meant to be: what would it feel like just to wander the world, knowing I could stand on my own two feet? I couldn't look at the glossy cover of a travel magazine or browse the travel section of a bookstore without a lump forming in my throat.

I began to resent the person I loved for keeping me from all those other possible lives. And so I left. I would come back, I said. I just had to get away for a few months.

At first we mailed each other letters. I sorted out coins and dialing codes to call him from far-flung phone booths. One of the earliest calls was from a box on a busy market street in Kota Bharu, Malaysia, where I was about to board a rattling colonial-era wooden-seated train that slogged across the peninsula, through thick jungle, ending up a day later in a nowhere town that lacked even charm. It was very important to me to take that train, I recall, to make a twenty-four-hour journey that I could have accomplished in five, a desire I can't fully explain now except to say that I had to go the long, hard way around. A hallmark of the wanderlust-plagued is that we favor experience over inherited knowledge, however sensible the latter might be.

The best kind of travel—the kind I wanted to experience—involves a particular state of mind in which one is not merely open to the occurrence of the unexpected, but to deep involvement in the unexpected, indeed, open to the possibility of having one's life changed forever by a chance encounter. After several months of phone calls, letters and even a fax or two, I determined that my tie to Stu, which is to say my tie to home, was not letting me be completely open to the world. I wanted to feel that any life was possible. I wanted to be different people, and just as much, to see what core remained as I shifted from skin to skin.

So I called Stu from a phone booth in Yeppoon, a sleepy Australian beach town near the Tropic of Capricorn. I had to cut my ties, I explained, adding that I did not want to get married and was not coming home. It was agonizing to hurt him, and frightening to think that we were over. When, after an hour, I stepped out of the phone box, night had fallen and a full moon was on the rise. (For a long time thereafter, the sight of a full moon would remind me how many months it had been since that phone call.) My friends—one old, two new—were waiting for me in a camper, and we drove through the night to a tin-roofed village called Airlie

Beach, where we parked on a hillside at around two in the morning, stretched out in the back, and slept. In the morning, I climbed onto the roof and surveyed a pink dawn and sailboat masts, feeling scared and free. That was consummation.

Was it just new horizons I wanted, or new men, too? I could no longer see a meaningful difference. My goal wasn't romance, but anything can happen when you open up to the world.

Fast-forward. There was the Australian I met just a few months after that moment on the roof of the camper, while I was a shoestring backpacker. Yet he was a home-bound sort. Once I left his country, I never saw him again, although spates of letters and phone calls cropped up for years, always teasing the idea of a reunion before one of us backed away.

There was the American I met while living in New York. I moved to London, and we continued to see each other, with one of us flying back and forth every month, and scores of emails and phone calls in between. One of his last gifts to me was a digital camera.

In London I began seeing an Englishman. We were masters of the romantic vacation, taking trips to Sicily, Croatia, and Scotland during which we mostly ate and made love. He went on to live in Moscow while I moved back to Seattle. Aeroflot, we discovered, operated a direct flight three times a week between the two cities. After many months apart we reunited in Mexico, and traveled restlessly together to Cuba. We broke up shortly after he joined me back in New York, when, for once, neither of us really had to be anywhere else.

Then I met the diplomat. By this time I had the distinct sense that something was wrong. I wasn't happy, and it had something to do with either my itinerancy or my love life, which were, as usual, hard to separate. My long-distance relationships were so thrilling, with their international rendezvous (Jerusalem, Barcelona, Hong Kong, etc.). Seeing my boyfriends in new places after pent-up months of no contact heightened the excitement. But could I—fickle wanderluster—maintain a flame with someone day in and day out? Wasn't growing up, as my stable friends suggested, accepting the fact that life wasn't a thrill ride every day? I swore to myself that there would be no more long-distance relationships. With that in mind, I moved in with the diplomat and followed him to Washington, then Paris. I had never tried following someone in this way before, for his needs, his career. Maybe that was the missing ingredient.

It was not. After more than a year in Paris, on an early December morning as the Christmas lights faded and festive dark turned to gray daylight, I loaded four suitcases into a taxi on Avenue Montaigne. I went back upstairs to take one last look at my ex-apartment. The living room looked too perfect, with its balconies, its marble fireplace, its fashionable but uninviting white sofa. I surveyed the emptiness, then locked the door from the outside and slipped the key back underneath. Another life was over, and I couldn't get back inside if I wanted.

I flew back to Vancouver, where my parents met me at the luggage carousel. My four suitcases represented the household I had acquired thus far in life. The most overstuffed among them split open between Toronto and Vancouver. The handlers strung it up in red and white tape, but when it arrived on the carousel, the rip still gapped ominously, contents poised to escape, the whole bundle looking dangerously close to explosion.

We took the suitcase to the Air Canada counter, where they provided us with an enormous clear plastic sack, into which I dumped the remaining physical artifacts of my existence: clothing, bags, boots, books. We gave the airline the broken suitcase, and four days later a new one, larger and sturdier than its predecessor, turned up on my parents' porch.

My life wouldn't be so easy to fix. I had woken up at the age of thirty-four to realize that I wanted to go home, only to discover that I had no idea where home was.

I felt numb all winter. I pinged around the world some more, to an assignment in New Zealand and then back to Paris for more work, all the while knowing I had to settle down for my own sanity. Finally, of the three great variables in life—work, home, love—I made decisions about the two in my power. I moved to New York City and abandoned freelance writing for a staff job, the kind with such novelties as a fixed location and health insurance. I signed a lease, with myself as the sole renter, for the first time in my life. Nervously at first, mindful of all the places and people I had run away from, I began to buy large things, such as a desk and a bed. They represented my growing confidence in my ability to stay put.

Months went by. Then a year, a year and a half. I didn't re-experience the soaring thrills of my earlier long-distance loves, but nor, thankfully, did I plunge back into the sense of loss and disorientation I had felt on achieving a perfectly rootless life.

One weekend I sorted through a box of old journals excavated from my parent's home, and a letter fell out. It was from Stu, dated Sept. 24, 1995—four months after I had left, and about two after I had made that full-moon call from the phone booth in Yeppoon. In the wake of my departure he, too, had abandoned Seattle, and was on a sailboat bound for points south.

Written on five small sheets of yellow notepaper, the letter read in part: "By leaving our safety net, we have thrown our souls upon the wind, exposing ourselves to all of the fears and dangers that we sought to protect each other from, and in doing so, we have made ourselves available to experience things that…border on the magical."

The letter stunned me, both for its forgiveness, but even more so for its understanding of the force that drove me away, and dominated my life for the next decade. I wanted to call him, but was too nervous. Would he even want to talk to me? What would we say? We had been in touch on and off, but not in the last couple of years.

I found his phone number listed in an online directory and, after hesitating for twenty-four hours, began to dial. It was our old number in Seattle. He answered, and a few weeks later, he boarded an airplane.

And so it began again, with a letter and an airplane, and continues now with emails and cell phones and JetBlue, scans and photographs, old-fashioned handwritten notes, and promises that no longer scare me. Whatever comes next, he's given me back at least one thing: the feeling that if I open up to the world, anything can happen.

≈ ≈ ≈

Elisabeth Eaves is the author of Bare: The Naked Truth About Stripping, *and an editor at* Forbes. *Her writing has appeared in publications ranging from* The Wall Street Journal *to* Sport

Diver, *and her* Slate *story "Eco-Touring in Honduras" was anthologized in the 2009 edition of* The Best American Travel Writing. *She was born in Vancouver, lives in New York, and is still not entirely sure if she wants to settle down.*

ॐ ॐ ॐ

Viajera Loca

The crazy traveler strikes again.

"*¡Bajo!*" yells the bus conductor. I look around hopefully, checking the other passengers' faces. Everyone else is asleep. I glance back at the conductor. He's definitely looking at me.

"*¿Aquí? ¿Estás seguro?*"

"*Sí, claro. Estamos en Mindo.*"

Could've fooled me. I look out the window into pitch black. "*¿Dónde está el pueblo?*" Pray tell, where in this nothingness would I find the town?

"*Bajo, bajo,*" he says, pulling my backpack off the shelf and shoving it at me. I take it from him and pick my way to the door, over parcels and sacks, past passengers falling over each other in a debauchery of sleep. I move carefully. Two hours of Arnold Schwarzenegger terminating in Spanish on the static-ridden bus TV has left me exhausted, and I don't want to step on any stray limbs. I climb down the stairs, rubbing my eyes as I peer into the blackness. Not a single light on this side, either. I turn back to the conductor. *"Por favor—"*

He stares fixedly ahead as the engine clanks into gear. The bus roars off.

I knew I should have left Quito earlier. I did try. I was told that the buses for Mindo Nambillo left every quarter hour, but I waited for an asphyxiating hour and a half by the queue of departing buses. The conductors, rounding up potential passengers with the fervor and conviction of stockbrokers running insider trading, kept telling me that the Mindo bus was due to arrive next.

This is supposed to be my "weekend off." After this, I have a language intensive course to revive my flaccid Spanish, and then I head into the Amazon to visit the communities I came to South America to write about. I figured Mindo would be a good place to start: I am covering the impacts of extractive projects (oil, gas) upon the lifestyles and traditions of the Amazon's indigenous peoples. Mindo Nambillo is one of the most biodiverse regions on the planet, and also the site of a controversial new oil pipeline. I wanted to enjoy the rain forest before donning my journalist hat. But now it looks like I may just mosey off into oblivion instead.

The night is clear and cool, the road screened by thickets of bush. These are the highlands, and around me rise the shoulders of the Andes, colossal and lush. I fish out my headlamp, then trudge about until I locate a small dirt road angling off the big dirt road upon which we stopped. The homemade sign reads HOTEL MINDO NAMBILLO, with an arrow. In that case the town, which I presume exists, must be that way too. And the road is even going down, which is reassuringly in accordance with the conductor's laconic instructions. I square my shoulders, adjust my headlamp directly ahead, and start walking.

They're right. My friends, my family. Everybody who loves me and tells me I'm crazy to travel alone. I am out of my mind. Nine o'clock at night, total darkness, and I'm in the middle of nowhere, Ecuador, wandering down a dirt road toward a town that either does not exist or is so far away I can't even see the lights. Are there animals in this rain forest? Of course there are animals. But are there animals that eat people? Probably. Unless they got wiped out by development. You know, the same kind of ecologically devastating development I'm here to write fiery prose about. I pray briefly and fervently that there's nothing around here capable of mauling a human being. No doubt I am a spineless hypocrite, but I really hope that the beasts around these parts got eradicated.

Presently I turn off my headlamp and relax into the walk. A crescent moon emerges from behind clouds, casting a wan silvering palm over the scene. Huge trees surround the road. I turn the corner and am heralded by an orgy of tiny flickering lamps: fireflies, leaping about in nocturnal exhilaration. And to my right—there it is! Mindo! A cluster of lights at the very bottom of the valley. It can't be less than five miles away. I keep walking, maintaining light conversation with the fireflies and various other whirring, clicking, buzzing critters filling the night with a steady drone. Let me tell you about Quito, little friends. Big city, *mucha gente*, several leagues from here.... Wait. Everybody just pipe down. I hear something—is it possible?

I turn as a car roars by. I reprimand myself roundly. Just plain brainless. Why wasn't I ready? I keep walking, debating the risks of hitchhiking. If one car came,

another will. I decide I'll flag it down with my pocket-
knife at the ready.

The next car is preceded by loud Castillano folk
music, assailing me in bursts as it careens down the
mountainside. I turn, place one hand on my hip, and
extend the other one, thumb up. I am brave. I am reck-
less. I am that character from the Tom Robbins book,
minus the deformed thumb.

The car pulls up. I hold my breath. The passenger
window rolls down. Tinny vocals swell the air, and a
round face emerges. I exhale in a rush, giving silent
thanks. It's a woman. Get in, get in, she orders, smiling
broadly. What in God's name are you doing out here?
The back door opens and I clamber in, next to three kids
who all stare at me open-mouthed. I balance my backpack awkwardly on my lap and pull the door shut.

Off we roar.

The woman turns around, still smiling, and introduces herself as Jenny. The driver—not my husband,
she whispers, no, no, my husband is a doctor—is Diego,
and the three children are Pepe, Maria, and Pablo.
They're still staring at me. Pablo's mouth has been open
so long he's beginning to drool.

"What are you doing walking on this road in the
middle of the night?" demands Jenny.

I explain.

"What? Are you crazy? Crazy traveler!" she says,
laughing uproariously. "Traveling by yourself? Why?"

How to explain the wanderlust that draws me, time
and again, to the solo journey? That I'm forced by
circumstance to be totally open? That there is no refuge from sheer experience? That every day is a new
adventure, every chance meeting a wee blessing? You're

the reason, I want to say. You, Jenny, and Diego, and the fireflies, and Maria with her pigtails, and even that accursed bus conductor.

"I'm a freelance writer," I settle on.

"Ah, *sí, sí,*" she responds, brow furrowed in complicity. That explains it.

There is a pause, predictably brief.

"But alone, at night, on this road?" Diego asks, turning to face me. His features are bunched up toward the center of his face, like a knot on a balloon. The car careens into the blackness as he scrutinizes me.

"Yes," I say, pointing a forefinger at the road, hoping he'll get the hint.

He gives a soft whistle of incredulity, turns back.

I exhale.

"¡Eres una viajera loca!" shrieks Jenny, shaking her head and giggling.

I hear this a lot from locals—particularly women—and right now I'm inclined to agree. She grins as I nod and shrug regretfully—*sí, soy loca*—and the conversation moves on. Jenny explains that she and her husband are the new owners of a small hotel-restaurant in Mindo—the Café Mindo—and I am ceremoniously invited to stay. I accept, gratefully.

The hotel portion of Café Mindo is small—three rooms, to be precise, on the second floor—and my room is currently occupied by a couple of the kids. Diego, who manages the café, shuttles their stuff out apologetically, and I settle in. I am on the verge of collapse, but Jenny urges me downstairs. I tramp down to join them at one of the wood tables comprising the café portion of Café Mindo. Jenny smiles voluptuously, her eyes crinkling into mere cracks above the swells of her cheeks.

She pats my hand. "So, tell me everything about San Francisco."

I am about to embark on my two-minute summary when the door creaks open. A new arrival—tall, handsome, black, and wielding an ancient guitar—shoulders his way in, peering about timidly. He smiles at Jenny, holds out his arms, and she is up, out of her chair, kissing him extravagantly on the cheeks. *"¡Mira!"* she shouts. *"¡Aquí esta Ramiro! Ramiro, Marisa. Marisa, te digo—¡Es una negrita, pero todavía es artista!"*

It takes me a moment to rise; I am thrown off-balance by the blatant and apparently routine racism. *He's black, but he's an artist nonetheless.* I smile at Ramiro, and we give each other the customary peck on the cheek. We all sit down, and Diego, tiny and hunched, shuffles a chair up to join us. Ramiro picks up his guitar and begins to tune the blackened strings. We wait expectantly. Then he settles it on his lap and starts to sing.

Aye. Voice like late summer sun, fingers like driving rain. Voice like thunder, fingers like grass stealing its way out of the dirt. I slump in my chair, a puddle of gratitude. Ramiro, amigo, sing it. Sing it, brother.

Jenny nudges me. I open my eyes to a tall glass. Rum and something sweet and fizzy. She pushes it at me again and again. *Toma, amiga, toma.* Drink, my friend.

This woman is a force of nature. I'd rather get drunk than argue with her.

Ramiro sings folk songs of love and loss. Loss and love. Love and loss. There are no other themes, it seems. What else is there to sing about, in truth? Love and loss pretty much sum it up, I conclude, as my body tingles pleasantly with the rum. We are clustered around him now, listening, each adrift upon the paper boat of our own love-and-loss ruminations. The other tables are unoccupied, but the lights blaze. Come to Café Mindo. We are an island of warmth and song, a small glowing oasis for wayward travelers.

Instead, Maria, Pablo, and Pepe, who have been playing outside, come banging in the front door. Pablo sidles up to Ramiro and attaches himself to his knee. Thumb in mouth, eyes black pools, he stares adoringly up at the musician. Pepe grabs Maria's hand, pulls her to him, clasps her in his chubby arms. The two of them waltz around the room, giggling and occasionally lurching into an ill-placed bench or table.

The song—a lament about an incurable cheat—draws to a close. Jenny hands Ramiro the rum and leans toward him, batting her eyelashes. I'm not sure I've ever actually seen anyone bat their eyelashes. "Something happy, Ramiro," she murmurs. "Something upbeat." Her eyelashes blur.

Ramiro takes a healthy swig of the rum. He smiles at Jenny, winks, and strums a few major chords. She laughs long and loud, opens her mouth, and issues a warbling soprano. What Jenny lacks in skill she easily makes up in enthusiasm. Hand on chest, eyes screwed tightly shut, she belts it out. I back my chair up a little, hoping she doesn't notice. To my left, Diego is somehow drifting off to sleep.

The song draws to a close, and Jenny's voice leaps an octave in a rousing finale. Diego shudders awake, eyes snapping open in alarm. I wonder briefly about the neighbors. We all applaud, Pepe and Maria pausing to bow and curtsey. Jenny smiles, puts her arm around me. "Isn't he good?" She gestures at Ramiro.

"*Sí, sí,*" I nod vigorously. "*Increíble.*"

Ramiro stares modestly at the floor. He fiddles with his guitar, picks out a slow dirge. Jenny sighs deeply. Her hand returns to her chest, eyes drawing slowly closed. "How could you leave me, my love?" she croons. "Where did you go, after this world? If I cross the seas, will I find you?" I watch with mounting affection as the odd tear slides down her face. The woman wears her heart smack-dab naked-splayed on her sleeve. If only we all could. If only. Wars would freeze mid-battle, opposing soldiers dropping their weapons to chant duets. Trials would unfold in four-part harmony. Oil company CEOs would abandon post to belt out Andrew Lloyd Webber, oil workers leap athletically into Busby Berkeley sequences....

Feeling my gaze, Jenny opens her eyes and smiles. She takes my hand, lifts it to her thigh, clasps it in a sweaty, urgent grip as the song wrenches out of her. When she finishes, we all sigh heavily. Loss and love. Love and loss. Who can guess the torments we have suffered through? Who can know the heart's hidden ways, who can understand what led us each here, at this very—

A low, throaty keening slices the silence. Diego is slumped over double in his chair, sobbing. Jenny looks at me with wide eyes. "His girlfriend," she stage-whispers. "She died after ten years together." She nods meaningfully as this sinks in, then rises to sit next to Diego. She lifts his head to her shoulder, arranges his skinny arms about her. He sinks into her chest, weeping. Maria and Pepe come close, run their small hands across his heaving back. Ramiro stares glumly at the floor.

We sit together quietly as this man releases all that has been pent-up inside his tiny frame. He hurls himself in desperate, rhythmic assault against Jenny's generous bulk. She coos softly, a wordless murmur of comfort, stroking his head, his back. Gradually his sobs ease into a soft wail. Jenny pulls slowly back, wipes his sodden face with gentle hands. *Estás bien,* Diego, she says tenderly. You're O.K. You're with us here.

Diego nods. He settles into his chair, back hunched, hands moving over his face like an infant discovering the sense of touch. Jenny looks at Ramiro, raises her eyebrows at his guitar. Ramiro's fingers flit over the strings, whittling a high, happy melody. He pauses, meets Jenny's eyes with a grin, and they both open their mouths and launch into song. Pepe grabs Maria and begins spinning her around the room again. Diego's hands are still covering his face, but his foot taps in time with the beat. I lean forward, opening my mouth to join this song I have never heard before. I discover that my cheeks, too, are wet.

Jenny reaches over and pulls me up, toward her. She takes me in her arms and leads me in a wild, reeling waltz. We thread our way through the furniture, gallop up the stairs and back, and return in time to applaud Ramiro's virtuosic finale.

Jenny leans in close, inches from my face.

"¿Marisa, mi amiga, crees en la reencarnación?" Do you believe in reincarnation?

"Sí."

"Pues," says Jenny, smiling so fiercely that her cheeks become small planets orbiting her chin and nose, "Well. I think we knew each other in a past life, amiga."

She is watching me closely.

I smile back.

Then we nod solemnly, laugh uproariously, and take one more spin across the floor as Ramiro's fingers melt those ancient strings into pure, unalloyed joy.

ℬ ℬ ℬ

*Marisa Handler—writer, activist, singer-songwriter, and speaker—
is the author of* Loyal to the Sky: Notes from an Activist, *which*
Booklist *called a "must read," and which won a 2008 Nautilus
Gold Award for world-changing books. Her journalism has
appeared in the* San Francisco Chronicle, San Francisco Bay
Guardian, Earth Island Journal, Salon, Alternet, *and* Tikkun,
Orion, The Sun, *and* Bitch *magazines. Marisa speaks and sings
about visionary social change all over the country. Find more,
including music videos and her album,* Dark Spoke, *at www.
marisahandler.com.*

Acknowledgments

Our first round of gratitude goes to the hundreds of amazing women who filled our mailboxes and inboxes with stories this year. Each submission was a joy to read: we regret that we could print only twenty-seven. Thanks also to Michael Yessis of World Hum, Tim Leffel of Perceptive Travel, and Robin Hemley and David Torrey Peters of the University of Iowa's Nonfiction Writing Program for sending winning essays our way. Laurie King of Travel Writers News and Anna Brones of Written Road, meanwhile, were instrumental in helping spread the word. Gracias.

Stephanie would like to extend her gratitude to James and Sean O'Reilly and Larry Habegger, for inviting her to join this project; Lucy McCauley, for her friendly counsel; Kevin Hopkins, for his witty teasers; and Christy Quinto, for serving as the series' wise midwife.

Final thanks go to Mother Road, who makes all journeys possible.

"The Suffer Fest" by Mary Caperton Morton published with permission from the author. Copyright © 2010 by Mary Caperton Morton.

"Not-Surfing New Zealand" by Colette O'Connor published with permission from the author. Copyright © 2010 by Colette O'Connor.

"The Heat Seeker" by Alison Stein Wellner was first published in a longer form on the Travel Channel's World Hum in May 2009. Published with permission from the author. Copyright © 2009 by Alison Stein Wellner.

"In the Half-Light" by Jennifer Percy published with permission from the author. Copyright © 2010 by Jennifer Percy.

"Design a Vagina" by Johanna Gohmann was first published on YourTango.com in September 2009. Published with permission from the author. Copyright © 2009 by Johanna Gohmann.

"Bosnian Blues" by Landon Spencer published with permission from the author. Copyright © 2010 by Landon Spencer.

"Grinding Saffron" by Beebe Bahrami published with permission from the author. Copyright © 2010 by Beebe Bahrami.

"Woman in the Wild" by Laura Katers published with permission from the author. Copyright © 2010 by Laura Katers.

"The First Day" by Jennifer De Leon published with permission from the author. Copyright © 2010 by Jennifer De Leon.

"Winter with Dogs" by Erika Connor published with permission from the author. Copyright © 2010 by Erika Connor.

"The Angel of Repose" by Marcy Gordon published with permission from the author. Copyright © 2010 by Marcy Gordon.

"Siliguri" by Megan Lyles published with permission from the author. Copyright © 2010 by Megan Lyles.

"To Italy, for Family" by Valerie Conners was first published on the Travel Channel's World Hum in May 2009. Published with permission from the author. Copyright © 2009 by Valerie Conners.

"The Moustache Brothers of Mandalay" by Shauna Sweeney published with permission from the author. Copyright © 2010 by Shauna Sweeney.

"Breaking Frontiers" by Maliha Masood was first published on www.PerceptiveTravel.com in April 2009. Published with permission from the author. Copyright © 2009 by Maliha Masood.

"Language Lessons" by Christine Buckley published with permission from the author. Copyright © 2010 by Christine Buckley.

"Holy in the Land" by Deborah Milstein published with permission from the author. Copyright © 2010 by Deborah Milstein.

"White Lady Scrubbing" by Sara Bathum published with permission from the author. Copyright © 2010 by Sara Bathum.

"An Ode to B-Cups" by Heather Poole published with permission from the author. Copyright © 2010 by Heather Poole.

About the Editor

Stephanie Elizondo Griest is the author of the award-winning memoirs *Around the Bloc: My Life in Moscow, Beijing, and Havana*; *Mexican Enough: My Life Between the Borderlines*; and the guidebook *100 Places Every Woman Should Go*. She has also written for *The New York Times*, *Washington Post*, *Latina Magazine*, *Texas Monthly*, *World Pulse*, *Poets & Writers*, and more than a dozen Travelers' Tales anthologies. As a National  Correspondent for *The Odyssey*, she once drove 45,000 miles across and around the United States in a Honda Hatchback named Bertha. She has won a Henry Luce Scholarship to China, a Hodder Fellowship to Princeton University, a Richard Margolis Award for Social Justice Reporting, and a Lowell Thomas Travel Journalism Gold Award for Best Travel Book. She lectures and performs around the globe but can always be found at her website, www.aroundthebloc.com.